Neverending Story

By

Carl Buckingham

ISBN: 9781916696686

Dedicated to the memory of Pat Sheldon, 1932-2010: a life-long book-lover.

Without change, life becomes a dull repetition of stale memories

1 The sun shone brightly

It all began in earnest on Monday October 1 1984 when I arrived in Preston to start a one-year journalism course at the town's polytechnic.

I had graduated from Middlesex Polytechnic, in North London, two years earlier and then spent two 12-month terms of office as full-time, elected Editor of the students' union newspaper at the poly.

This, though, was the start of the 'real deal' in my chosen career. The course at Preston, run by the National Council for the Training of Journalists (NCTJ) and with just 35 places, was one of only six of its kind in the country and acceptance - plus, of course, successful completion - virtually guaranteed a job in the newspaper world.

The NCTJ course was based in part of the polytechnic known as The Colonial Buildings, on old Victorian-looking structure (as the name would suggest) no more than five minutes' walk from the town's railway station.

As I entered for the first time, expecting to find myself among 34 complete strangers, I was a little surprised to see four people, standing together, whom I had already met

The course interviews had taken place six months earlier with hopefuls divided into groups of six, each of which spent a full day at the poly, completing a variety of written tests in the morning with formal interviews in the afternoon.

With so many applicants competing for so few places, I had, at the time, thought it unlikely that more than one, or two at most, would make it through from each set of hopefuls. But my group had obviously bucked the trend and this provided an obvious conversation-opener as I approached the quartet.

'Well, we did well, getting five out of six through,' I said.

'That's what we've just been saying,' replied the only female in the group.

Although we had all got on well enough back in early April, spending an hour or so at the nearby Adelphi pub in between the tests and the interviews, not surprisingly we all struggled to remember each other's names, but as the day unfolded it transpired I was in the company of Naomi Porter, Steve Barnes, David Barnes (no relation) and Ross McCarthy.

We heard talks from the course lecturer Alan McKenzie - a Scotsman and former Fleet Street sub-editor who had conducted April's interviews - and course head Julian Allitt and were given our timetables which, apart from journalism training, would consist of lectures in law and national and local government and learning shorthand.

In the afternoon we were asked, by Alan McKenzie, to compile a 500-word piece on our first day of the course as if we were writing it for a weekly newspaper.

At the end of the day I went to view the house I would be sharing with two under-graduate students I had yet to meet and who were not present when I arrived to finalise details with the owner Mrs Lewis. We agreed that I would move in the following evening when I would pay the first term's rent.

I then travelled down to Manchester to meet my journalist father, with whom I had stayed the previous night, after he finished his shift at The Daily Star at about 10pm.

My parents had separated when I was four, both had remarried by the time I was 10 and from the break-up until I was 18 I had no contact whatsoever with my father. Thereafter we met sporadically, usually in Cornwall where I had been brought up and where he had a holiday home.

Contact between us had dwindled in the two years prior to my acceptance onto the course at Preston, but when he heard news of my good fortune, on the North West journalism grapevine, he wrote to me during the summer.

This was quite a lucky stroke as my local education authority, Cornwall County Council, had decided, in its infinite wisdom, only to pay my course fees at Preston and not to provide me with a maintenance grant (their policy apparently being not to give such awards for postgraduate courses apart from teacher-training).

My father, who had not sent myself or my sister as much as a birthday card following the separation, uncharacteristically offered to help out by paying for my accommodation in Preston, perhaps because I was finally doing something he approved of by following his steps into journalism.

However, as he handed over a cheque for the first term's rent as we drank in the Land of Cakes pub that night, he added that I would have to find my own living expenses as 'I'm not providing money for you to piss it up'.

Such a comment seemed a little hypocritical from someone who had spent almost his entire adult life drinking himself into debt, which was part of the reason why my parents had split up. Perhaps the real reason for refusing to help further was the pressure he was being put under by his second wife, who strongly disapproved of him having anything to do with me at all.

The next day Alan McKenzie held a seminar where he returned our accounts of the first day on the course and told everyone, in front of the rest of the group, what he thought of their efforts.

He began by saying there were 'no hopeless cases', but it was clear, from several of the extracts he read out, that many were still some way from understanding the difference between an essay and a news report.

One student's opening paragraph began 'The sun shone brightly as I walked out of Preston railway station', while another, noting that The Colonial Buildings had not been decorated for quite some time, wrote of 'the allegedly-white-coloured walls'.

Few escaped criticism at all, but when it came to my turn Alan McKenzie simply advised that I 'needed to shorten my paragraphs a bit' but otherwise 'the standard of reporting is what I'd expect from someone with your experience' which, I suppose, was fair comment.

That night I moved into the house in Ashton, about a mile's walk from the poly, and finally met the undergraduates I would be sharing with for the next eight or nine months: Ian Hawkes, from Hexham in Northumberland, and Mick Rawson from Rotherham in Yorkshire.

They were both final year Humanities students, the same course I had taken at Middlesex, and both listed their hobbies as including drinking and football, which were usually the common denominators that ensured I got on with people.

As the first week progressed, those of us on the NCTJ course were gradually getting to know each other better and on the Friday it was loosely arranged that anyone interested would meet at the students' union bar for a few drinks the following evening.

I wasn't expecting a full turnout as many on the course lived in other towns in Lancashire and commuted to Preston during the week, while others had only five-day accommodation in the town and returned to their parents' homes at weekends.

However, I was a little surprised when only two other people turned up: Naomi Porter and James Barber, one of the non-graduates who made up approximately half the numbers on the course.

We waited in vain to see if anyone else showed up, commenting that those who had arranged the evening were among the absentees, and as the union bar was extremely crowded, later moved onto the less-cramped Adelphi pub for the rest of the evening.

I had spent more time with Naomi than anyone else on the course that first week, usually sitting next to her during lectures and coffee breaks. We seemed to click from the beginning and I was already entertaining the possibility that she might become more than a friend and colleague.

But I decided to proceed with caution as she was from Preston, and had just spent a year off there after graduating from Oxford University, so I suspected there might be a boyfriend lurking in the background who she hadn't yet told me about.

A matter requiring more immediate attention was my financial situation. Given my father's stated position on not helping with maintenance costs, the fact that my mother was in no position to give significant help and that what little money I had managed to save from my poorly-paid summer job in a Cornish bookmakers was already exhausted, I decided there was only one course of action I could take.

So on the Monday I signed on for unemployment benefit (which, of course, you weren't supposed to do if you were a full-time student) after blatantly lying about my details.

I certainly wasn't the only person on the NCTJ course not to receive a local authority grant, but as far as I was aware, David Barnes was the only additional would-be journalist claiming the dole; the others either living with or being supported by their parents.

The course I was finding straightforward with the exception of shorthand, which I not only found difficult but unnecessary as, being a fast writer and blessed with an exceptional memory, I found I could manage perfectly well without it.

This was never more clearly illustrated later that month when we produced Poly News, a twice-termly tabloid paper which was part of our coursework and was distributed free around the poly. My contributions were a lengthy interview with the National Union of Students' President Phil Woollas, when he visited Preston, and a report on an attempted donation by some members of the students' union to the National Union of Mineworkers, who were deep into what turned out to be a year-long strike at the time.

Both pieces won significant praise from Alan MacKenzie, others on the course and indeed many outside it, including my two housemates.

'Alan McKenzie certainly deserves praise for getting a good paper out like that when, less than a month ago, few of them knew how to write a news report,' I said to Naomi as we sat in The Adelphi the following Saturday night.

'Well, you were the star of the show, but you're going to have to do something about your shorthand,' she replied. 'Alan was saying that a lot of editors won't take people who haven't passed it at 100 words per minute, no matter how good they are in other ways.'

Naomi and I had continued to spend much of the time together during the first month of the course and had gone to The Adelphi each Saturday night. By now I was satisfied that there was no boyfriend, as surely she would have said something, and the following weekend, during a party at the home of Julian Allitt, the relationship I later learnt everyone on the course had expected to start for the past four weeks finally got under way.

Although things had moved to a conclusion in somewhat alcohol-fuelled circumstances that Saturday night, I had enough experience of such situations to suggest that we met again, in the cold light of day, at The Adelphi the following lunchtime.

Any lingering thoughts either of us might have had about the other only allowing things to begin because of drunkenness were soon dispelled and an interesting discussion ensued about the possible future.

We agreed that, while we didn't want to jump ahead of ourselves, if things were going strong at Easter, we would have to discuss what would happen if we were both offered jobs in completely different parts of the country towards the end of the course - something which was more than a possibility.

' I suppose whichever one of us finds a job first, the other one will have to try and find one in the same part of the country, but let's just see how we get on first,' I said. Naomi nodded in agreement.

After that weekend things settled down into a routine for the remainder of the autumn term. We had our first taste of magistrates' and crown court reporting and a second edition of Poly News was produced before Christmas.

Socially Naomi had her first introduction into my past life when we travelled over to Blackpool to attend the National Union of Students' conference, at the Winter Gardens, during the first weekend in December.

We met up with the Middlesex delegation, all of whom I knew well and which included four members of that year's students' union executive: Natascha Scott-Stokes, my successor as Editor of the newspaper, President Mike Crabtree and Jon Guite and Mark Hardy, two mature students with somewhat dubious past employment records who had become 'professional students' as indeed many of their ilk did in the polytechnic world of the 1980s.

A fine drunken day and night ensued. Naomi was well-received by my old friends before returning to Preston, by prior arrangement, early on the Saturday evening and by the time I crashed out on one of the Middlesex delegation's hotel room floors, at about 3.00am, I had consumed no less than 23 pints in the previous 15 hours - a personal record that still stands today and which I very much doubt will ever be equalled.

A less-successful venture, the following weekend, was my first meeting with Naomi's parents after I was invited to dinner at their home in the upmarket Fulwood district of Preston.

While there was not a hint of social snobbery about my new girlfriend despite her background - if there had been I very much doubt whether she would have been interested in the likes of me - unfortunately the same could not be said of her mother, a loud, brassy middle-aged character with dyed red hair and glasses and whose husband emerged as a nervous, hen-pecked wimp who only spoke when invited to by his other half and then usually only to agree with whatever she had just said.

I formed the impression, from that very first day, that whatever type I had been, or whatever I might have done or said, they would have found reason to have found fault and Naomi later confirmed that her younger sister's boyfriends had received a similar reception when introduced to Mr and Mrs Porter.

After a Christmas period satisfactorily spent with family and friends in Cornwall, I returned to Preston in early January. Only the first six weeks of the Easter term would actually be spent at the poly; the remainder seeing each of us on the course going on two three-week placements to work as reporters at weekly or daily newspapers.

Julian Allitt, who informed everyone where they would be going during that first week back, had devised a system where each of us could, wherever possible, choose the first newspaper we worked for, but would then have to go wherever we were sent for the second placement.

I had expressed a preference for The Western Morning News, the Plymouth-based title with which I was quite familiar as it was widely-read in Cornwall,, as the county's only daily paper, and had been taken by my grandparents for many years.

As I was the only person on the course with any connection with the South West - there were only four or five of us who could even claim to hail from south of Birmingham - not surprisingly I got my first choice which I doubt anyone else wanted because of the travel and accommodation costs involved whereas I, of course, could easily commute from my mother and stepfather's house in Cornwall.

For my second placement I was informed I would be working for The Burnley Express, a weekly title in an East Lancashire town that I had never previously visited. Naomi also got her first choice paper and would spend the first three weeks in Preston itself at The Lancashire Evening Post before going to a weekly in Chorley near Manchester.

Our first round of course examinations - two papers covering journalistic basics entitled Use of Language - saw comfortable passes for all but a handful of people in the group before we went our separate ways, placement-bound, at the end of the second week in February.

I travelled down to Cornwall on the Friday ready to commute the 50-odd miles from Truro, my home town, to Plymouth from the Monday. With the prospect of being away from Preston for three weeks, followed by another three travelling daily to Burnley and then a three-week Easter holiday back in the South West, I had no choice but to 'sign off' the dole and would be living off money my mother had borrowed from a friend, plus any expenses I might get from the two papers I would be working for during the following month-and-a-half.

My first day at The Western Morning News started off fairly quietly. I had set off from Truro very early in order to get to the office, in New George Street, by 9am. However when I arrived nobody in authority was around because the paper didn't go to print until 10pm and therefore none of the senior editorial staff started work until 10am at the earliest.

For the first hour or so I simply sat at a desk reading back copies of the paper and wondering how I could have been unlucky enough to develop a heavy cold, which had started during the weekend and now seemed to be getting progressively worse, on such an important day.

I was made to feel quite welcome when the News Editor, Jack Holman, and his deputy, John Owen, duly arrived. For the next couple of hours I was given press releases to re-write until the former suddenly threw a note pad to me (even although I already had one in my pocket) saying 'Right, here's a job for you - go with the photographer, he'll explain on the way what you're doing.'

It turned out we were going to a Plymouth hospital to cover the handover of a new piece of medical equipment by two television stars, Su Pollard and Matthew Taylor.

Although my task was really just a caption story, where I was only required to write five or six paragraphs, I could sense this was my big test of the first day. On returning to the office I wrote the piece, received no complaints about how I had done so and reverted to re-writing press releases for the remainder of the afternoon.

At one point the Editor Brian McArthur came into the newsroom, introduced himself to me and gave me the welcome news that I would be paid £50 a week plus expenses (about the same as the student grant I should have been getting but wasn't).

As my first day ended, John Owen said to me: "You've made a very good start, but you look like death warmed up.' My cold had worsened further and apart from regular coughing and sneezing, sweat was dripping down my face.

'If you're no better tomorrow, for goodness sake don't come in,' he added. 'It won't be held against you as we've all seen how ill you are.' Relieved by his words I didn't travel up to Plymouth on the Tuesday hoping the day off would speed up my recovery. I did venture out to buy a copy of the paper and there was my hospital picture-story, printed almost exactly as I had written it, prominently positioned on one of the early pages.

Although I was well used to seeing things written by myself printed in student publications, there was something slightly unreal about reading my work in a 'real' newspaper for the first time - especially one so familiar and which had been part of my upbringing.

I returned to the office on the Wednesday, the cold by now reduced to a persistent cough, and the following two-and-a-half weeks were extremely enjoyable if at times physically tiring given that I was making a round trip of more than 100 miles each weekday.

I had several more stories prominently placed in the paper and the editorial staff, at all levels, were friendly and helpful and invited me for a drink, at the nearby Bank public house, on more than one occasion.

Towards the end of my stay Jack Holman paid me the compliment of saying I 'wrote like a sub (editor)' which, in layman's terms, meant he thought that, for a beginner, I was better than he had any right to expect.

On my final day Brian McArthur called me into his office and said that while he didn't think he would have a staff vacancy that summer, if I didn't have a job to go to immediately after completing the course at Preston, to get in touch and he would find me some casual or temporary work.

There was further good news that day when I learnt that my old political grouping at Middlesex Poly had won a fifth consecutive victory in the students' union elections. I travelled up to London the following day to join the celebrations before completing the journey back to Preston on the Sunday ready to start my next placement, at Burnley, the following day.

My feeling of contentment and optimism that first weekend of March 1985 was quite easy to understand. Following my success in student journalism, both at

Middlesex and Preston, it seemed I had taken the first step up the ladder without any problem.

I really did believe, at that moment in time, that it was a case of 'Fleet Street here we come' in the next two or three years.

But if things had been that straightforward there would not really be a tale to tell.

2 'Anything but talent'

From my very first morning at The Burnley Express it became clear that the road to journalistic success wasn't going to be as free from obstacles as I had thus far believed.

Things began with a reverse scenario of my opening day in Plymouth when – due to a cancelled train between Preston and Burnley, then an extremely slow-moving follow-up service which stopped at a succession of small stations – I didn't arrive at my destination until around 10am.

This didn't unduly worry me as, firstly, I hadn't been given an official start time and, secondly, I had no control over the workings, or otherwise, of British Rail. However on arrival at the Express office, I overheard mutterings about having turned up 'late' on my first day.

Alan McKenzie and Julian Allitt had repeatedly drummed it into us, since the start of the course, that journalism wasn't a nine-to-five, Monday to Friday job – and my father and several people at Plymouth had reinforced that view – but the opposite philosophy seemed to operate in Burnley.

The atmosphere in the newsroom couldn't have been more different to the vibrant enthusiasm and friendly-but-intense bustle of The Western Morning News. Instead I found myself in a strangely-muted, apathetic and impersonal environment.

Perhaps, I thought, I was simply learning that things at a weekly newspaper were done more slowly than on a daily, but there was something more deep-rooted than that to the mindsets of many of those who worked there.

Most of the personal conversations I couldn't help but overhear in such quiet surroundings seemed to consist of almost-daily accounts of what people were going to have for dinner that night, where they were going to take the dog for a walk and what the latest happenings were in television soap operas. At Plymouth I hadn't heard a single word uttered on such subjects during the entire three weeks.

What made the situation even more frustrating was the newdesk's strong reluctance to give me work. Although the half-a-dozen or so stories I was given to cover were printed largely unsubbed – about the only positive note of my stay – this did not lead to an increase in assignments and the rest of my time at the Express was spent either accompanying senior reporters to court or council meetings or simply sitting at my desk reading the national papers because there was nothing else to do.

'Well, that's one paper I won't be going to when we finish the course,' I said to Naomi as we travelled down to Cornwall during the first week of the Easter holidays.

This was the first time I had officially taken a girlfriend to stay at my mother and stepfather's house (by 'officially' I mean with their prior knowledge and permission), but my family certainly took more of a liking to Naomi than her parents had to me. The first few days of the vacation went well as we undertook day trips to various parts of the county and she was introduced to some of my friends as we visited several Truro pubs.

Then Naomi was struck down with flu and confined to bed for several days before being well enough to travel back to Preston nearly a week later than originally planned.

I followed a few days later, arriving before the last weekend of the holiday to give myself time to 'sign back on' at the Unemployment Benefit Office after telling the people there that I been away on a training course for the past eight weeks.

The following Monday saw the start of the summer term at the poly and I was slightly encouraged to hear, from several others on the course, that they too had experienced 'one good one, one bad one' during their placements.

However the next day Julian Allitt approached me and asked to have a word in his office, where he produced a letter from Keith Hall, Editor of The Burnley Express.

'Well I don't know what went wrong, but he says you were the most disappointing pre-entry student to sit-in at his office for many years,' said 'JA', so nicknamed by many on the course as his mannerisms were so similar to the character 'CJ' in the 1970s television comedy The Fall and Rise of Reginald Perrin.

He then read extracts from Hall's letter in which I was described as 'disinterested' and 'regularly looking bored'.

I explained to 'JA' about the lack of work I was given, the fact that what I had been allowed to do was printed unsubbed and drew comparisons with my experiences at Plymouth, where my efforts had received nothing but praise.

'I agree that The Burnley Express isn't The Western Morning News, and I don't have a lot of time for Keith Hall. So I'm not going to read too much into this,' he replied.

'However I must say that you were one of the last people on the course I would have expected to have been the subject of a letter like this.'

Naomi had endured a similar experience at The Lancashire Evening Post where, despite receiving no complaints about her work, she constantly sensed an unspoken alienation towards her.

This appeared to be borne out when, upon returning to the poly, she discovered that the student who followed her to the Preston paper for a second placement – not, it has to be said, one of the outstanding people on the course – had been offered a reporter's job there later in the summer.

'Maybe it was my Oxbridge background at the LEP, and maybe it was your West Country accent at Burnley, but sometimes, even when you do nothing wrong, it's just that your face doesn't fit,' Naomi said to me as we sat in The Adelphi that first Saturday night of the summer term.

‘And then they’ll twist and distort half-truths to try and present you in a negative light,’ I replied.

‘Well yes, they could hardly blame you for looking bored and disinterested if they refused to give you any work to do.’

Several other students had been offered jobs at the end of the course – subject, in most cases, to successful exam results including shorthand at 100wpm – and the remainder of the term saw those of us who hadn’t yet found employment stepping up their efforts to do so.

A number of people, including Naomi, applied for a vacancy at the weekly paper in nearby Lancaster. However the Editor was a friend of a friend of my father’s and I was tipped off, early on, that they wanted a young non-graduate and the rest would be given interviews purely as a courtesy.

Then I learnt, from a member of my family, about a vacancy on The Falmouth Packet, around 10 miles from my home in Cornwall. I applied and, probably being the only ‘local’ anywhere currently taking a NCTJ course, was promptly invited down for an interview. It went quite well and they asked me to contact them again once I had completed my exams.

Unfortunately, they didn’t take anyone who didn’t have shorthand at 100wpm, which I knew I wouldn’t get – even though I didn’t admit that on the day in the hope they might later make an exception.

A week or so later Naomi and I were discussing the job-seeking situation with Alan McKenzie and he seemed sympathetic to our situation.

‘Sadly that’s the way it is with a lot of Editors,’ he said. ‘It’s always shorthand, age, whether you’re local – anything but talent.’

We completed our examinations, in law and local government, during May and again most people passed comfortably.

At the end of the month Naomi and I travelled down to Manchester one Friday afternoon for a few drinks with my father. It was the first time we had met since just before Christmas and I spoke to him at length about the jobs situation and how the placements had gone.

He, like Alan McKenzie, expressed cynicism, but from a slightly different prospective. 'At the lower end of the scale you'll probably find that the paper at Burnley was more typical than The Western Morning News,' he said.

'One thing you've both got to learn is that journalism, at a provincial level, isn't a profession overflowing with intellectuals.'

As we moved into June, Naomi and I were still among the jobless and, like many others on the course, wondering what we were still actually doing at the polytechnic. Our examinations were over, undergraduates from other courses were departing for the rest of the summer in their droves day by day, yet 'JA' seemed bent on stretching out our stay by organising a series of largely-meaningless functions and visits.

When these inevitably attracted poor attendances – just four people turned up for a talk by someone from the press office at a regional water company the day Naomi and I went to Manchester – he retaliated by sending letters to everyone on the course, warning that if there was further absenteeism he would write to prospective employers, recommending that they should not take certain people on.

One meaningful activity at this time came when we were asked to write reports on our placement experiences, copies of which would be forwarded to the Editor of each paper as well as being kept by 'JA' as reference for future work experience students.

After giving a glowing account of my time in Plymouth, I gleefully tore into The Burnley Express, telling it as it was but being unable to resist adding that 'the intellectual standard of conversation in the newsroom rarely rose above that heard in the average council estate laundrette'.

On the second Saturday in July, with almost every other polytechnic student long departed, our course was finally concluded with an end-of-year dinner where 'JA' unintentionally had large sections of the room in laughter by opening his keynote speech in true 'CJ' fashion with the words 'we haven't got where we are today…'

As the lease on my accommodation in Ashton had expired, I had little choice but to return to Cornwall, even though this meant probable long journeys to future interviews. Naomi, also still without a job, would remain living with her parents and we reiterated our agreement that when one of us found employment, the other would attempt to follow suit in the same part of the country.

I had written to The Western Morning News, keen to take up their offer of temporary work, shortly before leaving Preston, but then learnt, through the national media, that Brian McArthur was leaving to become launch Editor of Eddie Shah's national Today newspaper. I eventually received a reply from his replacement, recruited from elsewhere and therefore with no knowledge of me, politely saying there was nothing doing.

So it was in a less-than-contented frame of mind that I returned to Cornwall not even sure of what I was going to do until the inevitable, or so I had repeatedly been told, offer of a journalism job came along.

In previous summers, both while an undergraduate and the previous year while between Middlesex and Preston, I had worked for the bookmakers William Hill; an initial spell with them after A-levels had gone so well that I kept being invited back.

The problem this time around was I didn't know how long I was going to be in Truro – it could be weeks or months – and thanks to 'JA' artificially prolonging the final term in Preston, much of the summer had already elapsed and in all probability Hills would have already filled their seasonal vacancy. I therefore elected simply to transfer my Unemployment Benefit claim to my home county.

Those of us on the NCTJ course had devised a scheme, before we departed, whereby those who already had jobs would keep those who didn't informed of any vacancies they were aware of. After about a fortnight back in Cornwall I was told of one on a free weekly newspaper in Abingdon, Oxfordshire.

I made contact and travelled up, but the interview was a curious, non-descript affair which never built up any momentum and was over in less than half-an-hour. I also received another letter from The Falmouth Packet, who obviously hadn't yet filled their vacancy, asking if I had yet passed shorthand at 100wpm. I had just about scraped 70 and it now became clear that they weren't going to budge from their entry requirement.

Naomi, meanwhile, had been offered a week's work experience at the evening paper in Bristol, after which she came down to Truro for a long weekend, the social highlight of which was our winning the fiercely-competitive quiz at my local pub The Daniell Arms.

A week or so later I received a letter from her – my mother and stepfather didn't yet have a telephone – saying she had been offered an (albeit well-paid) job with the IBM computer company in Portsmouth. A former teacher of Naomi's, Jean Talbot, was now in charge of recruitment in one of IBM's departments and had spotted her name on a list of NCTJ students that had been circulated (by whom and why I never discovered).

Naomi accepted the offer, informing me that the job did involve some journalism and PR work, but I was still a little puzzled by her decision. It was only a few weeks since the course at Preston had ended and it seemed a little early, to me, to be thinking of non-newspaper permanent alternatives.

Perhaps it was the money being offered – or perhaps, after two years, she had simply had enough of living with her parents – but within a fortnight Naomi had begun work at IBM and was living in a flat in Southsea.

This coincided with my hearing about another vacancy, on The Isle of Wight County Press, a location which of course was just across the water from Portsmouth. I had some doubts as to whether I wanted to leave the British mainland, but given that things had reached the stage where I couldn't afford to be geographically fussy – and bearing in mind the agreement Naomi and I had made about one following the other to whichever part of the country they landed a job – I decided to apply.

An interview was arranged for a Monday lunchtime and I travelled up to Portsmouth the preceding Friday, spending the weekend with Naomi before going over to the island by ferry and then catching a bus to Newport, the reasonably-sized capital town where The County Press's main office was based.

The Editor, whom I only knew as 'Mr SA Rea' at this stage, seemed to be at an age not too short of retirement and spoke in strange, slow-but-deliberate northern drawl. He asked the predictable questions about the course at Preston – encouragingly not seeming too concerned about shorthand at 100wpm – and was curious about my role as Editor of the student paper at Middlesex.

He then told me something of the history of The Isle of Wight County Press, stressing that it was a totally independent publication and not part of a group as the majority of weekly newspaper were by that time.

Then, just as the interview was drawing to a natural conclusion, he suddenly said: 'Well, I've got one or two inquiries to make, but providing there are no discrepancies, I'll be in a position to offer you the job later this afternoon. Can you ring me at about four o'clock?'

I had no idea, and never did discover, what those inquiries were he had to make. He already had a printed testimonial from Alan McKenzie, so there was no question that I really was NCTJ-trained, and if he was checking on whether I had a police record (which I didn't) I don't know where he could have got the information confirming this in such a short space of time.

I even had my full travel expenses reimbursed in cash, unlike the interviews at either Falmouth or Abingdon. The offer was confirmed when I rang Rea after arriving back in Portsmouth and it was agreed that I would start work two weeks later, on Monday September 30, with the usual three-month probationary period.

The suddenness of the offer had taken me a little by surprise and it was only the next day, on the long train journey back to Cornwall, that everything began to sink in and I had time to reflect.

OK so geographically it wasn't ideal, but at least I was going to be as close to Naomi as I could reasonably have expected in the circumstances.

My overriding feeling, though, was one of having achieved a goal set more than 10 years earlier when, in my early teens, I decided that what I wanted to do, and indeed was going to do, was to be a newspaper journalist.

I might have been starting in a fairly humble division, but after the preliminaries at Middlesex and Preston I was now, so to speak, in the professional league.

3 Wight time, wrong place

Things started off quite quietly when I began work at The Isle of Wight County Press, although from day one I noticed that the paper was unashamedly stuck in the past.

It was not, at that time, unique in its old-fashioned broadsheet style – nor in its policy of not giving by-lines to reporters, even for the front-page lead story – but what I found particularly odd was that no Christian names were allowed in copy – everyone had to be introduced by their title and full initials and thereafter were referred to as Mr, Mrs or Miss (Ms, not surprisingly, was strictly banned).

There were, however, exceptions to this rule – children were called by their Christian names and, more confusingly, the island's member of parliament was always introduced as Mr Stephen Ross MP.

In an office as antiquated as the paper it produced, I was in a fairly small room with two other trainee reporters, David Leigh and Mandy Waltham, and seniors Phil Wolsley, Martin Ellis and Andrew Anderson. The Chief Reporter/News Editor position was vacant with a new person having been appointed and due to start work two to three weeks later. For the interim period Mike Sutcliffe, the Deputy Editor, was in charge of allocating stories to reporters and ensuring the strict house style was followed.

For the first few days I was given a mixture of weddings, obituaries and press releases to rewrite and picture stories to pick up on the phone.

On the Thursday evening I was set to cover my first parish council meeting – at Totland, on the far west of the island, where I was temporarily living while seeking a flat in Newport. However, shortly before I left the office that afternoon, I gained my first insight into the mentality of Rea.

The telephone on my desk rang and a voice asked to speak to Phil Wolsley, who sat immediately behind me. 'Hold on, I'll just see if he's available,' I replied, and turned to see that he wasn't as he was using his own phone. I was about to impart this information to the caller when the line suddenly went dead.

I did not, at first, think any more about it. I was still getting used to the County Press's phone system which was quite difficult to grasp as there was no way of distinguishing between internal and external calls and there were no extension numbers, which meant a certain amount of guess work when the receptionists, downstairs, tried to put calls through to specific reporters and when employees, generally, were attempting to ring each other internally.

About five minutes later I was asked, by Rea's personal assistant, to see him in his office. I entered, having no idea why he sought my presence, to be told it was he who had wanted to speak to Phil Wolsley and accused me of speaking to him as if he were 'the bloody tea boy' (because I had dared use the phrase 'hold on') and that my telephone manner had to 'bloody improve'.

'Don't worry, he's like that with everyone,' said David Leigh when I returned to my desk. 'If somebody new doesn't do anything obviously wrong the first few days, he'll soon think up an excuse to give them a bollacking.'

As my first few weeks at the County Press passed, I soon learnt that there was nothing unusual about Rea using the word 'bloody' and sometimes stronger language when telling people off. What was more astonishing – although admittedly in keeping with the 1950s culture in which the paper was stuck – was the Editor's tendency to both call and refer to people by their surnames, especially when angry.

The arrival of new Chief Reporter Mike Starke, a couple of weeks later, at least ensured that rest of the news desk had less day-to-day contact with Rea who then, towards the end of October, went on a fortnight's cruise holiday (an annual occurrence at that time of the year, I was told, which was eagerly anticipated by everyone else in the office). The more relaxed atmosphere under Mike Sutcliffe during those two weeks – without, significantly, any reduction in the efficiency of the editorial department – was immediately noticeable.

As Christmas approached, I wouldn't say I was happy on the Isle of Wight, but I was sticking it out. Mike Starke, an experienced journalist in his 40s with whom I was developing a reasonable working relationship, had given me two regular parish councils to cover, at Cowes and Wootton, and made overtures to Rea about my being allowed to attend some district and county council meetings.

This was dismissed out of hand as the Editor – still living in the newspaper world of 20 or 30 years previously when junior reporters began work at 16 and spent the first few months making the tea, rather than being graduates with a full year's journalistic training – made his position clear: only 'seniors' (reporters with two years or more experience) were allowed to cover the higher level councils and court cases.

Despite the generally strained atmosphere in the office, other than when Rea was away, the paper's archaic house style still provoked the occasional humorous spell of banter. I remember one debate, shortly before Christmas, when David Leigh and myself were wading through what seemed like a mountain of nativity play picture stories that had to be written up. After first ensuring that Rea wasn't within earshot, we asked Mike Starke if it was alright to call Jesus Christ by his full name or did we have to write 'Mr J Christ'? The Chief Reporter grinned, but as if then reminded of his own seniority, muttered 'I shouldn't let the Editor hear you say things like that'.

Naomi, in the meantime, had soon realised she had made a massive mistake in taking the job in Portsmouth, which had no journalistic element whatsoever, and, in early December, she informed me she was leaving, and taking a considerable pay cut, to go to The Aldershot News, in Hampshire, as a trainee reporter from early January.

I did not see this change having any serious impact on our relationship, which had now passed the year mark, as we would still be in the same part of the country, although it would be further for each of us to travel at weekends, when we usually alternated as to who went to stay with whom.

Around midway through Christmas Eve morning, when even those of us travelling to other parts of the country had to work until lunchtime, Rea sent word that he wanted to see me as my standard three-month probationary period was almost up.

'Don't worry, even he isn't going to sack someone on Christmas Eve,' said Mike Starke before I went in. 'Your staying on should be a formality as far as I'm concerned.'

And he was right, although Rea did say he found me 'an enigma' and reiterated what he told me three months earlier: that I would not be indentured, as trainee reporters usually were after completing their probationary spell, because I was older than 23 due to the two extra years I had spent at Middlesex. Instead I would be treated as an 'adult entrant'.

The festive holiday period was certainly different to what I had become accustomed to during my years in the student world when we had up to three weeks off. After not arriving back in Truro until 10pm that Christmas Eve – by bus, ferry and four trains – I had to travel back to the Isle of Wight on Sunday 29th ready to recommence work the next day.

Naomi came over to the island on New Year's Eve and we attended a party at Phil Wolsley's house. She was set to move to Aldershot that coming Saturday and had agreed to move in as a lodger with one of the paper's sub-editors, whose permission she would need to obtain, in due course, for me to stay with her some weekends.

During the second week in January Rea called all the editorial staff into one room to announce he was stepping down in three months' time, adding that 'you can all save the cheering until after I've gone'.

The retirement was not a total surprise. I never did discover his exact age, but he couldn't have been any less than 60 and had widely-known health problems including diabetes and arthritis.

After Rea left the room, following his sudden announcement, the look of undisguised joy on many faces was a sight to behold. Mike Starke – who, in the three months since he joined the County Press, had experienced several run-ins with the Editor – was grinning from ear to ear and one of the sub-editors was almost crying with happiness.

After phoning Naomi that evening, to give her the uplifting news, I made my first visit to Aldershot the following weekend and met her colleague and landlord, Martin Creasey, who said there was 'absolutely no problem' about me staying at his house some weekends.

Although a sub-editor, he was only a couple of years older than me; we shared a common interest in sport (he had been Deputy Sports Editor at The Aldershot News before becoming a sub) and he also knew Mike Starke, whose previous papers included the Hampshire title.

During February I had a week's holiday – we all had to take one week during the first three months of the year – and spent several days in London before travelling back, via Aldershot, the second weekend.

While in the capital I stayed with two friends from Middlesex, Stuart and Lynda Owens, whom I had known individually at the poly and whom had since married the previous summer.

Three or four enjoyable days saw me watch my football team, Tottenham Hotspur, play live for the first time since leaving Middlesex (lack of finance ruled out any such excursions during the year in Preston) and trawling pubs and student bars where I again met up with Mike Crabtree, now into his second term as President of the students' union, and Mark Hardy, unemployed after being thrown off his teacher-training course for constant absenteeism, along with two people I had not seen in more than 18 months: Jon Summers, the union's General Secretary during my final year at the poly, and Gill Crane, who currently held the same position.

I missed the hustle and bustle of London and, I thought that week, a return would certainly be a possibility when applying for my first senior job after completing my time at the County Press in about 18 months' time (leaving any earlier would prove difficult as trainee reporters were always expected to stay for two years even when 'unindentured').

One afternoon in March Mike Starke returned to our room at the County Press, following a meeting with Rea and other senior editorial staff, and called for hush.

'Well, do you want the bad news or the very bad news,' he asked. 'The bad news is that the new Editor, who was supposed to be starting here next month, has pulled out and won't be coming after all.'

'The very bad news,' he continued, 'is that the current Editor, after talks with the Managing Director, has withdrawn his resignation and will be staying on, probably for another year.'

At first there was a stunned silence in the room. For several seconds nobody spoke, then David Leigh said: 'This isn't a sick joke, is it?' Mike Starke replied that he only wished that it was.

Rea, determined to take his revenge against those whom he knew had been revelling in his pending departure, then embarked on a campaign of antagonism against most of his staff which was severe even by his standards.

Few escaped his wrath and, sure enough, my turn came a couple of weeks later. Like most of my so-called misdemeanours at the County Press, I had done nothing seriously wrong – simply not completed certain stories in the order Rea wanted them done, even though nobody had told me what to prioritise. My defence, that I wasn't a mind-reader, was rebuffed with the predictable 'don't bloody-well answer me back'.

But Rea's main target had become Mike Starke, despite his age and experience which included working freelance shifts on The Sun. Barely a week passed without the Editor screaming and shouting at him for one reason or another. Several of us heard our Chief Reporter mutter, more than once, that he couldn't put up with the situation much longer.

He was, however, still able to see a humorous side to the situation at times. One of my weekly tasks at the paper was to compile a historical piece, entitled Looking Back, where I picked one story from each corresponding edition of the County Press 50, 75 and 100 years earlier.

One week in May I chose, for the latter, an account of the annual open day at the island's lunatic asylum. 'Don't think he (Rea) will be very happy with that one,' said Mike Starke. 'I think you're getting a bit too close to the truth.'

The County Press was not, by any means, the only newspaper office not to be a totally happy ship. Naomi was having a torrid time at Aldershot, where the News Editor, an Ian Barron, told the Editor, at the end of her three-month probationary period, that he wasn't happy with the progress she was making and recommended a three-month extension before she was offered indentures (although Naomi was now 24, the 'adult entry' policy didn't seem to operate there).

What also was concerning me, in relation to my own predicament, was the policy of the Aldershot paper (and seemingly many others) of allowing trainees to cover district and county council meetings, and even court when necessary, and to complete prominent off-diary stories if they were people who found them, whereas at The County Press any such exclusives were automatically taken away and given to a senior. Not only did I find this professionally insulting, but it didn't bode well for my cv when I later applied for senior jobs.

'Well at least you're treated like adults in terms of what you're allowed to cover,' I said to Naomi when she came over to the island one weekend towards the end of May.

'Yes, but I still don't understand why they've got it in for me,' she replied. 'It's not as if much of my work is seriously changed by the subs. I think it must be because I went to Oxford.'

A week later I went down to Cornwall for my main holiday of the year – a fortnight to correspond with the first two weeks of the 1986 World Cup which, as it was being held in Mexico, would involve many late-night kick-offs.

Socially it went well as I combined seeing family and friends with a lot of drinking as England, after a poor start, reached the knockout stages of the competition.

However I also experienced, throughout those 14 days, a gnawing feeling in my stomach about having to go back to the Isle of Wight. It had got to the stage where I knew I could only stay there until I could work out what I was going to do next.

I returned to Newport to discover that Rea had formed the opinion that too much time and energy was being spent in the office talking about the World Cup and he ordered Mike Starke to ensure that all football followers were given an evening job on the Wednesday, when England were due to play Paraguay in the first knockout stage, and if there weren't enough obvious assignments to go around, to make sure he found some more.

I was told to cover the mouth-watering annual meeting of the Isle of Wight Scouts' Council which, luckily, was being held only a few minutes' walk from my flat in Newport. I turned up early and was delighted to discover that a pre-printed copy of the main report was available from the organisers, which I took away, to re-write the next day, and got home in time to see England win 3-0 and move into the quarter-finals where, of course, a few days later they would fall to Maradona's Hand of God goal. And God also only knows what would have happened if Rea had found out what I did that night, but he didn't.

Two weekends later, while in Aldershot, I learnt from one of Naomi's colleagues, David Thompson, that his previous paper in North London, The Enfield Advertiser, was looking for reporters, even though they hadn't advertised nationally, and he assured me that no Rea-like practices took place there. I knew this part of the capital well – one of Middlesex Polytechnic's sites was based there and I had lived in the town during my first year as an undergraduate – and promptly sent off a speculative application.

For Mike Starke, things came to a head at the County Press less than two weeks later, on Thursday July 10. A series of rows with Rea, which begun almost as soon as they arrived and continued throughout the morning, led to him taking an extended lunch hour, when he discussed matters with his wife, and then giving notice to Rea in the early afternoon.

The sub-editors and some of the senior reporters, who were based closer to the Editor's office than we were, later told us that, as the resignation was tendered, the shouting and language used, particularly by Rea, defied belief. The long and short of it was that Mike Starke returned to our room, packed his briefcase and left on the spot, whether of his own accord or by mutual consent none of us were really sure.

Nice business this journalism, I thought.

4 'No! No! A thousand bloody times no!'

Any hopes that Mike Starke's sudden departure might create a 'lull after the storm' – with Rea, at least for a limited period of time, keeping a low profile – were soon extinguished.

The next day he was, if anything, even worse than usual, screaming and shouting both at Martin Ellis, for putting a story in the wrong copy tray, and at one of the subs for not having completed a page, even although the copy he needed had not come through due to the confusion understandably caused by the sudden absence of a Chief Reporter.

Later that morning, following a series of meetings in Rea's office, an internal memo was circulated naming Clive Barton, a long-standing senior reporter, as the new head of news with Phil Wolsley as his deputy, although within a couple of hours rumours were circulating that both had accepted their new responsibilities somewhat reluctantly.

Since Rea's retracted retirement there had been several departures from the County Press. Andrew Anderson had moved to a weekly paper in the Midlands, Mandy Waltham left to get married and David Leigh, who was away on holiday at the time of Mike Starke's exit, had given a month's notice before departing and would soon be joining the Evening Argus, in Brighton, as a senior reporter. Although a couple of new trainees were due to start later that month, the editorial staff was somewhat depleted.

Shortly before I left the office that Friday afternoon, Rea came charging into our room and flung something down on my desk. 'No! No! A thousand bloody times no,' he screamed. This was one of his familiar catchphrases, apparently derived from a 1930s film and song which, of course, did not include the expletive.

As he left the room I picked up what he had returned to me. It was a story of mine, submitted to Mike Starke earlier in the week and cleared by him, in which I had the audacity to use a pun in the introduction – something that was generally discouraged but not forbidden at the County Press.

The next two days passed uneventfully. I had not arranged to see Naomi as she was on weekend duty at The Aldershot News. On the Sunday I reluctantly (as was always the case by now) prepared myself for another week at the County Press, but when I awoke the next morning, something inside me told me I simply couldn't work there anymore.

The next thing I knew I had packed a holdall, caught a bus to Ryde and ferry to Portsmouth and was on a train heading towards London. I had a good illness record at the County Press, only two days off in nine-and-a-half months there, and could easily have got away with phoning in sick if it was simply a case of needing a couple of days off to think things through. However I already had the idea in my head, even though my actions that Monday had not been planned over the preceding weekend, that my days at the paper were over.

After arriving at Waterloo I visited a couple of pubs and, from the second, rang Lynda Owens, asked if I could stay the night and said I would explain what was happening when I got there.

I stayed with the Owens, in their one-bedroom flat in Edmonton, that night, using the living room couch where guests tended to sleep. But things had changed since my last visit in February. Lynda was now pregnant and it was therefore not really conducive to have guests staying indefinitely in such circumstances. They suggested that if I wanted to remain in London more than a couple days, I go to Mark Hardy's flat, about a mile away, where there was a lot more space, and the following lunchtime I wandered down there. Being still unemployed he was predictably at home and said I could stay as long as I liked.

Before leaving Lynda and Stuart's flat I borrowed their typewriter to compose my resignation to Rea, which was posted later that day. I began the letter 'Dear Stephen' (his rarely-used Christian name) knowing that such anti-1950s informality would immediately enrage him and continued in a similarly-disrespectful tone, culminating in a suggestion that he book an appointment with a psychiatrist.

My next move was to contact the Enfield Advertiser, whose office was no more than a couple of miles away. I had heard nothing since my speculative letter more than a fortnight earlier but given my changed circumstances and new geographical location, I phoned Editor Lawrence Phillips and he asked me to call in and see him the following afternoon.

This temporarily raised my hopes of a quick and seamless transition from the County Press to another paper, and in a part of the country where I wished to return, but when I met Phillips I soon realized that such good fortune was not likely to be.

He was probably the vaguest interviewer I've ever encountered. Apart from having misplaced my earlier letter, the man in charge couldn't remember which paper I had been working for, didn't asked why I wanted to leave (I didn't tell him that, effectively, I already had) but did ask if I had any sub-editing experience as this was the area where they were most in short supply.

I wished I could have said that I did, but the only subbing I had done was in producing the student paper at Middlesex, which was a magazine format and some way removed from the 'casting off' system used on newspapers. Phillips said he would be in touch, but I wasn't holding my breath.

Although there was a positive irony that I was staying in Edmonton – my ancestral home of sorts as my grandfather was born and raised there, hence my family's traditional support for nearby Tottenham Hotspur – the accommodation in which I found myself left much to be desired to say the least.

One of two shabby, 1960s-built four-storey buildings in between two tower blocks, Hereford House was housing association owned and was occupied by a mixture of students, unemployed people and low earners.

Four others shared my temporary home: Mark Hardy, his long-standing girlfriend Mary, who had just completed a BEd (teacher training) degree, Tessa, another newly-qualified primary school teacher whom I had met a couple of times before, and Ruth, a second-year undergraduate whom I had never previously encountered and, like me, was an unofficial resident.

All were unemployed – Mark Hardy since the start of the year and the others since the polytechnic's summer term ended – although Mary did have a probationary teaching post lined up at a North London school from the September.

The amount of time the quartet had on their hands was, unfortunately, not directed into maintaining the property in a reasonably clean and presentable state. The flat was an incredibly-untidy tip which did not look as if it had been hovered for months and with a kitchen sink stacked high with unwashed dishes.

It was rare for anyone, other than myself, to rise before lunchtime and afternoons usually consisted of watching daytime television, the highlight of which was the strangely-excitable welcoming of a children's quiz programme called Blockbusters, before the drinking began in the early evening.

Although Naomi had mixed feelings about my departure from the County Press – admitting that she wouldn't have worked long for someone like Rea, but a little concerned about the manner of my departure – she was less than happy about where I was staying, having met Mark Hardy twice before and being singularly unimpressed.

'I can't see how living somewhere like that is going to help you get back into journalism quickly,' she said when I went down to Aldershot for a weekend at the end of July. 'If you stay too long living with people like Mark Hardy, you'll probably find yourself being dragged down to their way of life as the normal thing.'

'I've no intention of staying there too long,' I replied. 'But let's not knock it too much in the short term – it's rent-free and I certainly can't afford to move anywhere else for the time being.'

I knew that unless I got an extremely lucky break, as indeed I might have done with The Enfield Advertiser, there was going to be a 'dust settling' period where my priority had to be ensuring week-to-week financial survival before I could start making a concentrated effort to get back into my profession.

I was also aware that, because of the way I left the County Press, I would receive no unemployment benefit money for six weeks and therefore needed some sort of temporary work.

Apart from journalism, my only previous employment had been working summers for William Hill while a student. Bookmakers' shops tended to have a quick turnover of staff as, apart from managers, most employees were part-time and there was nothing unusual in someone taking such a job and staying only for a matter of weeks or months. Hills, however, had no branches in my part of North East London, so I obtained and completed an application form from a local branch of Ladbrokes.

Meanwhile some hope of a quick return to at least part-time journalism emerged in August. The Sports Editor of The Aldershot News was considering taking on someone two days a week and Martin Creasey – with whom I had got on with increasingly well during the seven or eight months Naomi had been lodging with him – had recommended me, correctly saying that Mike Starke – whom, of course, the Sports Editor knew – would provide me with a reference.

'It's not definite, as the Editor has to approve the financial side, and it wouldn't be full-time, but it would be a foot in the door,' Naomi said. I agreed, thinking that I could possibly combine such an opening with a part-time bookmakers' role in the Aldershot area.

Before I heard anything else from The Aldershot News, I was contacted by Ladbrokes. They offered me a job, with an immediate start, as a boardmarker in their shop at Palmer's Green, a short bus journey across the North Circular Road from Edmonton and where I had lived for a couple of terms during my second year at Middlesex.

I began work during the first week in September but when I heard, from a disappointed Naomi, that her Editor had decided not to take anyone on part-time, I knew that, having by now dismissed The Enfield Advertiser from my calculations, I had to start thinking about making a concerted effort to re-enter journalism by writing to papers every week.

However this would not be straightforward in the workshy world of Hereford House where there was no typewriter – the Owens had one I could use if an urgent need arose, but I really needed unlimited access to such a facility – and no telephone, not as unthinkable as it would be today, but even in the mid-1980s it was becoming increasingly unusual for any residence, even one occupied by students or the unemployed, not to have at least a payphone where calls could be received. Employers, in turn, were by now expecting employees, would-be or actual, to have a contact number.

Another problem was that Ladbrokes' regional office were deducting emergency tax from my pay, because I didn't have a P45 from the County Press, and while I was told that I would get it back 'eventually', in the meantime, even when working my day off, I was taking home barely enough money to get through the week, let alone being able to save for potential journeys to whatever parts of the country I might be granted interviews.

Moreover, while things had got off to a satisfactory start at Palmers Green, in terms of getting on with the work and my colleagues, after three weeks the area manager, without giving a reason, moved me to another branch in Phillip Lane, South Tottenham, close to where the Broadwater Farm riots had taken place a year earlier.

Whereas the atmosphere at Palmers Green had been as amenable as you could reasonably expect in a bookmakers – it wasn't dissimilar to that I had experienced while working for Hills in Cornwall – Phillip Lane was something else with a clientele largely made up of noisy West Indians armed with a daily supply of funny cigarettes and cans of Special Brew. When I pointed out to the manager that alcohol was banned from all Ladbrokes shops, he shrugged his shoulders and said he had been told to turn a blind eye to such activities as the takings would drop dramatically if such individuals were banned.

Meanwhile, back at the flat, Mary had begun her first teaching job, Ruth had left and Tessa was still unemployed. Mark Hardy, as if slightly embarrassed by both his girlfriend and guest resident now working full-time, decided to make his own small contribution to reducing the national unemployment figures by joining a Job Club (a 1980s government initiative where the medium to long-term unemployed regularly attended a drop-in centre where they received professional advice and the free use of telephones and stamps to look for work).

On a Wednesday evening in October, Stuart Owens called at the flat to give me a message from Naomi, who had his number, given the absence of a phone at Hereford House, in case she needed to get in touch with me quickly.

I had been scheduled to go to Aldershot that weekend and the message said that I should stay on the train an extra stop and get off at Farnham. She would meet me there and explain everything. Stuart believed she had found somewhere new to live, but didn't know any further details.

This news had me slightly puzzled as I wasn't aware that Naomi was looking for anywhere else to live. She had been with Martin Creasey for almost 10 months now, and I hadn't been told of any serious tensions between them.

Unable to wait until the weekend to unravel the mystery, I phoned Naomi at work the next day to learn she had agreed to a house share, for six months, with two of her paper's other reporters: David Thompson and Jo Petherbridge. The latter I had never met but had heard quite a lot about in the preceding months.

'This is all a bit sudden,' I said. 'I didn't even know you were looking to move.'

'Well I wasn't really, but Jo and Dave asked me if I was interested and I had to make a quick decision,' she replied.

I travelled down to Farnham after finishing work on the Saturday (a compulsory working day at bookmakers) and stayed until the Monday morning before returning to London and going to Ladbrokes, where I didn't start work until midday on weekdays, direct from Waterloo.

The new house, situated around 10 minutes' walk from the railway station at the top of a long hill leading out of the town centre, was extremely spacious and I finally met Jo Petherbridge, who was about the same age as Naomi and seemed OK. I was also impressed with Farnham, an extremely well-heeled town which couldn't have been more different to grimy and military-dominated Aldershot, even although the two places were less than three miles apart.

Throughout the weekend Naomi made a series of pointed comments about Hereford House and its inhabitants. She had refused to stay at or even visit the flat – the one weekend she had travelled up to London since I left the Isle of Wight we had spent the night at the Owens – and there was nothing new in her expressing displeasure at my temporary abode, but this time her comments were more persistent than usual.

Suddenly it dawned on my what Naomi was up to – part of the reason she had moved into the new house was to engineer a situation where she could get me out of the Edmonton flat, while at the same fulfilling the agreement we had made, in Preston, that as soon as it was practically possible for us to live in the same town we would.

Of course, this would be no permanent or long-term deal. Once I got back into journalism the arrangement would have to end unless I got a job within travelling distance of Farnham, which was unlikely, and, of course, they only had the house on a six-month contact while the owners were abroad .But it would be a step along the right road and immeasurably preferable to my remaining at Hereford House where, apart from anything else, there was always the possibility that the housing association officials might discover my unofficial presence.

I didn't see Naomi every weekend as my Saturday work commitments, and the fact that she sometimes worked that day herself, meant it wasn't always practical for me to travel down, but on this occasion I was scheduled to return the following Saturday as the Monday, November 3, marked our second anniversary together and we had agreed to celebrate it on the Sunday night. What better occasion, I thought, for us to discuss my move to Farnham.

On the Monday morning, after Naomi had gone to work and I was walking around the centre of Farnham before getting a train back to London, I passed a branch of Corals bookmakers and noticed that they were advertising for a boardmarker. 'If that advert is still there in a week's time I might well apply,' I thought to myself.

The following weekend went generally well. Both David Thompson and Jo Petherbridge went out on the

Sunday night, giving Naomi and I the house to ourselves for our anniversary dinner. As the meal progressed, I waited and waited for the subject of my moving into the house to arise, but curiously it didn't.

I started to wonder if there was some kind of obstacle I had overlooked. Jobs in bookmakers were ten-a-penny, so she knew I wasn't tied to London by work reasons, the house was certainly big enough to accommodate another person and there couldn't be a problem with the other residents as one I'd only met a week earlier and the other I got on with well enough.

The next morning, just before Naomi left for work, I decided to mention the job I had seen advertised in Corals. 'If it's still vacant I could apply,' I said.

'Well, yes, I suppose so,' she replied, before rushing off to get a lift to the office with Jo Petherbridge. As it turned out, the advert was no longer posted in the bookmakers, otherwise I might have walked in and inquired about it on the spot, but what was going on?

The suggestion that I take a job in Farnham had been greeted with neither joy nor negativity, but puzzlement – and that, in turn, left me perplexed.

Meanwhile a wind of change was starting to blow through the flat in Edmonton and it wasn't down to an improvement in the hygiene. Mark Hardy's relationship with Mary, while four years old, had been tottering on the brink for several months and more than once they had 'split up' only to then become quickly reconciled.

However when her starting work at the primary school coincided with an increase in his drunkenness and subsequent obnoxious behaviour – now almost every daytime as well as the evenings – her impatience at his refusal to find work, made worse by an attitude that he was doing nothing wrong, increased dramatically as did the frequency of the rows.

When even the hapless Tessa found a seasonal job with WH Smith from mid-November, the tensions grew still further and one night in early December, following a particularly bitter and prolonged shouting match, she packed a bag and stormed out, staying the night, we later leant, with Stuart and Lynda Owens.

Given that the relationship had 'ended' before, I did not read too much into this development at first, but when I returned from work the following day, I learnt that this time it really was the end: Mary had returned to collect the rest of her belongings, given notice to the housing association and was staying with the Owens until she could find another flat.

Unfortunately another relationship was by now taking a downward turn. While Naomi and I had our disagreements during our first two years together – as, indeed, all couples do – there had never been anything which could really be called a row, but these began during the approach to Christmas, mainly over her growing tendency to arrange social events in Surrey during the same weekends she knew I had other plans in London. Until that point we had always been able to sensibly compromise on what weekends we saw each other and what we then did, but it seemed those days were over.

I think Naomi thought she was making the point that she should be my main priority, while I took the view that if I was living in Farnham, which I should have been by then, such event clashes would rarely occur in the first place.

My dissatisfaction with Ladbrokes also deepened as – if not content with continuing to deduct emergency tax and turning a deaf ear to requests to transfer me from Phillip Lane to another branch – they then refused to allow me the week off between Christmas and the New Year, even though I had completed the three months required to gain holiday entitlement, saying they were too busy.

I promptly gave a week's notice to leave the Saturday before Christmas and subsequently arranged to be registered for work with an Edmonton employment agency, Reeds, from the first Monday in January.

After completing my last day at Ladbrokes, I went to Farnham for the rest of the weekend before travelling down to Truro on the Monday. On arriving I learnt that the city's popular Liberal MP David Penhaligon, tipped by many as a future party leader, had been killed in a car crash that morning. The whole community was in a state of shock and the death completely overshadowed the festive period.

I returned to London on December 30, taking with me a fairly-old portable typewriter which would at least ensure that I would be able to make widespread applications to newspapers in a way I had so far been unable to do since leaving the Isle of Wight.

By prior arrangement Naomi, who had gone back to Preston for a few days at Christmas, travelled up to the capital for New Year's Eve, which was spent at an utterly-dire pub in Edmonton with the Owens and a few others before we slept, as on previous occasions, at the aforementioned couple's home.

The next morning Naomi asked to see the flat in Edmonton where I had been staying since July. She knew that both Mark Hardy and Tessa were still away and, while it was empty, I think she wanted to see just how bad it really was.

I readily agreed as I knew that, firstly, she would be disgusted by what she saw and hoped that, secondly, this might shock her into insisting that I belatedly join her at the house in Farnham.

On the first count I was absolutely right; on the second there was still not a word – and I think I knew, deep down inside on that first day of 1987, that the invitation I so desired was never going to come.

And a Happy New Year to you too!

5 Waterloo

Unfortunately, the uninspiring events either side of Auld Lang Syne did not prove to be a false start to the New Year.

My first week with Reeds saw me sent to work, would you believe, in the commercial department at Tottenham Hotspur Football Club and although the people there were fine, there wasn't a great deal to do and, on the Friday, I was told they couldn't justify keeping me any longer. The agency then said they had nothing else immediately, but that I should stay in almost daily contact as employees were quite often required at quite short notice.

Then came the unexpected news that Tessa was leaving the flat, once her temporary work with WH Smiths ended in mid-January, to go and work as a nanny in Argentina of all places – not quite what her county council had in mind when they paid for her four years' training to be a primary school teacher and less than five years after the Falklands War into the bargain, but I suppose she couldn't be blamed for thinking anything was better than Hereford House.

The upshot of this situation was that two of the flat's three bedrooms would soon become vacant and the housing association was likely to fill them with people from their waiting list. Mark Hardy asked me if I was interested in quickly joining that list as existing tenants could express a preference for who they wanted to move in if a room became vacant.

My gut feeling was that, under no circumstances, would I be prepared to pay rent to live in such an environment, but I also had to bear in mind that any new tenants, whom presumably we wouldn't know, might object to me, or anyone else, living there unofficially.

While this, in turn, might enable me to gain a back-door entry into the house in Farnham (on the grounds that I had nowhere else to go) I decided to keep my options open and went through the motions of completing an application form, submitting it to the housing association and then waiting to see what happened.

The one positive note to an extremely-cold first month of the year was the newly-arrived typewriter, which I used to send off a raft of speculative letters to weekly newspapers, concentrating on those in London and the surrounding counties as, firstly, I didn't want to be too far away from Naomi if possible and, secondly, these locations would be cheaper and easier to get to if I was called to interviews. The early replies – no vacancies at present, but we'll keep your name on record – were not entirely unexpected. It was simply a case of keeping at it until I got a break.

Following a week without employment, Reeds sent me to the North London Waste Authority for general clerical work which was somewhat tedious but less than difficult. A plus point was that their office was only a 10-minute walk from the flat, which meant no fares or rush-hour traffic worries, and they were expected to need someone until the end of the financial year, which was two-and-a-half months away and meant a considerable period of guaranteed temporary employment while I stepped up my bid to re-enter journalism.

I went down to Farnham for the third weekend in January and went straight to work from Waterloo on the Monday before going back to the flat in the evening. There I was greeted by a disconsolate and even-drunker-than-usual Mark Hardy who looked up and said: 'Those two bloody dykes. The housing association have let them move in.'

I had to stop and think, for a moment, what he was talking about. Then I recalled, one evening the previous week, he had told me of two overt lesbians calling after being sent by the housing association to view the vacant rooms. However he also assured me that he had done more than enough to 'put them off' (not a difficult task, I thought, given the state of the flat) and that they would 'definitely' not be moving in. Famous last words indeed.

He did add that, since our new neighbours as such had moved in on the Saturday, they had kept a low profile and steered clear of the living room, where I slept, confining themselves to their bedrooms other than when using the kitchen or bathroom.

So while there did not seem to be any immediate pressure on me to move out, needless to say it was an unwelcome situation and had I followed my instincts, I would have contacted Naomi the next day regarding an overdue move to Surrey. Had the flat's new arrivals turned up a week earlier, that's almost certainly what I would have done but because I now had reasonably well-paid work lined up for several weeks I, fatefully, held fire and adopted a wait-and-see approach.

The answer was that nothing happened. The pattern set that first weekend by 'Van and Dyke', as the deviant pair were soon nicknamed, continued as apart from the occasional 'hello' on the stairs, they continued to ignore us and the living room. A co-existence of 'we won't bother you if you don't bother us' was soon established.

As winter moved towards spring, and the new 'arrangement' at the flat continued hand-in-hand with my work at the waste authority, for a while I largely forgot about the house in Farnham, other than when I visited every second or third weekend, as by now I had reluctantly accepted that I was never going to be invited to live there – not least as, by this stage, the three reporters' six-month contract, which was not renewable, would be up in a few weeks anyway and Naomi and her co-habitants were unsure of where they would living thereafter.

In March, after weeks of sending off speculative letters to weekly newspapers, I was finally invited for an interview at The Malvern Gazette in Worcestershire which, ironically, was one of the furthest-from-London titles I had written to.

My inevitable panning of Rea at the rendezvous did not backfire as the female Editor (still quite a rarity in those days) informed me she had reason to speak to the miscreant after taking on Andrew Anderson, who was now employed at another title in her group, the previous year.

'On the basis of that experience I can certainly sympathise with some of the things you've told me today,' she said, adding, however, that she had advertised the vacancy and had other people to see.

I felt that the day had gone well and although, after a wait of 10 days, I finally heard that I had not got the job, the experience, after more than six months out of journalism, had lifted my spirits and I saw it as simply the first step back on the road. Unfortunately Naomi did not see things quite that way.

I travelled down to Farnham, during the first weekend in April, to be greeted by a tearful rant, claiming I had 'blown' my career by leaving the Isle of Wight in the way I had and she doubted whether I would ever get back in.

Naomi's lot, at The Aldershot News, was still far from a happy one and her premise seemed to be that because she was sticking out an unpleasant situation, so I should have done. However the outburst seemed something of an over-reaction simply because I hadn't been offered a job after attending a single interview. Had it been the fifth or sixth such occurrence since the start of the year she might have had more of a point.

When the criticism extended to my personal circumstances, with a comment about 'sharing a run-down flat with an alcoholic and two lesbians', I would have replied 'well you know what the alternative could have been' had I not already been informed, before the rant started, that Naomi and her colleagues were leaving Ridgway Road, where the house in Farnham was situated, at the end of the month and were currently viewing potential replacements.

Naomi's description of Mark Hardy was, by now, almost becoming charitable. While I had always known, from our days at the poly, that he was a heavy drinker – as indeed was I and most of my male friends at Middlesex – it was only after going to stay at Hereford House that I realized the full extent of his alcoholism. However since he had split up with Mary, the word 'chronic' could accurately be added to his condition.

By now he was regularly starting to drink at eight or nine in the morning, managing to maintain his lifestyle with the aid of two credit cards. In those times it was unusual for these to be issued to anyone who didn't have a reasonably well-paid, full-time job, but he somehow managed to obtain one while a student and later added a second by lying about his personal circumstances.

The work at the waste authority ended, as expected, in early April and although Reeds sent me next to the x-ray department at a hospital in South Tottenham, this was only for a week's employment and the agency then said they had nothing else to offer me for the time being. Finding myself out of work coincided with Mark Hardy, in a drunken fit of pique one night, smashing up most of the living room in the flat (fortunately there was nothing of value to destroy). I then decided that enough was enough.

I received word from Naomi that she, Jo Petherbridge and David Thompson had found another rented house in Farnham, about a mile from Ridgway Road towards the outlying village of Wrecclesham. They moved in during the second half of April and I was due to pay my first visit there during the early May bank holiday weekend.

My plan was simple: I would tell Naomi that I simply could not continue living at Hereford House and either I was moving to Farnham or returning to Cornwall to continue my job-hunting from there. The geographical implications of the latter would, I hoped, prompt my partner into opting for the former, but then something happened, out of the blue, that enabled me to put such an ultimatum on hold.

A general election was called for the second week in June and I received a message, from Stuart Owens, that Nick Harvey wanted me to get in touch.

Nick, a former students' union president and close political ally of mine from our days at Middlesex, was standing as the Liberal Alliance candidate in the North London constituency of Enfield-Southgate and wanted me to help with the campaign, in particular with the writing of leaflets and press releases.

He was standing against none other than Michael Portillo, the prominent Conservative cabinet minister, and Nick explained to me, off the record, that he had no chance of winning the seat; his realistic aim being to push Labour into third place, which would be an excellent result for the party in London and one which should secure him a winnable seat at the next election.

This development was swiftly followed by my finding new temporary employment, through an advert in The London Daily News, as a computer imputer with British Telecom in central London. Suddenly I found myself very busy, daytime and evening, and put to one side my plans to leave the capital.

During my inaugural visit to Naomi's new house I did not, therefore, give the 'Farnham or Cornwall' choice I had originally intended, but instead explained that because of the election and the work at BT, which was expected to last until the end of June, I would be extremely busy for the next few weeks, but once these events were over, I was fully prepared to move to Surrey.

The new Porter residence, although pleasant enough, didn't quite have the appeal of Ridgway Road as it lay a good two miles from the centre of Farnham and was not therefore easily accessible for a non-driver such as myself. Moreover relations between both Jo Petherbridge and David Thompson and myself had cooled since Christmas, in tandem with my relationship with Naomi deteriorating, and I now had some doubts whether they would agree to me moving in (something that certainly wouldn't have been a problem a few months earlier when the initial tenancy commenced).

I therefore suggested to Naomi that an alternative could be just the two of us getting a flat together in or near the town. I had no idea how I would afford such a venture, but I wanted to see what her reaction would be. She replied that such a move might lead to friction with her two colleagues, but added that she would think over the situation.

It seemed as if both of us were making a determined effort to save our two-and-a-half year liaison, but then, a fortnight later, came a totally-avoidable incident when Naomi, out of sheer bloody-mindedness, attempted to arrange a Saturday afternoon out in Guildford (the nearest major shopping centre to Farnham) when she knew I already had plans to watch the FA Cup final, between Tottenham and Coventry City, in London that day.

Although Naomi was no football fan, she was fully aware of the occasion's significance to me. My attempted compromise – to go to Guildford the following Bank Holiday weekend when I would be able to stay in Surrey longer – fell upon deaf ears and she then compounded the problem by travelling to Guildford alone on cup final day, knowing I wouldn't be there, and then falsely telling her housemates, and other work colleagues, that I had 'stood her up'.

A heated exchange of letters followed in which we both said things we probably shouldn't have. Had I not been so busy, I'm sure I would have taken steps to resolve the situation sooner, but with the full-time work at BT continuing and the election campaign gathering momentum, it was not until three weeks after the cup final, on Sunday June 7, that we agreed to meet, on sort of neutral territory, at Waterloo station.

I had prepared myself for the possibility that things might have gone beyond the point of no return, but once we had adjourned to a nearby pub, which thankfully was very quiet, and spoken for an hour or so, it became clear that neither of us wanted the relationship to end permanently: what seemed to emerge, as the meeting progressed, was a choice between soldiering on or separating, as opposed to splitting up, for a limited period while both of us, and obviously me in particular, sorted our professional futures out.

The former was effectively ruled out when Naomi again rebuffed any suggestion that I move to Farnham, saying that, by this stage, she knew her housemates would veto my moving into the new house, while it wouldn't be fair on them for her to move out and share a flat with me – and, in any case, what guarantee was there that I could afford the high rents that were the norm in the Surrey town?

She did acknowledge that I should have been invited into Ridgway Road from the outset, but at the time she 'didn't think I wanted to' and 'wasn't sure whether I was being serious' when I suggested applying for the vacancy at the bookmakers in Farnham. In any case, it was too late to do anything about that now, she added.

And so we agreed to a maximum six-month separation. This would enable me to make an all-out attempt to re-enter journalism, but with two major tactical differences to my approach. To date I had followed the principle of writing speculative letters to papers as this was the way we had been told to do it in Preston. However Martin Creasey had suggested, when I last saw him a month or so earlier, that instead I should apply for specific vacancies listed in the UK Press Gazette, journalism's trade paper.

Although most of these openings were for senior and editorial management roles, which I would stand no chance of getting, there was, I had been told, an increasing tendency to advertise junior positions in this publication.

The second variation to my approach would be an end to any geographical limits to where I applied. Naomi had already decided that she was leaving The Aldershot News at the earliest opportunity once her indentures expired at the end of the year and the plan of action, loosely co-ordinated that day, was assuming I found a job within the allotted six-month period, she would attempt to find employment in the same part of the country (in effect a re-launching of our strategy agreed in Preston).

We concurred that, whatever happened, we would meet again, no later than December, to review progress and decide, depending on our geographical proximity and how we both felt after a period apart, whether the relationship would resume.

As we parted company that day my emotions were a mixture of sadness, that things had come to this, and relief that we had pulled back from the brink of splitting up permanently and there was still a good chance of salvaging the relationship.

A couple of days later Mark Hardy informed me that Van and Dyke were leaving the Edmonton flat and this solved the dilemma of where I based myself for the new job-seeking assault. While a return to Cornwall would have guaranteed use of a telephone and a day-to-day environment more conducive to seeking employment than Hereford House, being based in the far South West would mean increased travel costs, and probable overnight stays, when travelling to interviews. I was also aware that many Editors, if in receipt of several applications from similarly-qualified candidates, chose to interview those who had least far to travel.

The one positive thing about Hereford House was that it was in London – from where it was possible to complete a round trip to almost anywhere in England in one day – so, having been on the housing association's waiting list for several months, I again applied and this time they said I could move in (to a flat where I had been living unofficially for the past 11 months) once the two bedrooms became vacant.

The general election duly took place five days after I saw Naomi at Waterloo and Nick Harvey achieved his hoped-for second place in Enfield-Southgate in a poll that, nationally, saw Margaret Thatcher comfortably returned for a third term of office.

My work with BT ended, as scheduled, a couple of weeks later on the final Friday in June, although I was told to stay in touch with the agency as more of the same might be available in a few weeks' time.

I took the following week off to go down to Cornwall for the first time since Christmas, ensuring that I placed an order for the UK Press Gazette at an Edmonton newsagents (the publication could only be obtained in that way; individual copies could not be bought 'off the shelf') before departing to reflect on what had been a frantic and strange past few weeks.

After a good holiday in Cornwall (a little too good in terms of money spent) I returned to a much-quieter Hereford House, with just two of us now in residence and a third room vacant, to begin my quest to re-enter my chosen profession and, hopefully, salvage the relationship with Naomi.

While the first purchased edition of the UK Press Gazette contained no job vacancies I would have stood any chance of getting, I accepted this would the case some weeks. Of more immediate concern was the lack of temporary work available, either through Reeds or the agency that supplied the BT employment.

Most of the money that remained from that venture had gone on my first month's rent as an official resident of the flat. Subsequently I was almost broke by the second week back in London and was forced to 'sign on' for the first time in 10 months. Given my changed circumstances I would now be entitled to both housing and unemployment benefits, but it would, as always in these cases, take time for any money to come through.

While Mark Hardy and myself had never been in the position to lend large sums of money to each other, we regularly did so with relatively small amounts as we both tended to have short-term cash-flow problems while awaiting payments that were due.

It should therefore have been a matter of routine when, that second week back, I asked to borrow an unsubstantial amount to buy the next edition of The UK Press Gazette and fulfil other basic needs.

'Elaine says I'm no longer allowed to lend you any money or to borrow any,' he replied. Such had been the number of women he had drunkenly brought back to the flat, usually for one night only, since splitting up with Mary that I had to stop and think who Elaine actually was. I then recalled having been introduced to her in a pub during June: the two of them had met at the Jobclub and she was now working as a window-dresser for Boots.

It seemed that while I had been preoccupied with the full-time employment at BT, the Naomi situation, the General Election and then the break in Cornwall, what I had considered to be a liaison of little significance had developed into something more serious.

I nevertheless failed to see how, at such an infant stage of the 'relationship', his new girlfriend could dictate what happened on a minor, day-to-day basis at a flat she had not, to my knowledge, even yet visited, but it became increasingly clear, as the next few weeks passed, that he was becoming more and more under the influence of a partner who bore a striking resemblance to a young Barbara Windsor, without the cleavage, and whose drawly Essex accent added weight to the comparison.

The most astonishing development was her forcing him to look for a job and after several unsuccessful applications – not surprisingly given he had spent the previous 18 months doing nothing – my flatmate was offered employment at an Edmonton estate agents (this, I recall, was something of a boom industry at the time and there were numerous vacancies to be filled) and he began work in early September.

There had, meanwhile, been no improvement in my situation. I had begun receiving unemployment benefit, but the housing benefit office had cocked up my application and I already had rent arrears as I waited for them to sort it out.

There had also been relatively few suitable vacancies advertised in the UK Press Gazette - those that were all seemed to be in the north and I wasn't invited to any interviews – and despite being in regular contact with the employment agencies, no further offers of work were forthcoming.

While, at first, I toyed with the admittedly-fanciful notion that Mark Hardy's changed circumstances were indicative of him finally having turned over a new leaf, after a few weeks it became increasingly obvious that this was anything but the case.

After a reasonably-enthusiastic start at the estate agents, the novelty soon evaporated and he regularly started going in late. A week's feigned illness was, unfortunately for him, followed by genuine sickness which meant he was absent from the office for two out of three weeks while still on a probationary period. It also became clear that the unsuspecting Elaine was being kept in the dark not only on many of these work matters, but also of his drinking in pubs (something he had been given strict orders not to do) and sometimes entertaining other females on nights when the two of them were not scheduled to meet.

Despite this disloyalty to his supposed girlfriend, he still maintained that it was on her instructions that he was unable to lend me money, but by now I had serious doubts. He had always resented Naomi's dislike of him and her refusal to stay at Hereford House when she visited London. Moreover he knew how vital it was that I found a journalistic job during our allotted six-month separation. His real motive, it was becoming increasingly clear, was to obstruct and hinder my efforts, out of some peculiar sense of 'revenge', while simultaneously deluding himself that he had turned his own life around.

Although that autumn I did obtain an interview at a weekly paper in Eastbourne – a non-descript affair, like the one in Abingdon two years earlier, that never really got off the ground – thereafter I cancelled the UK Press Gazette as my financial situation had become so bad I knew that, until there was an improvement, I wouldn't be able to travel to any more interviews outside of London. Although my application for housing benefit had eventually been sorted out, by then my rent arrears were such that the lump sum I was owed, and subsequent fortnightly payments, were sent directly to the housing association.

Then I was set to start a significant period of temporary clerical work, through Reeds, only for the project to suddenly be cancelled as a result of the Black Monday stock market collapse. Nothing, it seemed, could go right.

I had already decided to return to Cornwall at Christmas, to try and reignite my career from there, when I finally received an offer of temporary work – at a photographic processing company on Enfield Highway. The job was scheduled to last for a month from mid-December and after the first week went well, I decided to stay for the entire period and postpone my return to

Cornwall, other than for a few days at Yuletide, until late January.

I had not, as arranged, contacted Naomi in early December as there was absolutely nothing positive to report, but neither did she get in touch with me. I nominally sent her a Christmas card, keeping the message inside vague and saying I would 'be in touch again soon'.

For some reason she did not send a card to my family home in Cornwall – which, her being unsure of my exact whereabouts, I thought would have been the safest option – but strangely opted to post her festive communication to Hereford House which I didn't receive until returning to London at the end of December.

It was then that I learnt of her departure from The Aldershot News a few days before Christmas and that she would be starting work as a district reporter with the Eastern Daily Press, in Norfolk, from early January.

Naomi made no reference to the reconvening of our relationship, neither hinting that it was or wasn't still on the cards, so there was nothing to be devastated about in that respect. However news of the Norfolk move meant that if there was any meaningful possibility of us getting back together, I would have to concentrate my job-seeking efforts on East Anglia, which wasn't really an option as, after being out of journalism for 18 months by now, I wasn't in a position to be geographically fussy.

If only, I thought, the flat's resident alcoholic (who was drinking as much as ever outside of working hours) hadn't deliberately obstructed my job-seeking those past six months, I might have found employment first and Naomi, who was in a position to be more selective about her next move, might well have followed me to the same region. Now the chance of that had gone for good.

Mark Hardy's estate agent bosses had extended his probationary period, shortly before Christmas, with a clear warning that his absenteeism record and general time-keeping had to improve. My last clear visual memory of him is one morning, about a week before I left London, when I entered the living room at about 10am. My soon-to-be-ex-flatmate was sitting in a chair eating cooked breakfast and when I inquired why he wasn't at work, where he should have been an hour earlier, he replied: 'I decided to have some breakfast first'.

He had been talking, in the preceding weeks, about 'wanting to settle down with Elaine', but how could this be compatible with staying on the inevitable road to dismissal from his job? As I said to him that morning: 'The only thing you're going to be settling down with soon is an unemployment benefit giro'.

And so, in late January, I returned to Cornwall, from where I knew I would have little chance of finding a job in the northern half of the country, but where at least I would have guaranteed access to the UK Press Gazette, a telephone and, if necessary, money to borrow for train fares to interviews. To be perfectly honest, the relief I felt when leaving the grimy Hereford House was as great as when I departed the Isle of Wight a-year-and-a-half earlier.

If you have found the past two chapters as depressing to read as I did to write, I will say only this: while this story has more than 30 years to run, is barely off the ground in terms of my career, contains many more twists and turns, ups and downs and strokes of both good luck and misfortune, never again would my life sink to the depths of those two dreadful years of 1986 and, in particular, 1987.

6 Seaside salvation

Stephen A Rea, the Ridgway Road fiasco and Boy Breakfast (aka Mark Hardy) notwithstanding, I knew from the outset that 1988 was going to be a make-or-break year and that if I didn't put things right, and quickly, my thoughts wouldn't be revolving around saving my career, but whether I still had a career to save.

Despite the obstacles and distractions of the past 18 months, the fact remained that I had attended just three interviews at newspaper offices during that period with one of those, at The Enfield Advertiser, occurring the same week as I left the Isle of Wight. Such a return, whatever the difficulty of my circumstances, was simply not good enough.

Curiously, I felt a strange sense of optimism about the future from the day I arrived in Cornwall in late January. I had never lacked confidence in my own professional ability and clung to the memories of how highly-thought-of I had been by Alan McKenzie, Mike Starke and generally by those at The Western Morning News – albeit that these positive points were now between two and three years old. Surely though, I told myself, things would be different now that the shackles were off and I could apply for jobs without restriction.

Before I had been back a week I was asked to attend an interview at The Sunday Independent, a regional title based in Plymouth. Their advertisement, in the paper itself rather than in The UK Press Gazette, had been spotted by my mother who sent a copy to me in London, from where I applied shortly before leaving, but giving my Truro address, which explains why I heard from them so quickly after my return.

While I had no intention of toning down my opinions on the Rea regime at the County Press, I knew that at this, and any subsequent interviews, I would have to explain why it had taken me so long to return to journalism. I decided to emphasize that personal circumstance (ie my relationship with Naomi) had prevented me from applying anywhere outside of London and the surrounding counties. While this was not entirely true during the second half of 1987, I could hardly say that I was virtually imprisoned in a squalid flat, without use of a telephone or guaranteed access to The UK Press Gazette, by a delusional and workshy alcoholic.

The interview at The Sunday Independent went reasonably well but I gained the feeling that the paper's unashamedly down-market tabloid style, with the emphasis on exclusive off-diary stories, was such a contrast to the County Press's straight-laced community format, and initials instead of Christian names, that the Editor believed I would find it difficult to make the admittedly-enormous transition. I disagreed, but at this stage of my career didn't have enough experience to be able to claim versatility as one of my strong points.

I had heard nothing further from the Plymouth title when, just a few days later, I was invited to travel up for an interview at The Leamington Courier, a weekly in Warwickshire. This was the first vacancy from The UK Press Gazette I had applied for and was only able to make the long journey to the south Midlands with a loan from my mother. This, of course, was the whole point of my being back in Cornwall: while at Hereford House, particularly during the final six months, I would probably have found myself in the ludicrous position of having to postpone or cancel such an appointment as I couldn't afford to travel there.

Again I was happy with the way I performed. A youngish Editor seemed quite sympathetic to my predicament on the Isle of Wight, pointing out that he didn't have the staff numbers to discriminate between senior and junior reporters in terms of what they were allowed to cover and, if taken on, I could expect to do a bit of everything.

What money I had saved from my temporary Christmas work at the photographic company had by now gone and my only source of income was coming from daffodil picking, something I had previously undertaken during Easter holidays while a student. It was no questions asked, cash-in-hand on a daily basis and, of course, there was no problem about taking a day off for an interview.

Two days after Leamington Spa, I returned from a day in the fields to find a message from my youngest sister, who still lived home, asking me to phone a David Banks at The Dawlish Gazette in Devon. They had advertised in The UK Press Gazette the previous week and after duly responding to the message I was on the road again the following Monday. I had been back in Cornwall just three weeks and couldn't believe the speed at which things were moving.

Although the advertisement clearly stated that the vacancy was in Dawlish, the interview was to be held in nearby Teignmouth, at the office of the company's free newspaper, as this was where David Banks – whom I assumed to be the Editor, although he hadn't specified his title when I spoke to him – was based. I had never set foot in either town, but was familiar with travelling through the area as each resort had a station on the Paddington to Penzance railway line. Dawlish, in particular, stuck in my mind as the trains ran alongside the beach.

David Banks was accompanied at the interview by News Editor Cedric Clough. They explained that their Chief Reporter was leaving to have a child the following month and would not be coming back. Since advertising for a replacement, the Dawlish office's other reporter had given a month's notice to join The Sunday Independent (so now I knew who had got that job) at the end of March, so they were now looking to fill two positions.

Cedric Clough asked most of the questions about my NCTJ training and what had gone wrong on the Isle of Wight, while David Banks – a softly-spoken, middle-aged individual who sounded much more like a businessman than a journalist – asked what I had been doing during the intervening 18 months and then moved onto some detailed questioning on my time as full-time Editor of the students' union newspaper at Middlesex Poly.

This somewhat surprised me as, while that experience had undoubtedly helped me get a place on the course at Preston, it had barely warranted a mention at any interview since as most editors didn't count it as 'real journalism'.

After asking about my dealing with printers and advertisers – and inquiring what it was like having permanent union staff members, most of whom were considerably older than me, working under me those two years – David Banks then moved on to my political standings – again something never remotely discussed at any previous interview – saying that he 'didn't want any trouble-makers setting up a NUJ (National Union of Journalists) branch'.

I replied that I wasn't a member of any national political party and that the broad-based anti-communist alliance I had been a member of at Middlesex had, in terms of student politics, been considered right-wing, although few of those involved would have been described as such in the outside world, particularly in the South West.

He seemed satisfied with my answer and, as the interview drew to a close, asked me if I would be interested, if appointed, in moving into the vacant flat above the office in which we were speaking. I was shown around the accommodation before leaving and certainly felt this was a good sign as why would he have bothered even mentioning the flat unless he was considering taking me on?

Three days later, as I returned home from flower picking, I could hear the phone ringing as I walked through the door. No-one else was in and I picked it up to be greeted by the voice of David Banks offering me the job. After a successful three-month trial period I would get the title of Chief Reporter and thereafter – in what was, it should be stressed, an extremely small set-up for a paid-for weekly paper – would be expected to deputise for Cedric Clough during holidays and illnesses.

'Far from being stopped from doing things as you were on the Isle of Wight, here we want someone who is ready to take responsibility and hold the fort,' he said.

I also agreed to take up residence in the basically-furnished flat, for although its décor was only marginally better than that at Hereford House, I couldn't afford to pay a large deposit anywhere else prior to starting the job and not having to seek accommodation would mean one less thing to think about in the run-up to the beginning of my new employment.

So not only had I managed to achieve in three-and-a-half weeks what I had never coming seriously close to doing in 18 months in London, but I would be getting a senior job into the bargain – although David Banks had added that I would only be paid at the rate for a second-year junior reporter until my probationary period was completed.

There was to be a three-week gap between my appointment and starting work and once the euphoria at the sudden upturn in my life began to level off into anticipation of the new challenge ahead, I began to ask myself how I managed to re-enter journalism so quickly once returning to Cornwall after such a long period of frustration when, for reasons already given, I was never really able to get a sustained job-hunting campaign going.

Undoubtedly there had been an advantage in applying at the time of the year I did. Most of the previous year's NCTJ intake would have fixed up with jobs by the autumn and there was less competition around in January and February (paradoxically, had I moved to Ridgway Road when I should have done, I could have taken advantage of this same situation 12 months earlier).

Otherwise it was simply a case, as anticipated before leaving London, of being in a day-to-day environment conducive to seeking employment with a telephone, no worries about access to The UK Press Gazette or having the money to get to interviews and none of the laziness, aimlessness, habitual drunkenness and general negativity that characterised Hereford House and its residents.

The irony of ironies came a week or so after I had formally accepted David Banks' offer when I was phoned and asked if I was still interested in a position at The Leamington Courier. It was nearly three weeks since the interview there, so I think I must have been the Editor's second-preference candidate and the first choice had pulled out. What would have seemed unimaginable two months earlier – me turning down a job because I already had one – had suddenly become reality.

Despite my largely negative memories of The Isle of Wight County Press, there had been some minor plusses – I gained some limited experience of council reporting and learnt a few things from some of the more experienced journalists such as Mike Starke – and I have never wiped the period from the record. Although Rea was one of the last relics of a dying breed of old-school tyrannical editors (at provincial level at least) I nevertheless considered my time there, like my much-shorter unhappy time with The Burnley Express, as part of a learning curve.

I wrote to Naomi giving news of the Dawlish development and while her reply expressed relief that I had finally been able to re-launch my career, she was still very much 'sitting on the fence' regarding what the future held for us.

I suppose this was understandable as, what with us both embarking on new ventures some 300 miles apart, there was now little chance of reviving the relationship for probably the next two years – and at least one of us could easily meet someone else during such a relatively-long period.

Those appalling last few months of 1987 had killed dead any hope of a short-term reunion, as we had originally hoped and planned, and all I could really do now was get on with my new job, maintain some sort of contact with Naomi and just see what happened.

I travelled up to Teignmouth, to take up residence in the company flat, on the second Friday in March ahead of starting work at the Dawlish office on the Monday. I developed a heavy cold that day and although that made me feel uncomfortable as I arrived, I saw this as possibly a lucky omen as my last successful journalistic experience, at The Western Mornings News three years earlier, had, if you remember, also begun with my suffering from such an ailment.

David Banks wasn't around and I collected the keys from the firm's advertising manager Pat Betts and later that afternoon met Belinda New, the reporter leaving to join The Sunday Independent, who that week had been covering for Karen Martin, the Teignmouth office reporter who was on holiday.

Friday afternoons in weekly newspaper offices are generally very quiet and I had quite a lengthy conversation with Pat Betts – a 40-something female based in Teignmouth who didn't, I soon realized, mince her words – in which I gleaned some interesting information about Dawlish Newspapers, the official name of the company.

It transpired that my first instincts about David Banks were correct: he wasn't, and never had been, a journalist. He was a printer by trade and his company had brought out The Dawlish Gazette until he purchased the independent paper a few years earlier.

The printing firm had since gone bust and his sole business interest was now Dawlish Newspapers, where his self-styled title of Managing Editor was confusing for, as

Pat Betts informed me, he rarely involved himself in editorial content of either The Gazette or The Teignmouth News, the company's free paper which he had founded, and in reality was the general manager or managing director who ran the company's finances.

The day-to-day boss, she added, was Cedric Clough, of whom she was less than complimentary, saying – somewhat surprisingly considering we had only just met and she wasn't a journalist herself – that I 'wouldn't have much to follow' if I was to deputise for him in the months ahead.

My cold had largely subsided by the next day when I had a good look around Teignmouth and then walked over to Dawlish, two-and-a-half miles away, on the Sunday. Both were medium-sized resorts which, I assumed, would become considerably livelier in the summer months than they seemed at present.

So, I thought to myself before setting off for my first day in my new job, I won't be deputising for the news editor, as I had been led to believe at the interview, but for the Editor. And all this following nearly a year at a weekly paper where I wasn't allowed to cover court or district council followed by 18 months out of journalism completely.

Now all I had to do was to make sure I came up with the goods.

7 Back in the groove

The first thing that struck me about The Dawlish Gazette office was how incredibly small it was compared to the premises of the three newspaper offices where I had previously worked and, indeed, those I had visited for interviews.

I entered the front door to find a reception desk separated from a small, three-desk newsroom only by a seven-foot-high partition. An open doorway led to another tiny room used by up to three typesetters and behind that lay a narrow strip where the Production Manager pasted up both The Gazette and The Teignmouth News. Outside his window was a little courtyard with a single toilet cubicle for use by all staff of both sexes.

'Well, this is very compact,' I said to Cedric Clough as we were reacquainted.

'Aye, it's certainly a lot smaller than anywhere I've worked before, but you get used to it,' he replied, adding that there was another very small room, separate from the main building, at the back of the courtyard which was used on Fridays by a part-time advertising sales rep.

My new Editor was, like Rea, a northerner who spoke in a slow and deliberate manner, but there the similarities between the two ended. Cedric, as I had observed at the interview, was awkward, at times a little nervous and often stuttered. I learnt, later that week, that he was 52, but he could easily have passed for being 10 years older and, from the outset, it was clear that he was terrified of doing anything to upset David Banks.

That opening morning started fairly quietly. At first it was just Cedric and I in the newsroom. An hour later we were joined by Joss Laver, the outgoing Chief Reporter with whom I would be overlapping for just a fortnight.

Belinda New was taking a week's holiday owed before her own departure in three weeks' time. The only other people in the building were a receptionist, Production Manager Chris Russell and two typesetters.

After a couple of press release rewrites, my first main story was an update on the town council's campaign to get Dawlish a traffic warden. Cedric nodded in approval as he read each of my submissions with no suggestion that I should have done anything differently. I was also pleased that, after 18 months or so out of the game, there was no rustiness on my part.

What had been an unruffled and controlled atmosphere changed in the early afternoon when a loud and scruffy middle-aged man suddenly appeared at Cedric's desk and was excitably telling him about something that had supposedly happened in Dawlish. I didn't take a lot of notice at first and only really started to listen when the Editor said 'perhaps Carl could go down with you and take a look'.

'So you're the new reporter,' the newcomer said. 'I'm Colin Wallace, the photographer here. Got a good story – The Royal's not opened today and the rumour is the owner has gone bankrupt. Wanna go down and see if we can find anything out?'

I accompanied my new colleague, who smelt strongly of drink, in his car, which reeked of fish, on the short journey down to The Royal Hotel, a building which had obviously seen better times, next to the town's railway station. I soon gathered that the establishment, despite its name, had operated solely as a pub in recent years. It was locked up, with no-one seemingly inside, and Colin Wallace suggested that the landlord, a Mike Bailey, might be found at a nearby amusement arcade he owned, but he was not there and a staff member said he had no idea where his boss was.

After returning to the office I discovered that Mr Bailey's home phone number was ex-directory. However I did manage to ascertain that he leased The Royal Hotel from a brewery, whose regional office in Bristol I rang only to be given a firm 'no comment'. Two days later the pub was still closed and empty and the owner still could not be contacted, so we ran the story along the lines of 'what's going on at The Royal?'

On the way back to the office that first afternoon, Colin Wallace said to me: 'The first thing you've got to learn about this place is that 9-2-5 is a joke. Just down here on a semi-retirement basis – knows nothing about news.'

'Sorry, who exactly is 9-2-5?'

'Cedric, who do you think. Called that because he thinks it's a 9 to 5 job – never works evenings or weekends.'

I also learnt that Colin was not a Gazette staff photographer – I would have been surprised if the company could have afforded such a luxury given the shortage of employees generally – but a freelance based at our office who also supplied pictures to The Herald Express and The Express & Echo, the evenings papers for Torbay and Exeter respectively.

His usual daily routine was to make an early morning run to those papers' offices, where photos would be required in good time for their lunchtime deadlines, before retiring to The Prince of Wales pub in Dawlish from opening time until afternoon closing at 2.30pm. He then spent the afternoons in The Gazette office, unless there was a job to rush off to, until his 'local' reopened at 5pm (all-day 11 to 11 pub opening was set to be introduced in England and Wales a few months later).

My first week at The Gazette office continued satisfactorily and although I contributed a significant number of stories, at no time did I feel under pressure – although I was aware that could change in a couple of weeks' time as no replacement had yet been found for

Belinda New and, as it stood, the editorial department would temporarily consist of Cedric and myself along with Karen Martin in the Teignmouth office.

First thing each Friday morning David Banks, Cedric, Pat Betts and Chris Russell held a meeting in the former's office where they discussed how the past week had gone and looked ahead to the next edition. Thereafter our Managing Director would make up the weekly wage packets and bring them over to Dawlish, his only regular visit to our office, for distribution shortly before lunchtime.

I had obviously figured in the discussions at that first Friday's gathering as, when David Banks handed me my pay, he asked if I was happy with the move I had made and when I replied in the affirmative, nodded and muttered 'good, good, good'.

The following Monday morning, with Belinda New back and therefore with the rare luxury of three reporters at the Dawlish office for just one week, I accompanied Joss Laver to her final meeting of Teignbridge District Council at its headquarters in Newton Abbot, a 10 to 15 minute train journey away. As Chief Reporter it would be one of my duties to cover the council's weekly meetings once we were fully staffed and I went along that day really just to familiarise myself with where to go, although I was briefly introduced to the council's three Dawlish members after proceedings had ended.

We returned to the office that lunchtime to learn that, at The Prince of Wales the previous night, Colin Wallace had been beaten up by Mike Bailey who had taken umbrage, I was told, not at what had been written about him in The Gazette, but The Herald Express, whom Colin had also tipped off about The Royal's closure and whose account had been penned by their Teignmouth-based reporter John Ware.

It seemed strange to me that Bailey – whom I learnt was something of a notorious local character – should vent his anger against someone who, at the end of the day, had only supplied pictures of the closed pub, but I gathered, from Belinda New, that there was a little bit more to it than that with a history of bad feeling between him and Colin.

Nevertheless I couldn't help wonder might have happened had Bailey been at his amusement arcade when I accompanied Colin there a week earlier. My first day in Dawlish could have been a really explosive one.

As March ended and April began, with Joss Laver and Belinda New departed, it was indeed Cedric and me holding the fort, although Teignbridge meetings were covered by Val Gale, a retired Gazette reporter who still helped out during holidays, until a new trainee reporter for the Dawlish office was found.

It was hard work – I was certainly doing well in excess of the 37-and-a-half hours we were supposed to complete each week – but I was enjoying it, taking over the sports pages in addition to my news reporting which included several front-page exclusives, most notably the proposed closure of The Rockstone hotel, one of the town's landmark buildings which the owner wanted to shut down and redevelop as sheltered flats (a popular trend in resorts at the time).

I also helped two parent-governors from Dawlish Infants' School launch a campaign, through The Gazette, to replace the crumbling 100-year-old building in which the seat of early learning was housed.

Adding to my upbeat mood was the hardly-surprising but appropriately-timed news that Boy Breakfast had duly been dismissed from his estate agents' job. I had reason to call his work number – I think it was something to do with my share of the previous quarter's electricity bill – and was told he no longer worked there and I would 'probably find him at home waiting to be repositioned'.

Nowadays such jargonised claptrap – as a diplomatic round-about way of saying someone had been sacked –

probably wouldn't raise too many eyebrows, but in early 1988 it sounded peculiar and I found myself asking the young man on the phone what he was actually saying in everyday English.

Perhaps this was my first experience of Americanisms in the workplace, but claptrap or not, it was still a richly-deserved fate for the most shameless workshy I have ever met, and while we had once been friends I now had nothing but contempt for him after the way he had deliberately obstructed my attempts to salvage the relationship with Naomi.

As is often the case in life, as one friendship ended another was beginning. The liaison between Colin Wallace and myself was a strange one: he was well over 20 years older than me, I was already aware of his reputation as a stirrer and someone partial to exaggeration (especially when drunk) and his negative professional opinion of Cedric could easily have led, unless I was extremely careful, to a clash of interests.

Colin was, however, well enough known around the town to be aware of everything that was going on and was a useful source of information providing you remembered to check out everything he told you. As our after-work visits to The Prince of Wales became more frequent, I learnt that, as a Londoner, he was a big Chelsea supporter and in addition to his work for The Gazette and the two evening papers, he was also the racecourse photographer at the Newton Abbot, Devon & Exeter and Taunton meetings.

Horse racing was a sport I had maintained an interest in since my student days working for William Hills, but I had never been to a meeting. So when he asked, in early May, whether I was interested in accompanying him, free of charge, to an evening fixture at Newton Abbot, I jumped at the chance and this venture was quickly followed by two after-work trips to Taunton as the National Hunt season drew to a close.

Colin knew one or two people connected to the stable of Martin Pipe, the Somerset-based champion trainer of the time, and the tips we received from this source enabled us to return from two of the three meetings well in profit.

My new friend and colleague was also a keen sea-fisherman – hence the smell in the car that had been so noticeable from the first day I met him – and he also asked if I wanted to go out with him in his boat one weekend. However this was one pastime that had never remotely interested me, so I politely declined.

Meanwhile, at the office, the time was drawing ever closer to my deputising for Cedric when he took a fortnight's holiday during the second half of June. There was still no new reporter in sight, although I was assured that Val Gale would help out as much as necessary during those two weeks.

Part of the pending challenge would be my lack of sub-editing experience. Although the publication I had edited at Middlesex Poly was constitutionally titled the students' union newspaper, its format had been that of a magazine, so although I was well-used to writing headlines, newspaper page design would be something completely new.

The truth was, however, that our Editor had no proper sub-editing training himself. The system in operation at Dawlish, probably unique to any paid-for weekly paper at the time, was that, after copy-subbing, Cedric simply wrote a headline at the top of each story and an instruction as to which page it should be placed. Then, after typesetting, it was left to Chris Russell to paste each page together and then indicate where gaps needed to be filled. In short there were no proper page plans.

This archaic state of affairs came about through David Banks' claim that he couldn't afford to employ a sub-editor in addition to Cedric, who was effectively the News Editor, and a Chief Reporter. The upshot was there was very little

Cedric could advise me about, on the production side, apart from guidance on headline point sizes.

Around two weeks before my turn at the top table, Karen Martin gave notice that she was leaving to go to The Express & Echo as a senior reporter. Although this would not affect the fortnight Cedric was away – those two weeks would, in fact, be her last with the company – David Banks now had to take urgent action to appoint trainee reporters and we heard that two juniors had been interviewed and would start work the Monday the Editor returned.

My first week in charge, though at times manic, went extremely well and we ended up going to print, on the Wednesday evening, an hour or so earlier than usual. Karen Martin, as I already knew, was a fast-working and competent reporter while Val Gale came in full-time during the first three days and her extensive knowledge of Dawlish and Teignmouth – where, you have to remember, I had still only been for three months – regularly came in useful. Colin – who, if the mood so took him, often dragged his heels with Cedric – co-operated fully and made sure I was never short of pictures.

'Well I think we better start off by congratulating Carl,' said David Banks at the Friday morning meeting which I attended in Cedric's absence. 'Excellent job done and finishing earlier than usual as well.'

Pat Betts – who, like Colin, consistently seemed to have it in for Cedric – muttered something along the lines of perhaps our Editor should extend his holiday by a few months, but David Banks ignored this comment and moved onto the next item on the agenda.

The second week went equally as smoothly and again we went to print early. One potential problem was not having an obvious page-one lead story for The Gazette, but Colin and I heard about some travellers, or hippies as they were sometimes still called, illegally camped on private land at Little Haldon on the outskirts of Dawlish.

We drove up there expecting a hostile reception, but the offered bribes of two bottles of cheap supermarket cider and a packet of cigarettes did the trick and the occupiers agreed to give us an interview and have their picture taken providing they only gave us their Christian names. The story not only made the front page of The Gazette, but was also the lead story on BBC Radio Devon's weekly review of the county's newspapers when my name was mentioned on air – something that was not only unexpected, but which sounded a little strange as I listened in.

The fortnight concluded with Karen Martin's leaving party in a private room at The South Devon Inn in Dawlish. An extremely enjoyable evening was had by all and at one point an admittedly-drunken Karen flung her arms around me and said I was 'the best thing that had ever happened to Dawlish Newspapers'.

Among the revellers were Cedric, seeming refreshed and relaxed after his two-week break and delighted at how well things had gone, and Julia Walsh, Karen's replacement from Merthyr Tydfil in Wales, who was introduced to everyone ahead of starting work on the Monday.

The one disappointment of my inaugural spell in charge had been the news that the second new trainee reporter, who I think was from Scotland, would not now be coming because of a serious illness in her family. It would therefore be a case of 'as we were' at the Dawlish office for the time being.

The shindig at The South Devon took place, I couldn't help but note, on July 1 – four years to the day after I left Middlesex Poly. That weekend I reflected on the ups and downs since 1984 and despite the exceptional start at Dawlish – Hereford House to Acting Editor in less than six months was no mean feat – I had to admit to myself that, certainly since leaving Preston, I had not achieved what I had anticipated professionally. There was also, of course, the unfortunate now-year-long separation from Naomi, with whom I was still sporadically in contact, but it remained unclear whether any reunion was realistically on the cards.

To look at my career, so far, in football terms, you could say I was someone, tipped for first division honours three years earlier, who was now captain of a fourth division team.

Fortunately, I thought to myself, journalism is a much longer vocation than football and although I seemed to be doing things the long way around, at least now I was firmly back on track.

8 All work and low pay

Although David Banks confirmed I was now officially Chief Reporter, by way of an internal memo on the final day of Cedric's absence, he then decided to pour cold water on everything that had been achieved during that heady final fortnight of June by refusing to move me onto senior pay until I had completed a year with the company.

'That's not what he said when I was appointed in March,' I said to Cedric, who had been tasked with giving me the news. 'He indicated then that if I proved myself capable of doing the Chief Reporter's job I would get a pay rise at the end of three months.'

'Aye, I know, but now he's saying that because you only did a year on the Isle of Wight, you have to do a year here before you can be considered a senior in terms of pay,' replied my weary-looking Editor who, I had learnt, received little more himself than a senior reporter would expect to be paid at most other weekly papers. 'I'm afraid there's nothing I can do. He's in charge when it comes to all money matters.'

This really was a case of David Banks having his cake and eating it: I was Chief Reporter in name and role but not when it came to salary. I must have been the only reporter in the country who was expected to stand in for the Editor (itself unusual enough) while technically still a junior.

During July I spent a couple of days each week in the Teignmouth office while Julia Walsh was with Cedric, in Dawlish, learning the workings of the company before taking over Karen Martin's role full-time. I didn't mind the change of scene for a limited period, albeit that I found it a little strange to be working in the same building as I lived, and I again picked up some interesting information from the unsubtle-as-ever Pat Betts, this time on the full circumstances surrounding my appointment five months earlier.

It transpired that another candidate – a woman in her late 20s who had previously been an Assistant Editor on a magazine in Hong Kong – had been offered the job on the spot, but had then burst out laughing when David Banks told her how much she would be paid. This opened the door for me, not being in a position to turn anything down on money grounds, to step in.

The mindset of my Managing Director was now becoming ever clearer: as part of his endless quest to do everything on a shoestring, he had selected applicants for interview who had past experience of putting a publication together – a student newspaper in my case and the magazine work of my short-lived rival – but because these ventures would not be recognised as 'real journalism' by the NCTJ, he was under no obligation to pay the going rate to whoever he appointed.

The carnival season then arrived – in Teignmouth during the final week of July and in Dawlish three weeks later – and I was amazed by the almost universal excitement with which these events were greeted, not only amongst locals but also the many holidaymakers who loudly boasted in shops, pubs and our offices how they had booked their annual summer holiday, to coincide with one or other of the carnivals, for the past 10, 15 or 20 years and travelled down from Wales, the Midlands or the North for events that took place over several days before the Thursday night processions.

Indeed, such was the interest that our Dawlish office had its only Saturday opening of the year, at the end of Carnival Week, so that visitors could order reprints of photos before they returned home.

It was around this time that Mike Taylor joined Dawlish Newspapers as an assistant to Chris Russell. This was a new position as, I had been told, previously David Banks had stepped into the breach when our Production Manager was on holiday or ill, but now it seemed those days were over. Where, we all wondered, had the money come from to increase the company's staff by one? A couple of weeks later we got part of the answer.

Belinda New was finally replaced, but only by a part-timer junior reporter. Andy Botterrill, who lived in Exeter and was NCTJ-trained, was about the same age as me, but didn't want to work full-time as he claimed to be too busy writing freelance articles for magazines.

His employment on Mondays, Tuesdays and Wednesdays enabled me to finally take over Teignbridge Council meetings from Val Gale and with Julia Walsh now firmly embedded into her role in the Teignmouth office – our department now as fully staffed as it would ever be while David Banks was in charge – things finally settled into a routine after months of uncertainty.

At the end of September I again stood in for Cedric, this time for just a week, and although things again went smoothly, this time there were none of the raised eyebrows and hearty congratulations that characterised my earlier spell in charge. Already people knew what to expect and from now on my replacing the Editor in his absence came to be considered the norm.

I soon discovered that Mike Taylor, a 20-year-old from Teignmouth, was both a drinker and a football fan – albeit of Arsenal, which led to a certain amount of banter between us – and soon we began not only going to the pub at lunchtimes, but to Saturday matches at the likes of Plymouth Argyle and Exeter City. When Colin returned from his annual month-long holiday abroad in November, we became a tavern-going trio, gradually becoming known by many as 'The Gazette crowd'.

Unfortunately as my social life in Dawlish expanded, as I made more and more contacts, so it became increasingly difficult to manage on junior pay. While the landlord of The Prince of Wales, Ray Martin, allowed me a 'slate' which meant I could usually scrape through to payday on Fridays, this only created a vicious financial circle and the situation seemed ridiculous, to myself and others, considering the seniority of my position and the amount of responsibility it involved.

At the office I was also becoming a little weary of the endless unpaid overtime which, at first, I had been happy to undertake as the enthusiastic 'new boy' looking to make a positive impression. David Banks attempted to justify his predictable refusal to pay overtime by recommending we took time off in lieu on Thursdays and Fridays, but there was rarely time to take more than an extended lunchbreak even on these relatively-quiet days.

Moreover while Andy Botterrill had taken over covering the tedious Kenton and Exminster monthly parish council meetings, the fact he was part-time meant he was exempt from working Thursday to Sunday inclusive while Cedric – to some extent justifying the 9-2-5 nickname bestowed upon him by Colin – also refused to work evenings, other than the mandatory staying until the paper was finished on Wednesdays, or weekends – even when someone else was on holiday or ill.

The situation was exacerbated by the Editor being quite happy for me to take on some of his responsibilities – I had helped with the subbing on Wednesday evenings since my first stint in charge and had completely taken over, and was indeed expanding, the sports pages – yet nothing was ever offered in return.

I was beginning to forge a particularly-good relationship with Dawlish Town Football Club, whose first team played in the premier division of the Western League. I had covered their two prestigious pre-season friendlies, against Football League sides Chelsea and Watford, and club officials were so impressed by the reports that they made contact and asked if I was interested in covering the team on a match-by-match basis.

This I had to decline as, first and foremost, I was employed as a news reporter and was already working enough unpaid overtime. There could also be practical difficulties for me, as a non-driver, travelling to away games often as far away as Somerset and the Bristol area, while midweek games were a non-starter as these were usually played on Wednesdays, our press day, when I had to be in the office.

Instead I encouraged club representatives to submit reports not only from all four senior teams, but from the under-11s up to the under-16s as well. This they did and, as other junior clubs in the area noticed this and began to send in accounts of their matches, The Gazette's sports coverage mushroomed from barely a page when I arrived to more than two by the end of the year.

My first Christmas in Dawlish was memorable for two happenings. The first came at the company's staff lunch at an out-of-town pub/restaurant called The Stables. Chris Russell, a born-again Christian and devoted family man, had strong views about alcohol and had regularly criticised what he saw as the 'pub culture' existence of Colin, Mike and myself.

Yet at this particular event he was the one who became embarrassingly drunk – and on no more than two or three pints which, I suppose, was a lot more than he was used to. The incident provided many a moment of merriment among Dawlish Newspapers staff – not only on the day but for many months to come.

The second piece of festive fun started off as a harmless spoof story which evolved into something far more meaningful because of the Lockerbie terrorist attack that took place shortly before that Christmas. Brummie Dave, a middle-aged character who frequented most of Dawlish's pubs, was notorious for telling appalling jokes, especially while under the influence. The imaginative article in The Gazette described him as one of the Midlands' top alternative comedians who would be performing a stand-up routine in The Prince of Wales on Christmas Eve lunchtime.

However, in light of what happened to Pam Am flight 103 over Scotland, semi-fiction became fact as Brummie Dave agreed to carry out the stunt to raise money for a nationally-launched fund to help families of the Lockerbie victims. He raised about £150 and the story spread to the Exeter and Torbay evenings, although they didn't seem to grasp, in their accounts, that he wasn't a bona fide comedian.

The New Year began with one of the most bizarre – and in some ways one of the funniest – episodes that I have ever witnessed at any newspaper office. A part-time vacancy arose in the all-female typesetting room and the best-qualified applicant was Don Bunce, who had recently taken a voluntary redundancy after doing the same job, for more than 20 years, at The Express & Echo.

However news of the pending appointment was greeted by horror by Lindsay Lavalle-Grimwood and Maggie Smith, the two most senior typesetters, who promptly went to David Banks and said they didn't want any men working in the room.

Had it just been that our Managing Director complied with this blatant request for sexual discrimination – such workplace practices, although diminishing, were still fairly commonplace in the late 1980s – the whole matter might not have remained a topic of conversation for more than a few days, but David Banks then compounded the problem, after taking on a far less-experienced female typesetter, by offering Don Bunce a part-time vacancy in the advertising department – an area of newspaper work where he had absolutely no experience.

The result was one of those 'truth is stranger than fiction' scenarios. The new advertising rep for Dawlish – an extremely-inarticulate middle-aged individual who spoke in a loud-but-mumbly Devon accent and punctuated almost every sentence with 'bloody' – constantly had those of us within earshot in fits of laughter as he attempted to sell adverts over the phone. His usual introductory line went something like 'Dawlish Gazette and Teignmouth News here. Wanna advert do-ee. 5x2 only cost-ee few bloody quid'.

Pat Betts, being based in Teignmouth, was at first slow to catch on to just how bad his telephone manner was, but as the complaints from would-be clients he had approached increased, so did the rows between Don Bunce and his department head. He also regularly forgot to contact potential advertisers, whose names he had been given by Pat Betts, and upset production staff by making a complete mess of his page plans. Chris Russell, with behaviour again not befitting a born-again Christian, once referred to him as 'a ****ing idiot'. The only surprising thing about Don Bunce's sacking was that he somehow lasted more than four months in the job before the axe fell.

Meanwhile my own stay with Dawlish Newspapers almost became a relatively short one when, close to my first anniversary with the company in March, I was approached, via Colin who had recommended me, by The Herald Express, which had a vacancy for a senior reporter. I met Jim Parker, the News Editor, informally in a pub in Torquay and although we got on reasonably well, the stumbling block was driving which, he pointed out, was a compulsory requirement at The Herald and no exceptions could be made.

Colin later told me that, had it not been for my lack of a licence, I would definitely have got the job and I began to seriously consider whether my next career move should be into full-time subbing, where being car-less should not prove a handicap.

By way of some compensation I did get the promised pay rise, of 20 per cent, after completing a year in Dawlish, but was still only on a basic wage of £150 a week, considerably less than many senior reporters at other papers who did not having subbing responsibilities, let alone deputise for the Editor. At least now, however, I could get through to Fridays without having to use a 'slate' at the Prince of Wales.

I was not, as it turned out, to be the only journalist in South Devon that year to be affected by the lack of a driving licence. A few weeks later Colin lost his for 12 months after being stopped by the police after concluding a lengthy drinking session at The Blue Anchor in Teignmouth.

It was, it has to be said, a 'fair cop' – Colin probably spent more time behind the wheel while under the influence than he did when sober, but for someone whose livelihood was so dependent on being 'on the road', and often at very short notice, he was now facing something of a dilemma. Coming to the rescue was Kevin Nowak, a Dawlish bar-fly and former carpenter in his 30s who had been on benefits since suffering back problems a couple of years earlier.

He was paid, cash in hand, to drive Colin around while the ban lasted which often meant that Kevin, in order to gain access to certain events, had to masquerade as a journalist. The most comical of these occasions came at the Devon County Show when Colin's driver, using Andy Botterrill's pass, had to 'sign in' at the press tent. When he removed the pass, and used it as a guide to spell out 'Botterrill', those on the reception desk looked on in amazement as here, they thought, was a reporter who couldn't even spell his own name.

Things had now become so routine-dominated at Dawlish Newspapers that the second half of 1989 passed quite quickly. A replacement for the unfortunate Don Bunce apart, there were no staff changes and everyone seemed quite settled in their roles.

Apart from The Herald Express, where I had been invited to apply, I had not attempted to move elsewhere as I was aware of newspaper journalism's unwritten rule – you were expected to stay in any full-time, staff position for two years, but thereafter it was perfectly acceptable to move on.

As that two-year mark began to approach and I pondered the future, I was also aware that Naomi, too, would soon be in a position to move on again if she so wished. We were still in semi-regular contact by letter and phone, but tended to merely exchange news rather than discuss whether the resumption of our relationship was still a possibility. It was a peculiar situation as while we had never formally split up on a permanent basis, it was now over two years since we had seen each other.

We had a prior agreement that if either of us became seriously involved with anyone else the other would be informed – so as there was no guesswork in that respect, I decided to take the bull by the horns and would ensure that 1990 would be the year when we resolved the issue of our 'limbo period', one way or the other, once and for all.

9 Break-up and make-up

Inside the Christmas card I sent to Naomi at the end of 1989 was a letter stating that as I had almost completed the obligatory two years at Dawlish Newspapers, I would be prepared to move to East Anglia in the near future providing I could find a job there – assuming, of course, that she planned to stay in the region herself. Going there on a purely speculative basis was not an option as savings were not something that went hand-in-hand with the wages paid by David Banks.

I travelled down to Truro on Christmas Eve to find a card from Naomi that had obviously been written and posted before she received mine. I knew she would be at her parents' home in Preston during the festive period, which was not the ideal place to ring her, so I decided to leave things until I returned to Devon and would await a response to my letter there.

Remarkably, in the first edition of The UK Press Gazette of the New Year, a vacancy was advertised on the sports desk of The Eastern Daily Press, one of the papers in the Norwich-based group Naomi worked for. I wrote off without waiting for a reply to my Christmas proposals as the deadline for applications was only a few days away.

The Great Storm of January 1990 provided us with a busy few days at The Gazette office as trees, roofs and greenhouses came tumbling down throughout the area and, in one of the remote villages on the outskirts of Dawlish, a fatality occurred when a farmworker was crushed by a pile of falling logs. Because of the chaos caused by the emergency services being inundated with 999 calls, and therefore not having time to release anything to the local media, news of the tragedy did not become common knowledge for two or three days. We only found out because a chance conversation Cedric overheard in a shop, but then got the story printed before either of the evening papers had, if you'll excuse the expression, got wind of it.

As to whether I was going to be storming into Norwich that year was still unclear. I eventually received a reply from Naomi, but her belated letter was sending out contradictory messages. On the one hand she wrote that she had effectively decided our relationship was over for good two years earlier when she moved to East Anglia and that we 'couldn't turn the clock back'. On the other hand she admitted to having 'put the letter away for a week', between writing and posting it (hence the delay to her reply), so she was sure she was making the right decision (why would that course of action have been necessary if she had made up her mind two years earlier?).

A fairly lengthy telephone conversation between us followed, but still she was vague and contradictory at times and I couldn't understand what she really wanted or was saying. The matter was then brought to a temporary close by the news that I had been unsuccessful in my application to The Eastern Daily Press. That I hadn't been shortlisted for interview I found a little surprising, but this may have been on geographical grounds given the distance from Devon to Norfolk. Naomi had no 'inside information' on the matter, saying she wouldn't even have known about my interest had I not told her. Exactly what would have happened had I got the job I'll never know.

A couple of months later I had another stab at getting onto a daily paper, on the sports desk of The Scarborough Evening News, and this time I did get an interview. I submitted an application after hearing that the North Yorkshire paper had been all set to take a trainee reporter from The Mid-Devon Advertiser, the nearest thing The Gazette had to weekly opposition as the Newton Abbot-based title nominally published a Dawlish edition even though they had no presence in the town and their paper rarely carried any up-to-date Dawlish news.

The MDA, as it was known, had stopped their trainee going to Scarborough as he still had six months of his indentures to complete and that, or so everyone at The Gazette thought, should have opened the door for me as the evening paper was obviously prepared to take someone from so far away. However I reserved the occasion for probably the worst performance I've ever given at an interview.

It was my first formal interview for just over two years and having travelled up on the Thursday I had to hang around the town until late afternoon the following day before meeting the Editor and Sports Editor, but there was something more to it than that. I simply felt unsettled and ill-at-ease, not only at the interview itself but throughout the day.

Remembering how fired-up I had been, and how well I had performed, at the three interviews in early 1988, the transformation in my performance was difficult to explain. Perhaps my moving to Yorkshire was just destined not to be.

As the summer approached, with me now having entered my third year with Dawlish Newspapers, I had two weeks' holiday booked to coincide with the World Cup finals taking place in Italy during June. I had planned to spend the bulk of this time in Truro, but about a week or so before the vacation began I received a letter from Naomi, saying she had been in Devon the previous weekend, to attend a former colleague's wedding, and had called at the flat above the Dawlish office on the Saturday morning, but I hadn't been at home.

She had, of course, got in a muddle over the two towns as it was the flat above our Teignmouth office I occupied (an elderly woman, with no connection to the company, lived above the Dawlish premises). It was a peculiar mistake to make as Naomi had spent the past two years writing to me at my Teignmouth address.

But why, I kept asking myself, had she called at all? I was suddenly overtaken by a compulsive urge to resolve matters once and for all and decided that part of my pending holiday would be spent travelling up to Norwich and seeing Naomi face-to-face rather than the less-than-satisfactory letter and telephone communications we had been restricted to for the past three years.

I could only make the visit with her agreement as it was physically impossible to complete a round-trip from Devon to East Anglia in one day; I could not, on Dawlish Newspapers wages, afford to stay in bed and breakfast on top of the train fare and subsequently would need Naomi to put me up for at least one night.

When I phoned and, without beating about the bush, stated my intention to visit, my proposals were accepted with less questioning than expected. I think, like me, she knew the 'limbo' period couldn't be allowed to continue any longer.

As the World Cup was about to begin, and to describe Naomi as a non-football fan was something of an understatement, I knew I had to arrange my trip so as not to coincide with any of the tournament's more significant matches. Therefore after Mike, who was also on holiday, and I enjoyably watched Scotland lose to Costa Rica followed by a more sobering 1-1 draw between England and the Republic of Ireland on the Monday, the first weekday of the competition, I travelled up to Norwich the following morning with the intention of staying two nights and one full day before returning on the Thursday.

We discussed both the past and present during those two evenings – Naomi had to work on the Wednesday daytime while I amused myself exploring a city I had never previously visited – and the upshot was that the relationship, although effectively over three years earlier the way things had turned out, had now officially ended.

Although we both regretted that it had ever become necessary to split up in the first place, temporarily or otherwise – and agreed that the Ridgway Road fiasco had been a calamitous mistake for which each of us had to take part of the blame – there was a mutual, weary acceptance that a line finally had to be drawn under the relationship.

We did agree to maintain occasional contact, at least until such time as one of us again became involved in a serious relationship, and as I made the long journey back, it was a strange feeling, after five-and-a-half years, to unequivocally be a free agent again – although I had seen very little in Dawlish and Teignmouth during the previous two years to suggest that a suitable replacement would be easy to find. It would be better, I thought, to move onto the next stage of my career, which hopefully would be much better paid, before starting to think along those lines.

After a couple of days back in Devon, I spent the second week of my holiday down in Truro. The football gathered momentum and became extremely memorable as England, after a sluggish start, went on to reach the semi-finals, but even now when I listen to the tournament's anthem, Pavarotti's Nessun Dorma, it reminds me not only of the most enjoyable World Cup I have witnessed (being a little too young to remember 1966 in any great detail) but of the sad but inevitable outcome of my visit to Norwich.

A few weeks later came another of those incidents that could only have happened in the occasionally madcap world of Dawlish Newspapers. One morning I was smoking a cigarette in The Gazette office's rear courtyard – to where David Banks had banished those participating in the habit a few months earlier – when I suddenly heard a commotion and Colin appeared in the doorway, summoning me with the words 'quick, in here – fight'.

Although his description of what was happening was, true to form, a little exaggerated, I was nevertheless greeted by an extraordinary scene. Lindsey Lavall-Grimwood and Marilyn Adams, the office receptionist, were standing head-to-head screaming and shouting abuse at each other in a part of the building where members of the public might have walked in at any moment, but amazingly none did.

It was unclear at first, to those of us who hadn't been present from the outset, what the row was actually about. By the time I got within clear earshot the combatants – each of whom, it should be stated, were in their 40s – had moved on to more general insults, each claiming the other was the most unpopular person in the office, and then to more stereotypical woman-to-woman bitchiness with comments about 'dyed hair' and 'the amount of make-up you wear I didn't think you needed any more'.

That final remark gave me the first clue as to what had caused the scene. I learnt, later in the day, that a rep had left some free make-up samples at reception and the two women each saw it as their prerogative to distribute these amongst the rest of the office's middle-aged female fraternity. What was almost as astonishing as the incident itself, and the unbelievably trivial reason for it, was the sight of spectator Ruth Banks – our Managing Director's normally goody two-shoes daughter whom he employed as the Teignmouth office junior, but who was in Dawlish that day – sprawled on the floor in an uncontrolled fit of hysterical laughter while most other employees stood in open-mouthed amazement at what was going on.

I, and others, wondered whether Miss Banks' daddy would take disciplinary action against the two feuding females, given that the incident could easily have been witnessed by visitors to the office, but for a while it was unclear whether he had even been made aware of what had happened. It was only a few months later that Pat Betts, as ever the only person who David Banks automatically confided in, told me that each woman had been warned, by telephone, not to let it happen again.

Shortly after what became known as 'the no making-up incident', Julia Walsh gave a month's notice to join the Evening Herald, in Plymouth, as a senior reporter. Her departure was not unexpected as she had taken, and passed, her NCTJ examinations in the spring, but it meant, after two years of no staff changes, there would soon be a new face in the editorial department.

I first met Louise Knox when she called at the Dawlish office, to introduce herself, the Friday lunchtime before starting work. She was only 19, having taken a pre-entry course immediately after A-levels, and certainly looked no older than that, but possessed, I noticed from that first day, a maturity that defied her years.

Our new trainee was to work a two-week overlap with her predecessor, which meant most of her early days with the company would be spent in the Dawlish office, mainly under my tuition, and I continued to be amazed by how quickly she picked up the required journalistic style, local geography and even the eccentricities that made Dawlish Newspapers the unique organisation that it was.

If she had a fault it was her natural self-confidence sometimes led to a lack of thought before putting her mouth into gear – her loud criticisms of Cedric's often sub-standard headlines resulted in some shaking of heads amongst some of the company's older, non-editorial employees who, from early on, found her a little too full of herself – but I took the positive view that it was a good sign that someone of such a young age, and only just starting off in the game, could recognize a bad headline for what it was.

After Louise moved to the Teignmouth office, to take over from Julia Walsh, our professional relationship continued to blossom – so much so that some wagging tongues within Dawlish Newspapers suggested that we might have become more than just colleagues. However there was no truth in these rumours: quite apart from my policy not to mix business and pleasure, she was 10 years younger than me and, more importantly, had brought a steady boyfriend in tow from her home town of Chard in Somerset.

Continuing the wind of change, as 1990 drew to close, was David Banks' announcement that computer technology would be replacing typewriters and typesetting the following year. This revolutionary step in the world of newspaper production had begun at the nationals in the early 1980s and had since slowly filtered down to the provincial press, but had not yet reached, as far as I was aware, any weekly title in Devon or Cornwall.

Given my ambition to move into full-time subbing, computer technology was something I was keen to learn and, I thought to myself, surely it would be easier to do so in an environment I was already familiar with. The alternative was moving to somewhere that already had computers and then having to learn how to use them on top of the usual tasks of familiarising myself with the requirements of a new paper and getting to know colleagues and the local geography.

So although 1990 began as the year I was sure would see my departure from Dawlish Newspapers, events had conspired to produce a scenario that at one time I could not have envisaged: a fourth year working for the South Devon company was now on the horizon.

The next few months were, as it turned out, largely uneventful as the work of our editorial department once again settled into an organised routine. The main local news story of early 1991 came at Teignbridge Council's annual budget meeting, in February, where the debate to decide the size of the following financial year's community charge – or poll tax as the ill-conceived and short-lived levy was more commonly known – degenerated into a screaming and shouting free-for-all. Rank-and-file members at one point approved an amendment cutting the proposed figure – the highest of any district council in Devon or Cornwall – only for senior officers to intervene, with threats of 'departments closing down overnight', which scared some of the rebels into changing their votes. This, in turn, was enough for the council's ruling clique to narrowly win the day.

My front-page report of that meeting was one of the most enjoyable leads I ever wrote for our two papers. It included verbatim accounts of abusive clashes in the chamber and was well-received by Cedric, many of the councillors who voted against and the public generally, who exacted their revenge in that spring's local elections when several long-serving councillors who had backed the exorbitant tax lost their seats.

Only David Banks seemed unhappy with my work. An admitted supporter of the community charge, he mildly admonished Cedric for allowing 'bias', both in my initial report of the meeting and in a follow-up article in the next week's editions.

Returning to matters of which he had a greater understanding, our Managing Director announced, a couple of months later, that computers would be arriving in August and, in anticipation of this, he, Cedric, Chris Russell, Mike and myself travelled down to the offices of The Devon and Cornwall Post in Launceston – one of the few West Country weeklies to already have the new technology – to see it at work.

I foresaw few problems, but Cedric was more than a little apprehensive about the pending changeover, muttering, on the way back, that he would consider retirement 'if only I could afford to'.

It was during a week's holiday in July that I learnt that my father might have lung cancer. After taking early retirement from The Daily Star in 1988, he returned to his home county of Cornwall and was living with his second wife in the north coast village of Crantock. Although he had not been totally happy about the manner of my departure from the Isle of Wight, relations between us had improved after the progress I had made at Dawlish and we tended to meet at The Globe public house in Truro three or four times a year, usually when I was on holiday.

He explained that he had started coughing up blood and his wife, a former nurse, had immediately arranged a hospital appointment and he was now awaiting the results of x-rays and other tests.

'Well, if I have got it then it's my own fault, 'he said, with obvious reference to his 70 or 80-cigarettes-a-day habit in Fleet Street during the 1960s and 70s before 'downgrading' to cigars in more recent years.

The possibility of him having the disease came as quite a shock as his 60th birthday was still three months away and it was only two years since the last of my grandparents, the grandfather on my mother's side, had passed away, albeit at the very good age of 89. I had not anticipated any further happenings of this kind within my family for a good few years to come.

The most optimistic thought in my head that day was the fact that my grandfather had smoked for more than 60 years and lived so long – proving that the habit didn't necessarily mean an early end – so perhaps it wasn't lung cancer.

The computer switchover duly took place at Dawlish Newspapers the following month and was, as far as I was concerned, the best thing ever to happen on the production side of journalism. We were now totally in control of our own priorities, instead of waiting for typesetters to reproduce what we had already written, and for the first time it became possible to provide totally accurate page plans, instead of rough guides, which made the jobs of Chris Russell and Mike a lot easier.

The papers were now usually ready to go to print by between 5pm and 6pm on Wednesdays, a good couple of hours earlier than before, and while Cedric, as expected, found the changeover difficult, he managed to grasp enough of the new system to keep his head above water and did not flounder in the way many had anticipated.

I rang my father's home in early September, knowing that by now he must have had the results of his x-rays and tests. His wife, with whom I had not had a proper conversation for many years, answered and there was an immediate and instinctive mutual understanding that, whatever our differences, we would have to put them to one side for the time being as she informed me that he indeed did have cancer of the left lung and had already begun having chemotherapy treatment at a hospital in Plymouth.

I again met him at The Globe when I was next on holiday in October. Judging by his appearance and relatively-upbeat mood, no-one who knew him would have guessed that anything was wrong. He told me that the treatment had gone as well as could be expected and after a break he would be returning to Plymouth for the next phase in a few weeks' time.

However when we next met, a couple of days before Christmas, I noticed that his outlook was distinctly more pessimistic. He was vague and evasive when I asked how the treatment had gone, saying he was 'still waiting to hear', and as we parted company, his final words to me were 'oh well, I suppose where there's life there's hope'.

So 1991 ended with a certain amount of trepidation on my part, not only because of obvious personal concerns, but having taken on board, very comfortably, the transition to computerised journalism, surely, I told myself, the following year would be the one when I finally departed Dawlish and moved on to bigger and better-paid things.

But while I did not anticipate the New Year being yet another that was largely a repeat of that which had preceded it, nobody could have predicted what actually was to happen in 1992.

10 In the name of the father

My pub preferences in Dawlish had changed during 1991. Although The Prince of Wales remained the usual lunchtime haunt of Colin, Mike and myself, in the early evenings I was now drinking regularly at The Marine Tavern, a former guest house converted into a pub the previous year on the town's seafront.

The new inn was owned and run by Jeffrey Easterbrooke, who was elected as a Conservative member of Dawlish Town Council in the May and who had become an increasingly-useful contact as the year progressed. I had grown tired of The Prince of Wales' evening culture of pinball, darts and card schools while The Brunswick Arms, the nearest the resort had to a trendy, young persons' pub, also no longer had much of an appeal, possibly because I had now passed 30 and most of those frequenting the joint were late teens to early 20s with very few customers in my own age group anywhere in sight.

I had originally started using The Marine Tavern – which was modern, refurbished and seemed to attract quite a few office workers and businessmen types - out of curiosity, but since befriending Jeffrey Easterbrooke had become quite a fixture there by February 1992 when, one Friday evening, I received a telephone message there asking me to ring an aunt. The relative in question was my father's sister, with whom I had enjoyed only occasional contact over the years, and the unexpected nature of the communication instantly left me in no doubt as to what the news was going to be.

I called her a short while later that night to be informed that my father had been in a hospice for the past couple of weeks and the doctor had advised that his sons – myself and one from his second marriage who was away at university

– should be informed that the end was nigh. I asked my aunt whether it was worth my travelling down to Cornwall while he was still alive, but she replied that there was no point as he could no longer recognise anyone. I gave her my home phone number and a further call, 24 hours later, confirmed the inevitable.

My father's second wife – tearful and anxious for 'bygones to be bygones' when I phoned her on the Sunday morning – was soon back to her usual self, putting a death notice in The Western Morning News that made no mention of myself or my sister from our father's first marriage and then instructing the vicar to give a similarly-selective account of his life during the funeral service. I had taken on responsibility for writing the obituaries for the appropriate Cornish weekly papers, so a full list of my father's offspring was recorded somewhere, but thereafter I never had any contact with his second wife again.

At the funeral wake I got into conversion with Nigel Blundell, a former colleague of my father at The Daily Star, who seemed to know exactly who I was and what I did and asked me to let him know if I came across any interesting stories from my patch in Devon. He had to leave early, to get a flight from Newquay Airport back to London before that night's paper went to print, but before departing handed me a business card which revealed that he was no less than the Star's Deputy Editor – a potentially-useful contact indeed.

The main talking point when I returned to Dawlish was the news that staff would receive just a two per cent across-the-board pay rise that spring. In previous years David Banks had worked out his own merit-based increases, which saw some people getting a lot more than others, but now Dawlish Newspapers' parent company, the Farnham-based Tindle Newspapers, had started imposing uniform rises across its various titles – so there would be no more pay increases for me of between 10 and 20 per cent, which

I had received in each of the past three springs, although as Naomi had said to me a couple of years earlier, '20 per cent of not very much still isn't a lot'.

I and several others, including Cedric, at Dawlish Newspapers hadn't even realised, until the previous year, that the company was fully owned by the Tindle empire. David Banks always portrayed himself as the sole proprietor but we discovered, once head office started standardising the way its newspapers were run, that our self-styled Managing Editor had been bought out and then employed by the big bosses at Farnham around a year before my arrival.

That same week I was contacted by Nick Harvey. I had not heard from the aspiring MP - or, indeed, anyone else from my Middlesex Polytechnic days - since 1988, but Prime Minister John Major had called a general election for early April and Nick was now the Liberal Democrat candidate for North Devon.

This was a quite-winnable seat, but Nick correctly anticipated that I wouldn't be able to take time off to help him and was more interested in whether I could be of assistance to Richard Younger-Ross, the Lib-Dem standing in Teignbridge whom I already knew reasonably well. Unfortunately I had to decline the invitation as I had a good working relationship with Jeffrey Easterbrooke and other Conservative councillors in Dawlish and Teignmouth (neither town had any elected Labour local government representatives) and, I pointed out, it would compromise my position as Chief Reporter if I was seen to be publicly taking sides in the election.

The following Monday lunchtime I returned to the Dawlish office following a Teignbridge Council meeting and, as I walked through the middle part of the building used by the typesetters, noticed an unopened pot noodle prominently displayed on top of a printing machine.

‘What on earth is that doing there?’ I asked Chris Russell, who was standing nearby.

‘Oh, Maggie brought that in this morning,’ he replied, raising his eyebrows. ‘It’s past its sell-by date and she wanted to know if anyone wanted to buy it for 50 pence.’

Such behaviour was not out of character for Maggie Smith as the frumpy, middle-aged typesetter had a deserved reputation at the office for penny-pinching and trying to make a tiny profit in the most inappropriate of circumstances (she once brought in some home-cakes, left over after a party, and attempted to sell rather than give them to her immediate colleagues).

That evening the bemused trio of Colin, Mike and myself, in The Prince of Wales, discussed Maggie Smith’s behaviour and came up with the idea of placing a classified advert, in both The Gazette and The Teignmouth News, offering the stale grocery item for sale at ’50 pence or nearest offer’ and adding the seller’s home phone number. Enlisting the help of Marilyn Adams, to ensure our handiwork got through the typesetters without the knowledge of our intended victim, the advert duly appeared on the Thursday and we eagerly awaited news of whether the Smith household received any responses. As it turned out, more than 70 people rang.

I don’t recall hearing of a single caller who had serious intentions of buying the pot noodle. Most were mickey-takers who demanded to know the snack’s flavour or late-night drunks, ringing in groups from pub payphones.

There were also spoof callers, including Marilyn Adams who, using a disguised Welsh accent, offered to swap the advertised item for some frozen pancakes, and Ray Martin, pretending to be a concerned official from the council health and safety department.

That weekend, while reviewing what had occurred, I thought about Nigel Blundell and wondered whether The Daily Star would be interested in such a quirky story. I typed up an account and sent it off to the Deputy Editor, who phoned to acknowledge my contribution on the Tuesday morning, saying he would pass it onto the news desk, 'to make of it what they will'.

I received a further call that afternoon, this time from an excited Star reporter named Virginia Hill, who had taken over what she described as 'a fantastic story' that would probably be the following day's page three lead. I told an amused and astonished Colin and Mike what to expect the following day, but no-one else at Dawlish Newspapers was aware what was going on until they saw 'Maggie's old noodles drive 'em all potty' emblazoned across the third page of the national tabloid on the Wednesday.

Maggie Smith had not reported the original advert to David Banks – probably because she was aware that several people were involved in the prank and that everyone else in the company found it hilariously funny – but this time there was no such holding back. Reports soon reached us of the angry typesetter threatening to go to a solicitor and even the Press Council, even though the story was substantially true and, as Colin later put it: 'if she hadn't brought the pot noodle into the office to sell, the whole thing would never have happened.'

Unfortunately, but not really surprisingly, it soon became clear that our Managing Director was very much on Maggie Smith's side. Although I had so far only admitted my involvement to two people, and the story's by-line had gone to Virginia Hill, there seemed to be absolutely no doubt in anyone's mind who was responsible (probably because I was the only Dawlish Newspapers employee deemed capable of such a stunt).

After we had put that week's paper to bed on the Wednesday evening, a glum-looking Cedric turned to me and said: 'David has rung me about what was in The Daily Star today. I'm afraid he wants you to take a few days off while he gets to the bottom of it and decides what to do.'

Since the introduction of computers at the office the previous summer, I had done so much voluntary, unpaid overtime that I was quite happy to follow this path providing the time off was in lieu and not holiday. Because I lived in the flat above the Teignmouth office, where David Banks was based, I could foresee this causing some awkwardness, so decided to go down to Truro and await further instructions.

My family – apart from my mother who, of course, had been married to a journalist for several years – and friends in Cornwall found the whole series of events I described very difficult to comprehend, but on the Monday I received a letter from the Managing Director asking me to attend a disciplinary hearing on the Friday morning. I returned to Teignmouth on the Thursday evening, arriving back just in time to cast my vote in that day's General Election, an event that had largely passed me by through being superseded by other happenings.

I awoke the next morning – having sat up into the early hours watching the Conservatives win an unexpected fourth consecutive term of office and Nick Harvey becoming the MP for North Devon – ready to attend the disciplinary hearing in David Banks' office. Cedric, who was present in his capacity as the most senior editorial member of staff, has already informed me, in an 'off-the-record' telephone conversation a few days earlier, that the most likely would be an official written warning.

David Banks began by insinuating that I, and I alone, had been responsible for placing the original advert in The Gazette and The Teignmouth News, which was total nonsense. When I commented as such, he asked who else had been involved.

'If you were able to discover that I was involved, surely you have found out about the others,' I replied, adding that every Dawlish Newspapers employee, with the exception of Cedric and Maggie Smith, had known about the advert before our papers went to print.

Rather than respond to this information, David Banks instead moved onto The Daily Star article. I explained about meeting Nigel Blundell at the funeral and how, after submitting the story, things had moved so quickly that there had been no time for second thoughts. Also, I explained, once you submit an article to a national tabloid paper it is then often out of your hands how or when they use it.

The Managing Director maintained that he had never known that my father was a former Fleet Street journalist, or even that he had died recently. The second point I found hard to believe as David Banks was a stickler for checking up on staff members' absences from the office and I had been away for two days to attend the funeral. He then added: 'I don't think if your father would be very proud of you if he was here now,' which, I thought to myself, was the exact opposite of what most other people had been saying during the past week or so.

We then moved onto the more predictable 'had it not been for your length of service and previous exemplary record…' before I was officially informed that I would receive a written warning that would stay on record for one year.

Strangely, though, the warning would not specify that I had written a derogatory article about another member of staff, but that I had sold a story to a national paper in breach of my contract, which stated that I could not write for other publications without the company's (ie David Banks') permission.

There were two problems here. Firstly I had never been given a contract in my four years with the company, possibly because of the uncertainty of exact job title during those first few months with Dawlish Newspapers while I was proving myself worthy as being named Chief Reporter and as an able deputy to Cedric. Secondly I had spent the past two-and-a-half years as part-time, voluntary programme editor for Dawlish Town Football Club, a role that David Banks had never been aware of, let alone given his permission for me to fulfil.

'Surely ''other publications'' means all other publications, not just national newspapers,' I said to Cedric as he drove me over to the Dawlish office after the hearing.

'Aye, you'd think so, but I don't suppose he's interested in unpaid work for local football clubs,' he replied.

And so I returned to work and it was almost as if the entire episode had never happened as the usual day-to-day routine at Dawlish Newspapers was quickly re-established. Maggie Smith and I – who had only ever rarely conversed, and then only on work matters when we had to – continued to mainly ignore each other and there was no outward hostility from anyone else.

I was informed that some non-editorial members of staff, while finding it hilarious that the advert had attracted 70 replies, thought that sending the story to The Daily Star had been going too far and that I had deserved my written warning. David Banks, incidentally, issued an internal memo that week, stating that free adverts in our titles were, from now on, strictly forbidden to company employees without the permission of himself or the relevant department head.

If my re-emergence at the Dawlish office caused less consternation than I possibly anticipated, the same could not be said outside of work. All sorts of stories and rumours had abounded around the town – and, indeed, in the offices of our rival papers – during my week-long absence: that I had been sacked, resigned with immediate effect (impossible, even if I had wanted to, because of the lack of savings accrued during my four poorly-paid years with the company) and the even more fanciful notion that The Daily Star had been so impressed with my contribution that they had offered me a full-time job, starting straight away.

Even Jeffrey Easterbrooke and his staff seemed pleased but slightly surprised to see me when I paid my first visit to The Marine Tavern following my return. It seemed that a part-time advertising rep from The Mid-Devon Advertiser – who occasionally frequented the pub and was appropriately nicknamed Pinocchio – had given them a completely misinformed, inaccurate version of what had happened and had implied that I had already parted company with The Gazette.

But although I had not departed, I and everyone else knew that my days with Dawlish Newspapers were now definitely numbered and that I would be moving on once I found another full-time job. I had only stayed as long as I had because of the previous year's changeover to computers, the pay was never going to improve meaningfully and the Pot Noodle incident, as it became known in the town and in South Devon journalistic folklore for many years to come, had probably ensured that I wouldn't now be favourite to succeed Cedric in the unlikely event of his standing down before his 65th birthday, which wasn't for another eight years anyway.

I expected to leave sooner rather than later. Although my previous attempts to move elsewhere had been unsuccessful, they had also been sporadic and highly selective ie the daily papers at Torquay, Norwich and Scarborough. I had not, at any stage since 1988, considered applying to other weekly papers, but the sudden change to my circumstances meant this would no longer be the case and, in a way, I looked forward to my first concentrated attempt to seek fresh employment for four years.

11 Saints follow sinners

I never expected my 1992 hunt for alternative employment to yield results as quickly as my last all-out push four years earlier – that, I had long-since concluded, had been a mixture of good fortune and applying at the right time of year with perhaps a little destiny thrown in – but I certainly didn't envisage spending more than a few months, at most, making applications.

In applying for sub-editors' jobs, I knew from the outset that, in terms of my cv, I wasn't going to appear particularly experienced as I had never worked as a full-time sub, although since we had switched to computers at Dawlish it certainly felt like it. However I had no wish to return to full-time reporting, not least because I knew that any such move would be hampered by my lack of a driving licence.

My first interview was not long in coming. At the end of April I was invited to make the long trip to meet the Editor of the oddly-titled Royston Crow in Cambridgeshire and although I thought the proceedings had gone quite smoothly, I was not offered the job. Still, I said to myself, the position had been advertised nationally and to be asked to travel such a distance indicated that I had been seen as a strong candidate. It was just a case of being patient.

Shortly afterwards I was asked to work a subbing shift at The Western Morning News, to whom I had written a speculative letter a few weeks earlier. I found the Plymouth office a much-changed place from seven years earlier and recognised only one face from my productive spell there while a pre-entry student.

The Editor, Colin Davidson, was obviously drunk when I briefly met him before starting work that afternoon and there was an overall strange atmosphere coupled with an even-stranger subbing system called Talbot Newswrite which was very different from the Applemac/Quarkxpress we used at Dawlish and, I had been repeatedly told, most provincial newspapers either already had or would soon be getting.

The shift was well-paid and when I inspected the paper the following day, none of my work had been altered, but I didn't hear from them again. Perhaps this was my first lesson that the old adage 'never go back' applies as much to journalism as to other walks of life.

As we moved into summer another unsuccessful interview followed at the office of a very downmarket series of tabloid titles in Egham, Surrey. I was receiving replies to every vacancy I applied for, but many Editors wrote that they had been inundated with applicants and could only interview so many.

I then decided to take a break from job-hunting as Cedric had a fortnight's holiday coming up in August – the events of March and April had not precluded me from deputising for him, probably because David Banks realised there was no-one else capable of filling the role – after which I had a week's holiday in Jersey planned with three friends from Cornwall.

The vacation had been booked several months earlier, before the Pot Noodle incident, and would be my first venture outside Britain since a primary school trip to Belgium, Holland and France. The jaunt had only been made financially possible through a rare act of generosity from our Managing Director who, when switching from the company's antiquated policy of paying wages weekly in cash to monthly by cheque at the start of the year, realised that this would cause most of his employees cash-flow problems. He therefore offered each of us a loan, equivalent to a month's salary, to make help them make the transition and to be repaid in 10 equal monthly instalments.

I had continued sending the odd article to Nigel Blundell at The Daily Star – making sure these stories were from outside the Dawlish and Teignmouth area so they would not come to David Banks' attention – and at the end of July I received another cheque from the national paper which surprised me as I hadn't realised any more of my submissions had been printed.

It turned out because the story had only been used as a 'filler' there had been no need for anyone to contact me and contribution's smaller prominence was reflected in the amount paid – only a third of the £75 I received for the Pot Noodle extravaganza.

Once the summer holiday period was concluded I resumed job applications and interviews followed at weekly newspapers in Barnstaple, North Devon, in October and Luton, Bedfordshire, the following month. The latter was, I reflected as I travelled back, the most positive encounter with a prospective employer yet – both the Editor and the Chief Sub-editor had been in fits of hysterical laughter as I recounted the sad story of Maggie Smith after they asked why I wanted to leave the employment of David Banks.

However I received a letter from them, a couple of weeks later, informing me the company's higher bosses had decided not to fill the vacancy and they were 'therefore unable to offer me the job'.

That sounded like the nearest miss yet, but why, I wondered, was it taking so long. Perhaps it was just good competition, but there was also my lack of full-time subbing experience and the growing realisation that holding a senior position on a Tindle newspaper did not carry as much weight outside the company as it did within. I certainly hadn't anticipated spending a fifth Christmas with Dawlish Newspapers, but that was the reality as a very strange year drew to a close.

There was an even more peculiar start to 1993 when I received a letter from a small weekly newspaper group in Scotland asking if I was interested in their vacancy for a Chief Reporter who would also be expected to deputise for the Editor. This was puzzling as I hadn't applied for the job and never did discover where they got my name from.

For the first and only time in my career I agreed to attend an interview only if the company agreed to pay my travelling expenses. The £90 train fare was about half of my usual weekly wage, but they agreed to cough up and I caught the train from Teignmouth to Stranraer – a journey so long that it started and finished in total darkness as an entire daytime passed – where I spent the first of two nights in a guesthouse before continuing the trek by bus to The Galloway Gazette office the following morning.

Any realistic hopes of my taking the position soon dissipated when the old question of driving arose, something I thought they would have checked on before inviting me all that way for an interview. The geography of that part of South West Scotland, with distances of up to 30 miles between the three rural towns the newspaper group covered and poor public transport, made it impossible for anyone to do the job without a car.

The location was in any case, I had decided, too remote. Had the vacancy been in a Scottish city, on the main railway line, it might have been different. As it was, the only positive aspect of my long haul was that I had been north of the border for the first time – and with someone else paying.

The broader picture of finding a new job was getting worrying. The fifth anniversary of my appointment at Dawlish Newspapers had now arrived and in a few weeks it would be a year since the Pot Noodle incident – and still I was stuck where I no longer wished to be.

Moreover Cedric had informed me that there had been mutterings of discontent, from David Banks, over the amount of time I had taken off to attend interviews during the past few months. This was, true to form, a ludicrous assertion as I was still working considerable unpaid overtime and the two weekdays I had been absent for the Scottish trip were holiday allowance carried over from the previous year. But such petty antagonism added to the pressure I felt under.

For the next few weeks there were no suitable vacancies. Then, in mid-April, The UK Press Gazette ran an advertisement for a sub-editor at The Southampton Advertiser – the only problem being that it was a temporary position for three months only. Yet something possessed me to apply: I'd worry about the consequences of the vacancy's non-permanence later; for now it represented another chance of getting away.

I didn't have to wait long to be invited to an interview and as my middle sister and her partner lived in Southampton, I stayed with them overnight before meeting The Advertiser's Editor Steve Davies on a Friday morning.

A very intense and direct speaker, and much younger than most of the other editors I had encountered, he outlined the complicated situation at his company Southern Newspapers. He was being seconded to The Southern Evening Echo, the daily paper based in the same building, as Campaigns Editor, later in the year. His replacement, from within the company, had been lined up, but he would be bringing his own sub-editor with him. Therefore a recently-departed sub from The Advertiser could only be replaced temporarily until the changeover took place.

As the interview started to draw to a conclusion – and I expected to hear the familiar words 'I've got other people to see, but I'll be in touch shortly' – suddenly Steve Davies offered me the job. 'But I want someone who can start almost immediately –how about the week after next? If you want a few hours to think about it, give me a call this afternoon.'

I explained that I would have to check with my sister and her partner whether I could stay with them, as finding a flat with just a three-month lease could prove difficult, and also asked whether there was any possibility of the work lasting longer than the advertised period.

‘Knowing the politics of this place, it might be longer than three months, but as things stand at the moment, there’s no chance of the job becoming permanent. It’s up to you if you want to take a gamble,’ he replied.

After speaking to my sister I accepted the offer and, come the Monday morning, David Banks arrived at his Teignmouth office to find a week’s notice under his door. The response from Cedric and most other people in Dawlish was ‘we’re amazed you’ve stayed this long’, but my now almost ex-Managing Director, angry that I had not given the month’s notice required in the contract I had never received, sought revenge by phoning Steve Davies and informing him of the Pot Noodle incident – a move that earned him, I would later learn, a blunt and to-the-point rebuke from The Advertiser's more-enlightened Editor.

My last day with Dawlish Newspapers, on Friday April 30 after five years and seven weeks’ service, turned into a night to remember, although that is precisely what I couldn’t do when it came to the latter stages. The festivities began in the mid-afternoon, when Roy Bolt, the football club’s vice-president, called into the office with a farewell bottle of scotch which was consumed before Colin, Mike, Louise and myself departed for first The Prince of Wales and then The Marine Tavern.

Various other well-wishers joined us at different stages of the evening and, when my brother arrived at the Teignmouth flat to drive me and my belongings down to Truro the following morning, I was still under the influence and several of my possessions were inadvertently left behind as I hazily and hurriedly completed my packing.

Fortunately it was a bank holiday weekend which meant two days to recover before catching the train to Southampton on the Monday to start work the following day. What I had been expecting to happen for three years – on and off for the first two and continuously for the past 12 months – had finally taken place and, at last, the next stage of my career had begun.

Subbing at The Southampton Advertise was more technically-challenging than at Dawlish, as the paper had a much more professional design, but the overall workload was nowhere near as great as I was now employed in an office that was properly staffed. There were four reporters – Nick, Zac, Julie and Armie – and very little of their work needed to be heavily subbed There were also no late finishes with it being extremely rare for anyone to be at their desks much after 5pm.

After five years of working in a small, pokey office with no proper segregation between journalists and non-editorial staff, my new surroundings couldn't have been more different. The large city centre building, known as Above Bar, must have housed around 200 people in all.

We had very little contact with anyone from The Southern Evening Echo, apart from the odd time-of-day conversation in the smoking room or the bar – the only newspaper office I've worked in to have such a facility – where I was happy to join my new colleagues most lunchtimes and early evenings.

Steve Davies, whom I learnt was only in his early 40s and had worked as a reporter for The Daily Mirror in his 20s, was fascinated by the shoestring manner in which Dawlish Newspapers was run, asking me one day how David Banks had got away with paying me so little.

I informed him that Cedric, as Editor, only received around £200 per week basic and went on to describe the general working conditions, including the single outdoor toilet cubicle for use by up to 15 people of both sexes.

'He certainly wouldn't get away with that up here,' said my new Editor, shaking his head. He was not the first person, from outside of the South West, to suggest that certain practises at my former company would not be tolerated in a more urban environment.

I was still in regular contact with Louise and Mike in Dawlish and learnt that the former had taken over my role, which is what I had hoped would happen, with a new trainee reporter hired for the Teignmouth office.

However David Banks once again decided to put a dampener on a generally-positive situation by refusing to pay Louise the same amount as me because she had failed some of her NCTJ proficiency exams the previous year and was awaiting the results of retakes. So I had lost my unwanted record of being probably the lowest-paid Chief Reporter in the country.

Once I got used to my new environment, the three months at Southampton passed quite quickly and without any noteworthy incidents. My time with The Advertiser was an interesting learning curve, being so different from Dawlish, and was certainly a useful addition to my cv as I had, for the first time, worked as a full-time sub-editor.

Socially things had been satisfactory, although never extending beyond activities with people from the office, and my only regret was that, in being employed from early May until the end of July, I had been unable to watch any matches involving Southampton Football Club, or Saints as they were universally known in the city, whose ground I had not visited since my early teens.

I returned to Truro at the beginning of August, temporarily out of work for the first time in five-and-a-half years, but with no regrets about the events of 1993 so far. The basic pay at Southampton, because it had been a temporary position, hadn't been massively more than at Dawlish, but because I had been paid as a freelance, no deductions had been made and this enabled me to save a reasonable amount.

My plan was to base myself in Cornwall and apply for jobs from there as I had in early 1988. On that occasion I was back for just seven weeks before moving to

Teignmouth and I wondered whether, this time, I would be counting my stay in weeks or months.

Little did I know that it would be three-and-a-half-years.

12 Back to the future

I had been back in Truro for five or six weeks, without seeing any particularly-suitable vacancies in The UK Press Gazette, when my mother saw an advert in the local West Briton newspaper, which was looking to recruit a part-time sub-editor.

The paper's long-serving Editor was Max Hodnett, who had worked with my father in Manchester during the late 60s and early 70s and been at The West Briton for such a length of time that, many years earlier, he had interviewed me for a trainee reporter's vacancy before I decided to take a degree prior to entering journalism.

I was particularly encouraged by the advert stating 'experience of QuarkXpress an advantage' as I knew most West Country weeklies had only recently installed the system or had yet to do so and therefore, I concluded, there couldn't be that many sub-editors around, and looking for work, who already had two years' relevant experience.

I applied, offering to work a trial period on a freelance basis, and was invited to attend an interview at the main Truro office, although the paper also covered the towns of Camborne, Redruth, Falmouth and Helston.

After being greeted quite amicably by Max Hodnett, who I calculated must have been in his early 60s, and his much-younger and recently-appointed deputy Robert Spratt, I learnt that the vacancy was not on The West Briton itself, but the free Leader series of papers the company distributed throughout their circulation area.

The part-time role would involve working 9am to 5pm on Fridays and from 9am until whatever time the four editions were finished on a Saturday. The Leader was then printed on Monday mornings.

When questioned about my career to date and why I had left Dawlish Newspapers, I did not mention the Pot Noodle incident – knowing that an old-school journalist like Max Hodnett, at a conservative broadsheet like The West Briton, would probably not see the funny side – but I did ask, given that the vacancy was both part-time and freelance, what the rules would be about writing for other publications, without mentioning the particular 'other publication' I had in mind. Providing there were no clashes of interests that would not be a problem, I was told.

My interviewers were pleased that I already had plenty of experience of QuarkXpress, admitting that their existing sub-editors were still in the early stages of learning the system, and we agreed a three-week trial period commencing the following Friday.

A few days later I was contacted by an employment agency, with whom I had registered a few weeks earlier, asking me to work two days a week, doing basic computer inputting at a health centre, until the end of the year. So suddenly I was effectively working full-time and off the dole less than two months after leaving Southampton.

I rang Louise, to inform her of developments, only to learn she had some equally-important news of her own. She, too, was to start work at her home town paper, in Chard, as a (properly-paid) senior reporter after giving a month's notice to a furious David Banks who now found himself with just Ellen Grindley, the trainee who had replaced Louise in Teignmouth, and Andy Botterrill who was part-time.

'Because Cedric has already had all his holiday this year, I think David's just planning to take on another trainee and muddle through until next year.' Louise said to me.

'But what if Cedric goes ill? What's he going to do – put a trainee who can't sub in temporary charge?' I asked.

'I think he's assuming that won't happen, given that Cedric is never off ill. He told me he can't afford to take on a senior and hopes, by next year, Ellen can be trained to deputise,' she replied. 'Anyway, it's no concern of ours anymore.'

On that there could be no argument and, after successfully completing my three-week trial at The West Briton, it was agreed that I would continue, two days a week, as a freelance. The Leader papers were a series of 'spoilers' – free papers with cheap adverts to stop rival companies moving into the area – and the editorial content consisted of regurgitated news from The Briton and Press Association features. So the work wasn't difficult – the reason I was doing it, I think everyone there knew, was to get a foot in the door and eventually move upwards to bigger things.

I soon became quite settled back in Truro. Although I had not lived in the city, holidays and temporary periods apart, for several years, and had not worked there since my last summer with William Hill almost a decade earlier, I had maintained many social contacts and soon became a member of two quiz teams – at Truro City Football Club and The Globe – as well as meeting different friends for a few drinks at regular times each week.

I even started to meet some desirable women in my own age group – something that, curiously, had never happened throughout my five years in Dawlish and Teignmouth – but these, unfortunately, were all married.

Contact between Naomi and myself had dwindled to little more than an exchange of Christmas cards over the past couple of years – the last time I could remember talking to her on the phone was to inform her of my father's death – but I wrote to her in late 1993, outlining the Pot Noodle incident, Southampton and my return to Cornwall.

This sparked a revival in communications between us. Still unattached and with the same company in East Anglia, although now a sub-editor herself, she seemed fascinated by what had happened to me during the previous 18 months or so.

The employment agency work ended, as expected, at Christmas and before we had moved far into the New Year, I was growing restless at only being able to work two days a week.

Although I had received no complaints about the way I edited the Leader series, Max Hodnett showed no inclination to use me on The West Briton itself, probably for no other reason than the subs' desk being fully staffed, but the money, even although it was proportionately better than at Dawlish, was not enough; indeed, had I not been living with my mother and stepfather, I would have found it extremely difficult to manage.

While I did not want to leave Cornwall for the time being – apart from being settled I was a little application-weary after spending much of the previous two years seeking jobs in various parts of the country – I could not allow the situation to continue indefinitely.

In the spring, just as I was about to again start scouring the pages of The UK Press Gazette for possible openings, I saw a local advert for a part-time sub-editor at The Cornishman in Penzance, about 35 minutes by train from Truro. I envisaged the successful applicant would be required for the early and busiest part of each week and therefore saw no reason why I could not combine such a role with subbing the Leader on Fridays and Saturdays.

Although The Cornishman and The West Briton were part of the same Northcliffe-owned Cornish Weekly Newspapers group, I thought it would be advisable to check that Max Hodnett had no objections to my applying. He did not and unusually, in response to my application, I was asked not to attend an interview, but to draw, by hand, a mock front-page design for the paper to be returned by post.

It was about this time that I got my second page-lead in The Daily Star: the tale of how a bookshop proprietor in

Truro called in health inspectors after customers complained about the smells coming from a pasty outlet across the street. Diplomatically, I told The West Briton's News Editor about the incident first, but as the reporter he allocated to the story had no idea how to handle such an off-diary matter, it wasn't properly investigated, The Star got an exclusive and I received £100.

I heard nothing from The Cornishman for about three weeks after submitting my page design and had I not been tipped off at The West Briton that I was the favourite to get the job, would probably have assumed, by this stage, that I had been unsuccessful. It was not until mid-June, around six weeks after the vacancy had been advertised, that I received a call from the Editor, Richard Van Hinsberg, asking me to start work in Penzance from the first Monday in July.

The position, he told me, would be Monday to Thursday until mid-September, while the staff subs were on holiday, and two days a week thereafter unless someone was on vacation or ill.

Aware that I would be working six days a week for the remainder of the summer, and therefore would have little time to do anything else, I went up to Dawlish in late June – only the second time I had returned since leaving 14 months earlier – and met Mike, Colin, Ellen Grindley (now Louise's replacement as Chief Reporter despite still being a second-year trainee) and Andy Botterrill in The Prince of Wales.

The latter, I learnt, was soon to leave not only Dawlish Newspapers but journalism generally to undertake a post-graduate teacher-training course in the autumn. My departure from the company, after several years of very few significant staff changes, seemed to have started a domino effect, with not only Louise departing, but Lindsey Lavall-Grimwood going to The Herald Express and none other than Maggie Smith moving to North Devon to run a guest house with her husband (jokes about the establishment's potential new-look menu were circulating for several weeks afterwards, I was told).

I informed the gathered quartet about the Penzance and Daily Star developments and received some interesting information in return. One of Cedric's trademark mountain-out-of-a-molehill headlines in The Gazette ('Plan to repel winged invaders' to describe a farmer using a scarecrow to intimidate birds) had been forwarded, allegedly by John Ware of The Herald Express, to The UK Press Gazette who had mockingly printed it on their often-sarcastic Dog Watches Dog page, adding 'that if the idea caught on, the farmer was likely to go into full-scale production'.

Although I usually saw an office copy of The UK Press Gazette, I had somehow missed that article. David Banks, however, had not been as unobservant and, I was told, had cancelled the company's weekly copy at a local newsagent and banned editorial staff from bringing the publication into either office.

The following week I began work at The Cornishman and things got off to an excellent start. Their subs had only been using QuarkXpress for a couple of months and were amazed at how quickly I churned out pages (which, of course, I should have been able to do, having used the system for nearly three years).

From my own point of view, the work was much more interesting than on The Leader, as I was dealing with up-to-date news, while Richard Van Hinsberg had a less-conservative attitude towards puns and jokey headlines than his counterpart at The West Briton.

The money I was now earning, combining the two part-time roles, was also considerably more than ever before (although there would, of course, be a reduction come the autumn when the busy staff holiday period ended in Penzance).

One lunchtime in early August I happened to be glancing through The Cornishman's office copy of The UK

Press Gazette and couldn't fail to notice that the Dog watches Dog page's lead article was a follow-up to The Dawlish Gazette 'scarecrow' story. Someone, it seemed, had leaked a copy of an internal memo from David Banks, banning the trade paper from company premises, and my former Managing Director found himself the subject of national ridicule in an extremely-unflattering article.

My own name was to appear in The UK Press Gazette shortly afterwards, but in completely different and unrelated circumstances. Someone – whether from The Cornishman or The West Briton I never discovered – nominated me for the publication's Headline of the Month competition after a Penzance maritime company's plans to build a smaller replica of an old lugger named 'Boy Willy' were described as 'New maritime group plans 54-foot "Willy"'. As one of the Truro-based subs commented: 'If you'd even tried something like that here, Max would have gone ballistic'.

Despite a national train strike leaving me relying on lifts and an extremely slow-moving bus service to get to and from work in Penzance for a period of three or four weeks, that summer of 1994 remains one of the happiest I can remember.

With a very low-key World Cup – England having failed to qualify and with the tournament taking place in the United States, most games kicking off in the early hours our time – my abiding memory of the time is instead Wet, Wet, Wet's chart-topping hit *Love is all Around,* from the film *Four Weddings and a Funeral,* which was at number one for 12 or 13 weeks. Even today when I hear that song, it instantly reminds me of the feel-good factor of my early days at The Cornishman combined with a social life that had been consistently enjoyable since my return to Truro.

After working six days a week solidly for three months, I decided that October would be the nearest thing I would get to a holiday that year and planned several excursions for the periods when I would not be required at either office.

I returned to my sister's home in Southampton for a few days, making up for the previous year's disappointment by watching a match at The Dell and calling into The Advertiser's office one lunchtime for a drink with the reporters who told me of their disillusionment at working for their new Editor now that Steve Davies had departed to The Southern Daily Echo, as it had now been renamed.

At the end of the month there was further football activity when, with some friends from Truro, I travelled up to London to see Tottenham Hotspur play West Ham United at White Hart Lane. It was the first time I had seen my team in action for more than two years thanks to all surplus cash being used for train fares to interviews during my final year at Dawlish followed by 12 months of working Saturdays (the day of the match was, in fact, my first Saturday off since I began editing the Leader series).

October also proved to be the last time I saw Naomi (although we would maintain occasional written communication for several more years to come) when we met in Exeter the week after I went to Southampton. She was holidaying alone in Dorset and we picked the Devon city as a 'halfway house' venue.

Having been in quite regular contact during the preceding months, there was no need to update each other on current activities and instead we talked reflectively about the past and where things had gone wrong between us, albeit less emotionally than when officially splitting up four years earlier, although it was clear to each of us that the other still regretted what had happened.

As I pointed out to Naomi that day, had we met up a week earlier it would have been 10 years to the day since we started the course at Preston (and, of course, when this tale began). However the irony of that statistic only really dawned on me in the years ahead once it became clear we would probably not be meeting again.

1994 had been a year when The UK Press Gazette had been a regular source of interesting information and that trend continued to the end as, in the December, I read of Nigel Blundell's departure from The Daily Star to concentrate on freelance writing. So now I no longer had a direct contact on the nationals.

Although I was settled, professionally and personally, I knew I had to aim for being more than just a reasonably well-paid freelance and decided to give Cornwall another year to see if either The Cornishman or The West Briton offered me a senior staff job. I was confident that either of them would if a vacancy arose - and the Penzance office would be my preference if I was given any kind of choice - but if nothing materialised during 1995 I would have to be on the road again.

13 You couldn't make it up

As had been the case at Dawlish six years earlier, the initial 'buzz' that accompanied my successful start at The Cornishman slowly levelled off into a routine and the early part of 1995 was not particularly eventful.

I was employed, on average, two days a week in Penzance along with Fridays and Saturdays in Truro and was already looking forward to the busier summer and a return to the six-day working week that would again see my bank balance rise sharply.

I still regularly received complimentary comments about my work at The Cornishman, particularly headlines, although it was sometimes felt that I went a little over the top. One story about an agoraphobic woman, who overcame her condition by taking up photography, was preceded by 'Photos get 'Her indoors' outside!' which prompted a letter of complaint from a member of the public, not the subject of the article, who found the headline 'in the most appalling taste'. Most people in the newsroom, however, found it amusing and Richard van Hinsberg, who signed off every page, could have asked me to change it but didn't.

An addition to my social life – where the two weekly quiz teams were now well into their second year – saw me again drinking regularly at The Daniell Arms. The pub, my 'local' throughout my 20s whenever I was in Truro, had been frequented by students, staff from the adjoining hospital and other professional workers, but had lost many of its customers in the late 80s, when the brewery refurbished and modernised several other city centre inns, and then when the hospital closed.

The Daniell had by now been in decline for several years with a string of short-lived landlords, very few lunchtime customers and in the evenings had become little more than a pool and darts bar (two activities which did not exist there in its heyday) and was very rarely busy.

However it was only a short walk from The West Briton office and during the second half of 1994 I had started going there on Friday lunchtimes – usually alone as the Truro paper, unlike those in Dawlish and Southampton, did not have a drinking school – and got to know the new landlord Dave McDonald who, aware of the pub's illustrious past, was trying hard to improve it.

One idea we discussed, of particular interest to me, were 'lock-ins' on Sunday afternoons when Premier League football was shown live on Sky. Although all-day (11am to 11pm) pub opening had been introduced in 1988, Sundays had not been included and bars were still supposed to close between 2.30pm and 7pm on the Sabbath.

The law was due to change in July 1995, when Sunday licensing hours would be brought into line with the rest of the week, and I put it to Dave McDonald that if he operated 'lock-ins' during the 1994-5 football season, many of those attending would continue to watch matches at the pub when Sunday afternoon opening became legal the following year.

The experiment worked well and I began using The Daniell on Sundays as well as Fridays and occasionally on midweek evenings if I had no other social commitments.

During one such visit, on a Tuesday evening in mid-May, I started talking to a character named Bob, a middle-aged Australian holidaymaker who was staying at a nearby hotel. We got on very well and he suggested another drinking session before he departed for the next leg of his English tour at the weekend. The following night I had a quiz engagement, so we agreed to meet again on the Thursday.

Quite late into our second evening at The Daniell, Bob was suddenly approached by an extremely-attractive woman in her 30s, with a strong but refined Liverpudlian accent, whom he obviously knew. I wondered how, given that he had only been in Truro for a few days, and as the three of us moved from standing at the bar to sitting at a nearby table, I learnt that the new arrival was also resident at the hotel, but was not on holiday.

She had recently moved down from the North to take over as manager of the city's Edinburgh Woollen Mill branch and was in bed and breakfast while waiting to move into a flat that was being refurbished.

And that was the night I met Pauline Jonas. The connection between us, from the outset, was unlike anything I had experienced since first encountering Naomi. On learning that I was a sub-editor with The West Briton she gave me her work telephone number, asking that I pass it onto the advertising department as a potential new customer – although I strongly suspected she wanted me to have the number anyway – and made sure she dropped into the conversation her recent break-up with a long-term boyfriend and the fact that she was now a free agent.

As the evening ended, I said farewell to Bob and arranged to meet Pauline in The Daniell on the Saturday night.

Things progressed positively but cautiously over the next few weeks. The same age as me, Pauline was certainly a fascinating character, having been a professional dancer in her younger days and also a bit-part television actress before entering retail in her late 20s. She had never been married and, like me, saw career development as the most important thing in the foreseeable future.

Pauline emphasised that – what with being in a new job in a completely new part of the country and having just ended a long-term romance – she didn't want to go rushing, head-long, into another heavy relationship. I, in turn, pointed out that for most of the next three or four months I would be working in Penzance four days a week, so not getting too serious too soon was fine by me.

During the second half of May and throughout June we saw each other about four times a week, usually in The Daniell, but occasionally going to other pubs or to restaurants for a meal. Pauline was scheduled to move into her flat in early July and until that happened our activities were going to be somewhat restricted, what with her living in the hotel and me abiding at my mother and stepfather's house.

Meanwhile I learnt in casual conversation at The West Briton – and it was ironic that I heard this here and not in the Penzance office – that Richard Van Hinsberg had submitted an expansion plan for The Cornishman to the Northcliffe regional bosses, and his proposals included making me a full-time, staff sub-editor. So, I thought to myself, things were looking up in all directions.

I was due to start my second full-time summer stint in Penzance from the first Monday in July and, on the preceding Friday, Pauline and I met after work and spent the evening drinking in The Daniell. The more we consumed, the more quiet and subdued she became – not the effect alcohol usually had on her – and when I asked if anything was wrong, she sighed, shook her head and muttered 'the problem with you is you're too nice'.

She wouldn't elaborate further, but then asked to leave the pub, even though it was only about 9pm and it was unusual for us to depart before closing time.

We had agreed, earlier in the evening, to go for a Chinese meal the following night and she duly arrived, seemingly back to her usual self, and made no reference to her strange behaviour of 24 hours earlier.

As we discussed the coming week, in which we both had a very busy schedule, it became clear that it wouldn't be possible to meet again before the following weekend when I would ring her from The West Briton office on the Friday to arrange what we were doing that evening.

Despite phoning the shop three or four times that day, I was told, on each occasion, that she wasn't there or was unavailable, although at least once I thought I could hear her distinct accent in the background. Puzzled, I made my way to The Daniell after work, half expecting her to be there, as she normally was on Fridays, or to arrive shortly afterwards. Instead I was greeted by Dave McDonald whose face dropped when he saw me.

It was around 5.15pm, the after-work regulars hadn't started arriving yet and the pub was empty apart from a couple sitting in the far corner. 'I'd better tell you this now, before it gets busy,' said the landlord. 'It's Pauline – she was in here last night with another bloke.'

The reality of what he was actually telling me didn't sink in at first. I started saying that I didn't have any objection to her having a drink with another man, although I was curious who it could have been as I knew her work colleagues at The Edinburgh Woollen Mill were exclusively female.

'No. I don't mean she was just having a drink with another bloke. I mean…well, do I have to spell it out,' he asked. 'I could have told you from the start what type she was, but I don't suppose you would have listened.'

I was in too much of a state of shock to answer and don't think I even stayed to finish my drink. I tried phoning Pauline at work on the Saturday, believing that I at least deserved some sort of explanation, but again she was always out or unavailable and I decided not to pursue the matter.

Contrary to what Dave McDonald had implied, I had realized, from very early on, what 'type' Pauline was, having had usually-brief experiences with her ilk when much younger. Where I got it wrong was in thinking that she would be different because she was older, what with being hundreds of miles away from home in a new job that offered no outside social life. I suppose I believed she would have been grateful to meet someone so soon in those circumstances as a lot of people in their mid-30s indeed would have been.

What was particularly galling was all the talk about having too much on her plate to become involved in a serious relationship. It had all sounded so believable. I later learnt, on the grapevine, that she had told people I was so different from the type of men she was used to going out with that she found the whole thing overwhelming and the relationship couldn't possibly have worked – although it seems a little strange that someone of her age and experience would take nearly two months to come to such a conclusion.

In the meantime, I decided to take steps, in the short to medium term, to minimise my chances of seeing her and opted to take a flat in Penzance, at least for the rest of the summer – an idea I had been toying with in the early spring before meeting Pauline put those plans on hold.

For the remainder of the busy holiday period I split my time between the two towns and offices, usually travelling up to Truro on Thursday evenings, to work Fridays and Saturdays at The West Briton, before returning to Penzance after dinner on Sundays.

I stopped going to The Daniell – no great loss as none of my friends had frequented the establishment for many years – and decided to take a break from the quiz teams after two years of unbroken participation. I was a little worried about Pauline spreading her wings, as she became more settled in the city, and starting to turn up at other pubs and clubs I regularly used.

But as the summer drew to a close, I was reliably informed that she had not been seen at those venues and cautiously and gradually, as the amount of work available in Penzance started to dwindle, I began to spend more time, socially, back in Truro.

In fact, I only ever saw Pauline once again – in a city centre off-licence a few months later when she turned her back and walked into a corner when she saw me coming in. By that stage I decided there was no point in trying to talk to her and made my purchase and left without looking in her direction.

Although left shaken by the experience, the one thing I was determined would not be affected was the way I did my job. True I spent too many working lunchtimes in pubs – a habit that hitherto had been slowly dying out due to a lack of drinking partners at either Cornish office – and at times I was uncharacteristically a little short-tempered, but as far as the finished product was concerned, nobody commented on any drop in standards.

In the late summer I had learnt, again at the Truro office, that Richard Van Hinsberg's expansion plans had been rejected by Northcliffe bosses and, at around the same time, it was announced that Max Hodnett would be retiring as West Briton Editor in the October, at the age of 62, to be replaced by Robert Spratt

This triggered a flurry of editorial changes: first the post of Deputy Editor was advertised nationally and a Gary Kaye was appointed from a weekly paper in Yorkshire; a senior West Briton sub-editor, miffed that he had not been offered the job, then left to join The Cornish Guardian, the third title in the Cornish Weekly Newspapers group whose head office was in Bodmin; he in turn was replaced by Jeremy Ridge, a long-serving district office reporter who moved to Truro as a trainee sub.

It was then confirmed that The West Briton's long-planned switchover from a broadsheet to a tabloid format would take place in November and Robert Spratt asked Richard Van Hinsberg if I could work at the Truro office as a full-time freelance during the busy transitional period and up to the end of the year.

The Cornishman's Editor replied I was available only during the weeks when he had no-one on holiday and between them they worked out a nine-week rota of where I would work. This suited me as I still had accommodation in both towns and it meant a substantial period of full-time work at a time of the year when my services would not normally be in such demand/

One Thursday afternoon in early December, during a week when I was working exclusively for The West Briton, Robert Spratt called me into his office and informed me that he planned to increase the size of the new-look paper in the new year and had been given permission to take on two additional full-time sub-editors – an advert had appeared in the paper that day – and was I interested?

I was already aware that, as part of the re-launch package, the Leader series was being discontinued at the end of the year and Robert Spratt emphasized that, because of the cost of taking on two new full-timers, he could not guarantee my continued employment as a freelance two days a week.

He added that he was 'aware of my record' at Dawlish Newspapers – presumably meaning my deputising for the Editor and not the stories I had sent to The Daily Star – and that he would be looking for someone to stand in for Gary Kaye as Deputy-chief Sub-editor. I asked for a couple of days to think it over and was told that was fine, as the advert had another week to run, but to let him know the following Monday.

The next day I received a call from Richard Van Hinsberg, who sounded worried and asked if it was true I was going to The West Briton full-time. Where he got that information from I don't know, but I replied that I hadn't made a final decision and explained about losing the Leader work, the verbal offer of becoming Deputy-chief Sub-editor and reminding him that The Cornishman didn't have any vacancies on the horizon anyway.

‘That might not be the case,’ he replied. ‘I’ve heard that Peter Heyman has applied to go there (The West Briton) as well,’ The journalist he referred to was The Cornishman’s Sports Editor and although he had very little experience of news subbing, I later learnt that Robert Spratt was anxious to get someone who could deputise for Rhod Mitchell, The West Briton’s Sports Editor, who operated as a one-man band.

On the Monday I verbally accepted Robert Spratt’s offer and then received another call from Richard Van Hinsberg, informing me that Peter Heyman had given a month’s notice to join The West Briton and that his job at The Cornishman was mine if I wanted it. I replied that while I would be sad to leave the Penzance office, being Sports Editor there could not compare with being Deputy-chief Sub-editor at The West Briton and I had to stand by my original decision.

It seemed peculiar that after waiting so long for one of the papers to offer me a full-time job, here I was with the choice of two on the same day. I saw the move I was about to make as a progression on the role I had fulfilled at Dawlish – this time on a much-larger scale and at the correct rate of pay. My career path was well and truly back on track.

A quite enjoyable Christmas period preceded my starting at The West Briton full-time with my family and friends both happy and impressed by my achievements. I received a card and letter from Naomi, informing me that she had finally found someone else – albeit through what she described as ‘an upmarket contact magazine’ – and she and her university lecturer fiancé planned to marry the following year. Like me she had patiently waited five years for the next right person to come along – unlike me, it seemed, her right choice had not proved to be the wrong one.

On Thursday January 3 the new sub-editing team began work at The West Briton and the following day an internal memo, from Robert Spratt, stated that no Deputy Chief-sub would be appointed as yet but, for the time being, those duties would be carried out jointly, in Gary Kaye's absence, by Jeremy Ridge – only a few months off the news desk if you recall – and Darren Norbury, a sub-editor with no NCTJ training.

You're right, for the second time in just six months I had well and truly been stabbed in the back.

14 That paper's surely *not* doomed (so I thought I'd get a job there)

I never discovered exactly why Robert Spratt misled me over my role at The West Briton. Certainly there was no age factor involved: some editors prefer to promote young, up-and-coming journalists, while others would rather have maturity and experience, but neither applied here as both Jeremy Ridge and Darren Norbury were, like me, in their 30s.

I suspected the paper's Editor might have been anxious to obtain my services as back-up in case Jeremy Ridge – whom, it soon became apparent, was his first choice and was simply being guided along by the more-experienced but less-ambitious Darren Norbury – eventually decided that such responsibility was not for him. However, a less-charitable story circulating around the office was that Paul Roberts had hired me simply to score a point against Richard Van Hinsberg and The Cornishman and never had any serious intention of making me Deputy-chief Sub-editor.

I had nothing whatsoever against Jeremy Ridge – a likeable person whom, even before his surprise elevation, I thought showed a lot of potential as a sub – although I, and several others at The West Briton, wondered why, if he was supposed to be editorial management material, had he been left relatively-languishing as a district office reporter for so many years.

Under different circumstances I might have been prepared to bide my time at The West Briton and see what developed. The pay was quite reasonable (around £6,000 a year more than I had been getting towards the end at Dawlish) and my social life in Truro had now settled back into its old routine following the disruption caused by the Pauline Jonas affair and move to Penzance.

But from the moment I read Robert Spratt's momentous memo, the recurring thought going through my mind, on almost a daily basis, was that I could, and should, have been Sports Editor at The Cornishman - and had I followed my gut instinct, instead of being taken in by The West Briton Editor's deception, that is precisely what I would have been doing. Finding myself jettisoned into a job I not only didn't want, but more importantly had never even applied for, was certainly not the anticipated outcome of my patient wait for a suitable senior, full-time position with Cornish Weekly Newspapers.

Adding to my dissatisfaction was the day-to-day atmosphere of smiling, sycophantic subservience amongst the sub-editors at The West Briton. The paper's pagination had been increased during the re-launch with a number of supplements and while the paper had seven or eight subs, around double that of the smaller Penzance office, each week was a never-ending treadmill of churning out pages where the leads were normally press releases and decent off-diary stories as rare as staff leaving the office at the time they were supposed to each evening. Yet nobody ever complained, even privately, about the never-decreasing hours and workload.

Robert Spratt, whose motto might well have been 'quantity not quality', seemed obsessed with the technical and design side of the job to the detriment of the paper's content. His staff seminars on Thursdays, the nearest we had to a quiet day, were usually farcical as, when reviewing that week's edition, he made no reference to quality of stories or headlines, but instead endlessly scrutinised whether line rules around adverts were properly joined up and paragraphs indented by precisely the correct number of millimetres (matters, of course, to which the average reader would be totally oblivious).

I was due to sign a contract, and become a fully-fledged editorial staff member, at the end of March, but things came to a head about a week before that. Late on a Tuesday night, after being at the office since about 8am, I was given a page to finish off that contained no news, but the likes of tide times, cattle market prices and other valuable pieces of local information. Everything should already have been copy-subbed, while being typed into the system, by a character named Jon Barrett, an ageing former sub who, because of health problems, had recently been demoted to an editorial assistant and imputer. My job was simply to make the copy fill the boxes on the templated page.

I thought no more about the matter until the Friday morning when Gary Kaye showed me a memo he had received from Robert Spratt, who was away from the office that day, saying he wanted to see the sub 'responsible' for the page in his office at 9am on the Monday.

The communication also included a number of hysterically-critical comments about minor design points that, once again, the average reader would not have noticed. True, there were some factual errors in the page's content, but as I did not have access to the original documents from whence the information came, such things could not have been checked at my end.

But to be summoned, school-like, into the office of, in my opinion, a second-rate Editor – who had taken away, through his devious behaviour, the full-time job in Penzance I had patiently awaited for 18 months – was the final straw.

The only thing he saw of me on the Monday morning was my signature on a letter of resignation, with immediate effect, which ended with a quote from Sir Arthur Conan Doyle about 'mediocrity recognising nothing higher than itself'.

I took a week off away from Cornwall, spending a couple of days in Preston – my first return since completing the NCTJ course nearly 11 years earlier – and then some time in Dawlish, staying at The Marine Tavern, where I saw, amongst others, Mike and Colin, but did not say anything about what had happened.

I had not visited the Devon town, or had any real contact with anyone there, since the previous summer and being unsure as to what I was going to do next, I simply said that my situation was unchanged and I was still working for both Cornish titles as a freelance.

The three reasonably-well-paid months I had spent at The West Briton, following on from a profitable second half to 1995 as a freelance, meant I had no short to medium term financial worries, but what were my prospects of getting back in at The Cornishman?

The Sports Editor's position had, of course, long since been filled, while my old position of relief sub-editor had been taken over by one of the paper's former production workers, all of whom had been made redundant the previous year when Northcliffe moved production and printing of its Cornish titles to a new, purpose-built centre on the outskirts of Plymouth, which was also the new home of The Western Morning News.

My replacement had, needless to say, no prior journalistic experience and I had heard from Peter Heyman, shortly before I left The West Briton, that Steve Crossman, The Cornishman's Chief Sub-editor, was less than impressed by the re-employed newcomer's efforts. This offered a chink of light and I wrote off to Penzance stating that I was again available as a freelance.

I pre-empted any reply by taking another flat in Penzance, this time in Morrab Road, just a stone's throw from The Cornishman's office. I had not told my family and friends exactly what had taken place at The West Briton –

simply that it hadn't worked out and that I was returning to the paper I should never have left in the first place.

I had been back in the town about a week, still having heard nothing from The Cornishman, when I bumped into Steve Crossman one lunchtime. He confirmed they had received my letter and that, as far as he was concerned, using the ex-production worker was 'unsatisfactory', but that Richard Van Hinsberg was being 'intransigent' on the matter and had ruled that while he was prepared to use me again as a relief sub, this would only be when more than one person was away from the office.

And so a largely-boring late spring and summer developed. I worked only a handful of days at The Cornishman, usually when Richard Van Hinsberg was away at Northcliffe meetings while someone else was on holiday, and spent most of the rest of the time propping up the bar at The Lugger, a seafront pub where I got to know the staff (particularly a barmaid named Michelle) quite well.

The only other highlights were football's European Championships, where England reached the semi-finals on home soil, and Wednesday nights when I returned to Truro to join the one pub quiz team of which I was still a member.

Around this time it was widely reported that The West Briton had won a regional award as best weekly newspaper – although reading the comments of the judges it was obvious that it had done so purely because of its size and not its content – and at this point in time, I must confess, it did seem as if Robert Spratt's editorship was totally vindicated. Because hardly any of the Truro paper's editorial staff lived in the city, I had not seen anyone since my departure. I had, however, heard via The Cornishman grapevine that there had been further mutterings of discontent about Spratt's style of man-management.

Towards the end of August I befriended the couple in the flat below me. Paul Edmund was a photographer of around my own age who had worked for one of the national music papers in the 1980s, but now concentrated on weddings. His partner Jenny Rose was a special needs teacher who did not actually live in Morrab Road (she had her own flat elsewhere in the town) but spent much of her time there.

Through them I got to know more people in Penzance and reached an agreement with Paul on the use of his phone, both for incoming and outgoing calls, after the communal payphone on the stairs ceased functioning.

In the September I opened a copy of The Cornishman to see an advert for a full-time sub-editor which was, even more surprisingly, repeated in The UK Press Gazette a few days later. I rang Steve Crossman and was told that Nigel Salmon, a long-serving sub, had joined the exodus to The West Briton, presumably, like Peter Heyman, because the Truro paper paid more. I said I would be applying and asked why the vacancy was being advertised nationally.

'I don't know – it's not something he (Richard Van Hinsberg) has done before,' Steve Crossman replied. 'He's got a bee in his bonnet that it's something he's got to do this time. Penzance is a long way for people to travel to interviews and we certainly don't want people coming here thinking it's a semi-retirement job in Cornwall. We'll have to see what the applications are like.'

I was a little perturbed that I had only found out about the vacancy through seeing an advert in the paper. I suppose I could understand Richard Van Hinsberg being a little miffed over my turning down his offer the previous year, but he was fully aware of the reasons why and my actions hadn't prevented him from re-employing me, albeit on an occasional basis, that summer.

A couple of weeks later, in early October, Paul Edmund knocked on my door and informed me that 'the Editor of The Cornishman' was on the phone. As I walked down the stairs to take the call I inevitably thought 'this is it – he's going to offer me the job', but it turned out that he simply wanted me to work three days the following week when he was at a Northcliffe conference and Nigel Salmon was taking his final week's holiday due before joining The West Briton. What had raised my expectations was that it was usually Steve Crossman who phoned when they needed me for relief work, but on this occasion, for some reason, Richard Van Hinsberg had decided to do so himself.

In his absence, no-one at the office the following week mentioned the vacancy or asked whether I had been offered the job. On the Tuesday lunchtime I briefly returned to my flat to find a letter from the Editor, presumably written and posted before he went to the conference, informing me that my application had been unsuccessful, but that I had been 'seriously considered' and 'should not be discouraged from applying for any future vacancies that might arise'.

I later learnt that a sub-editor from the Wolverhampton-based Express & Star, an evening paper, had got the job, so I suppose the successful applicant, on paper at least, must have been a strong contender. However, the whole thing smacked of Richard Van Hinsberg manufacturing a situation where he would not have to take me on – and several of The Cornishman's editorial staff shared that view.

There was no doubting, however, where the real blame lay - one disgusting lie, probably concocted solely to score a cheap point against a rival title in the same group, had now cost me not one but two full-time positions at what for more than two years now I had considered to be my own newspaper.

Practicalities dictated, however, that I now had to abandon The Cornishman 'dream', and probably any realistic possibility of continuing my career in my home county, and get a job elsewhere as soon as possible. By now I was almost continuously overdrawn at the bank and using credit cards to supplement my meagre earnings from the

Penzance office. I started applying for anything in The UK Press Gazette I thought I stood the remotest chance of getting, irrespective of geography.

The following month I read that Robert Spratt was leaving The West Briton, to become an assistant editor at The Western Morning News, after just a year in charge. Some saw this as another step up the ladder for a journalist obviously on his way to big things – and an extremely-boastful interview published in the Cornish Weekly Newspapers titles suggested he saw matters that way himself – but I was not so sure. It was very unusual for someone to edit a weekly newspaper for just 12 months, unless health issues were involved, and the reaction in the larger Truro community, following 22 years with Max Hodnett at the helm, was one of 'he didn't last very long, did he?'

Shortly before Christmas I was asked to attend an interview at The Bath Chronicle which proved unsuccessful, although I was pleased to have been shortlisted after hearing the evening title had received around 80 applications.

Yuletide saw me with more than a month's rent arrears as well as a large overdraft and I did not receive a card from Naomi, for the first time since we had met 12 years earlier, which led me to assume that she had followed through with her marriage plans and no longer considered contact with me appropriate.

Following a few days back in Truro over the Christmas, I returned to Penzance to spend New Year's Eve with Paul Edmund, Jenny Rose and some of their friends and an extremely-drunken night ended with none of us getting to bed much before 4am. However not since the dark days of Hereford House, a decade earlier, had the turning of the year been accompanied by such a gloomy and unoptimistic outlook.

January did little to lift my spirits. I received my first written warning over my rent arrears and there were no suitable full-time jobs advertised in The UK Press Gazette, although I did apply for a maternity leave cover at The News, the daily paper in Portsmouth.

The month's solitary piece of enlightenment came in a different section of The UK Press Gazette. The Dog Watches Dog page had been informed of some derisory comments Robert Spratt had made about The Western Morning News, including whether the paper even had a future, at one of his Thursday seminars while West Briton Editor the previous year. The sarcastic article – headed 'That paper's surely doomed (so I think I'll get a job there)' – certainly made amusing reading.

If ever there was evidence that one phone call can change the course of a decade – and, by consequence, a much longer period – it came on the evening of Tuesday February 4. At around 5.15pm Paul Edmund knocked on my front door, saying there was 'someone from a newspaper in Jersey' wanting to speak to me. My neighbour was already slightly the worse for drink, despite the relatively-early hour, and as I made my way downstairs I thought he must have made a mistake as I hadn't been in contact with anyone in the Channel Islands.

But it was indeed The Jersey Evening Post Editor, Chris Bright, who informed me that he was looking for a freelance sub-editor, for up to three months, who could start work almost immediately. Puzzled, I asked where he had got my name from and was informed that it was someone from The News in Portsmouth (they obviously weren't going to employ me themselves, but deemed I was an experienced enough candidate to pass my name on to others).

As the conversation gathered momentum, my potential new employer seemed pleased that I had visited Jersey before (on holiday four-and-a-half years earlier) and that I had previous experience of working for an island paper.

Yes, I could start a week Monday and most certainly yes, pay equivalent to £20,000 a year (considerably more than salaries at either The Cornishman or The West Briton) would be acceptable. I was asked to confirm my interest in writing and, subject to a satisfactory reference from Richard Van Hinsberg, a renewable monthly contract would be sent to me by the end of the week.

My head was still spinning after the unexpected call ended. Chris Bright had explained his paper's dilemma – his deputy had a hospital operation coming up, one sub had badly broken her arm and would be off work for possibly months, another had a month's holiday in Australia booked and a further member of the desk was due to retire shortly. Even so, it had all come so out of the blue, and in such an unlikely destination, that it was still hard to take in.

The following morning, before posting my letter to The Jersey Evening Post, I found myself going to the library, across the road from the flat in Morrab Road, and comparing the address and details of the paper from Willings Press Guide against what I had scribbled down the previous evening. I don't think I really believed the whole thing could be a wind-up (who would do it and why Jersey?) but it all seemed so unreal I instinctively found myself double-checking.

Further research revealed The Jersey Evening Post to be an extremely-profitable concern. Its circulation was around 20,000 a day (on an island with a population of around 80,000) and the paper's parent company, The Guiton Group, owned a string of newsagents on the island, the distribution rights for all the UK's national newspapers there and made a profit of between two and three million pounds a year.

A further phone call from Chris Bright, having received my letter, confirmed the offer on the Thursday evening and a contract duly arrived on the Saturday. I was also informed that the paper would pay for my flight and arrange a hotel as my initial accommodation.

For the next few days the comment 'you're going *where*?' was frequently heard as family, friends and former colleagues learnt the news. I rang Steve Crossman, thinking he would have already have heard of my good fortune from Richard Van Hinsberg, but strangely he hadn't, although he wished me well and asked me to let him know once I was back in the country.

I moved my belongings back to Truro in stages, so as not to arouse the suspicions of the flat's letting agents, whose office was only a few doors away. Because of my by-now enormous rent arrears, I didn't want them to know of my departure before I had completely moved out.

My final night in Penzance was spent with Paul Edmund and friends, watching England disappointingly lose a World Cup qualifier to Italy, before removing the remainder of my possessions the following day and then deciding what I would be taking in the two suitcases that would be accompanying me to the Channel Islands.

And on the morning of Valentine's Day I caught a flight from Plymouth Airport in some ways still half expecting to wake up.

15 The famous five go fishing

The sense of familiarity I felt when arriving in Jersey early that Friday afternoon was quite remarkable considering my only previous visit to the island had been a largely alcohol-dominated week's holiday in August 1992.

I took a taxi from the airport to the Almorah Hotel in St Helier, the accommodation the paper had arranged, where an itinerary for my first two days at The Jersey Evening Post had been left for me to collect.

I learnt that I would be joined by another freelance sub – John Bowen, who had recently left The News in Portsmouth – and that the Monday and Tuesday of the following week would consist of us attending a series of seminars, visiting various locations, learning about Jersey's geography and political history and, perhaps most importantly, the legal and governmental differences between the island and the UK. We would then start work properly on the Wednesday.

I spent the weekend re-familiarising myself with St Helier and some of its pubs and getting to know the hotel's owners Peter and Karen, a couple in their 40s who were originally from Yorkshire but had lived on the island for many years.

They were very friendly and the fact that I got on with them well from the outset in no small way helped me settle into a situation that inevitably seemed a little strange given the rapid succession of events – it was, remember, still less than two weeks since I received the first, out-of-the-blue phone call from Chris Bright.

The Jersey Evening Post – which, I would soon learn, was referred to by all as The JEP – had its office at Five Oaks, to the north of St Helier and about half-an-hour's walk from the hotel. An open-plan building housed an editorial department of around 50 and, in total, between 150 and 200 employees. Apart from The Southampton Advertiser, it was the only office I had worked at where the paper was printed on the premises and one of the early experiences I found a little odd was seeing, in print, a page I might have only finished subbing a few minutes earlier.

After spending the first few days doing a bit of everything, subbing-wise, from the second week I was asked to compile the paper's two world and national news pages, using Press Association copy, where the emphasis was very much on including stories that had broken between midnight and our 1.30pm deadline and would not have been in that day's national papers.

I also helped out regularly on the sports desk while the afternoons saw the subs drop down a couple of gears, following the lunchtime deadline frenzy, and prepare features pages for the following day's edition.

As the weeks went by things continued to progress smoothly and satisfactorily. I found no problem in adjusting from weekly to daily deadlines and my headlines were already starting to draw praise from Chris Bright and other senior editorial staff members.

After the first month I had been offered a new contract taking me up until early July. The JEP were keen to keep me for this longer-than-expected period as John Bowen had decided that island life was not for him and had returned to the mainland once his initial month's contract expired.

The money was so good that not only was I living comfortably, but clearing my credit card debts as rapidly as they had built up during the second half of 1996. What helped further was that I was only required to pay the first £100 per week for the hotel with The JEP quite happy to foot the rest of the bill. I had never worked anywhere before where money was simply no object and the whole experience seemed on a different planet to the penny-pinching world of David Banks and Dawlish Newspapers where I had still been employed only four years earlier.

Outside of work my two main drinking partners were Graeme Currie, a single Liverpudlian in his early 30s who was The JEP's only staff sub not to hail from the island, and the much-older Neil Bradbury, a Mancunian from the paper's sportsdesk who had worked with my father at The Daily Star in the early 1980s and remembered him well. The three of us regularly frequented St Helier pubs after work while Graeme and I usually spent Sunday afternoons watching Premier League football on Sky at The Sports Bar, a modern pub in the centre of the town.

I was having my post redirected from Cornwall and among the birthday cards I received in March was, surprisingly, one from Naomi, informing me that she was indeed married and living in Cambridge, where her husband taught physics. I had not been too upset by the absence of a Christmas card three months earlier, thinking that convention decreed that contact with 'exs' ceased once one was wed, but, possibly after discussing the matter with her partner, she obviously had second thoughts.

I sent her a postcard, giving news of the upturn in my fortunes, and received a reply, a few weeks later, in which she expressed astonishment at this latest development in my 'rollercoaster' career.

As we moved into May – with the main news back in the UK being a landslide Labour general election victory ending 18 years of Conservative rule – I received my second shortlisting in The UK Press Gazette's Headline of the Month competition. This time it related to the ending of an outbreak of Colorado beetles on the island – which I titled 'No more beetles – have they let it be/' – although I never found out who nominated me, although I was fairly certain it was one or both of Graeme and Neil.

Around this time Lis Perchard, The JEP's Chief Sub-editor, confirmed that her desk was soon to be back to full strength and I would not be needed beyond early July, but would I be interested in returning, on a longer contract, at the end of the year, when one of her subs was due to retire?

I had no idea what was going to happen when I returned to Cornwall, although I was planning to contact Steve Crossman as we had agreed in early February, but said there would be a good chance that I would be interested in a second stint at The JEP.

I said my farewells to all at the paper, and indeed to Peter and Karen at the hotel, during the first weekend in July and flew back to the mainland hoping, even though I was certainly not short of money, that it would not be a case of 'after the Lord Mayor's show' with little or no work being available at The Cornishman or elsewhere.

I was not to be disappointed. On the Monday morning Steve Crossman rang, asking if I could work Tuesday and Wednesday of that week, and as I caught the train down to Penzance the following day and made my way up the main street towards The Cornishman office, there was a strange feeling of not only being back in familiar surroundings but also wondering if the previous five months had really happened.

I quickly rejoined my two quiz teams, each of which had kept going in my absence albeit with various personnel changes, and generally, amongst family, friends and colleagues, many a tale of life in Jersey was both sought and happily given.

The Cornishman had nobody off the following week and I was waiting to hear when they would need me again, but on the Monday I did receive a call and when my mother informed me that it was a John Pearn on the phone, I immediately recognised the name. He had been Editor of The Cornish Guardian during my first stint with Cornish Weekly Newspapers and had then succeeded Robert Spratt at The West Briton the previous autumn.

He explained that he was going to be short of sub-editors for the next few weeks and was I interested in working for him as a freelance, possibly until the end of August?

I asked whether this would generate a clash of interests with The Cornishman, but was told he and Richard Van Hinsberg had already discussed the situation and had agreed that The West Briton would have first call on me for the remainder of July and throughout August, then I would be required at Penzance during most of September when several holidays were booked.

I agreed to meet John Pearn on the Wednesday afternoon, once The West Briton had gone to print, with a view to starting work the following day. I suddenly realized that he had said nothing of the circumstances of my departure from the Truro office the previous year and decided that, rather than spend the next 48 hours wandering what he might ask, to get the subject out of the way now.

'One thing I should mention is that, as you probably know, I worked for The West Briton before and, well, it didn't end very happily,' I said.

'Well that was before my time,' he replied. 'I've spoken to several people about you and checked into your background and I'm quite satisfied that you can do the job,'

I recalled hearing that, when he was Cornish Guardian Editor, John Pearn did not get on at all with Robert Spratt and that was something else that was obviously counting to my advantage.

A generally warm welcome greeted my unexpected return to the Truro office. There were several new faces, on both the news and subs desks, but apart from a couple of predictable suspects, those I knew seemed quite happy to see me again and Jeremy Ridge even quipped that I was 'more than 15 months late' (for the meeting with Robert Spratt).

I was also informed that The West Briton's previous Editor had stayed only a few months as an assistant editor at The Western Morning News before Northcliffe high command shunted him off to run one their monthly magazines somewhere in Devon and never to be heard of in the newspaper world again (whether The UK Press Gazette article played any part in his downfall I never did discover).

I spent most of the next seven weeks working full-time in a much-improved atmosphere at the Truro paper. There was a sudden three-day return to Penzance in early August when Richard Wardle, the sub from Wolverhampton who replaced Nigel Salmon, had to rush back to the Midlands following the death of his father and John Pearn agreed to 'lend me back' to The Cornishman for the busiest part of the week.

I gratefully took the first week in September off, realising that it would be my first full seven days without employment since travelling to Jersey almost seven months earlier, and the break coincided with the aftermath of the death of Princess Diana in Paris on the Saturday night. Every local and regional newspaper filled its pages with pictorial tributes from when she visited their area, but the media coverage generally became so saturated that this was something I was quite happy to miss out on.

Three weeks followed doing holiday cover at The Cornishman. During my final Friday afternoon there, just as I thought the summer relief subbing season had reached its natural conclusion, I was asked by Richard Van Hinsberg if I was interested in working the following Tuesday and Wednesday at The Cornish Guardian in Bodmin, which like The West Briton a few weeks earlier was one sub down while awaiting the arrival of a new staff member. I said 'why not' and was given the number of the Editor, Alan Cooper, to ring and confirm my attendance.

I caught the train, the following Tuesday, to Bodmin Parkway, about three miles from the town centre. One of the subs, by prior arrangement, picked me up and drove me to the office before returning me to the railway station in the evening.

As we travelled to work he asked me if I had worked for The Cornish Guardian before and as I replied 'no' it struck me that this was the paper where my father began his career, back in the 1950s, before progressing via The Western Morning News to the nationals.

I was not, however, expecting there to be any editorial members of staff who remembered him as someone aged 18 then would be in their late 50s by now and had they still been at the same paper it probably would have set some kind of national long-service record.

I went on to work three consecutive Tuesdays and Wednesdays in Bodmin, which were completed to everyone's satisfaction, but I knew that, as we were now into October, work at any of the Cornish Weekly Newspapers titles would not be plentiful from now on and I wondered what I was going to do next.

During my penultimate week at The Cornish Guardian I saw an advert for a full-time sub-editor in Kingsbridge, a small town buried in a remote, rural corner of Devon known as the South Hams. I had never visited that part of the county before, but in order not to put all my eggs in one basket – given the uncertainty of how much work would be available at Cornish Weekly Newspapers during the winter and in case the call to return to Jersey never came – I despatched an application.

The Kingsbridge Gazette was owned by Tindle Newspapers who, I had been informed by Mike Taylor shortly before going to the Channel Islands, had parted company with David Banks the previous year and appointed a general manager to bring all of its South Devon operations – in Newton Abbot, Dawlish, Totnes and Kingsbridge – under one umbrella. Consequently. this was about as close as I could get to returning to Dawlish

Newspapers, four-and-a-half years after departing, without actually doing so.

In keeping with the way the year had gone (where as soon as one source of work started to dry up another would appear) I received a phone call from Kingsbridge the day after finishing at The Cornish Guardian and made the two-and-a-half hour journey, by train and then rural bus from Totnes, on the Friday.

I was interviewed by Editor Brian Cooke, whose 24 years at the helm exceeded even Max Hodnett's length of tenure in the top job, while Mike Roberts, the aforementioned group general manager, popping in for part of the proceedings. They explained how short staffed they were and given that I had nothing more definitely lined up in Cornwall, asked if I could work a week's trial as a freelance from the following Monday.

I pointed out that my non-driver status would make it impractical for me to commute from Truro, and we would have been talking about a 150-mile daily round trip even if I had possessed a car, but they replied that was no problem – they would foot the bill for bed and breakfast. Such a generous offer immediately made me wonder whether the financial antics of David Banks at Dawlish Newspapers had really been as typical of Tindle companies as I had been led to believe.

The first week at my fifth newspaper office that year went well. I was asked to compile the sports pages, which seemingly no-one else liked doing, and wrapped them up in two days before moving onto news on deadline day and then the company's free newspapers on the quieter Thursday.

The following lunchtime I was offered a three-month contract by Brian Cooke with the option of then becoming a permanent staff member if I did not go back to Jersey. This timescale suited me down to the ground as by the time the three months had expired, I would definitely know, one way or the other, whether a Channel Islands return was on the cards.

I quickly settled into the routine at Kingsbridge, taking a small flat there after the company paid for a second week in bed and breakfast. My colleagues were a friendly crowd and I soon joined the drinkers – Deputy Editor Ron White, sub Trevor Drew, Chief Reporter Philippa Thompson and a couple of production staff – for their early Thursday evening sessions in the hotel bar next to the office.

My only misgiving was the remoteness of the town – an hour by bus to either Totnes or Plymouth, the nearest railway connections, with no public transport links at all on Sundays between October and March. However, I became a regular at the Creek's End pub, which showed live football on Sky, and felt reasonably settled as an extraordinary year drew to a close.

But during the second week in December I received a phone call from my mother informing me that the Editor's secretary in Jersey had tried to contact me. I was subsequently asked not only to return to The JEP, but with the possibility of a year's contract once an initial settling-back-in period had been completed.

With a certain amount of sadness, I informed Brian Cooke that I would not be staying on once the three-month agreement expired in late January. He acknowledged that, as Editor of such a small weekly title, he wouldn't remotely be able to match The JEP's financial offer and agreed I ought to get some more experience of working for a daily title onto my cv. I was welcome to return to Kingsbridge, providing they had a vacancy, at any time in the future, he added.

I had often heard it said that runs of good and bad luck in one's life have a habit of evening themselves out over the years. I had experienced nothing but bad luck during most of 1995 and 1996, but after the remarkable events of 1997 – which, of course, had started off so pessimistically – I had to finally admit that those who expounded this theory might well have been right.

16 The long walk home

I returned to Jersey on the last day of January, a Saturday, ready to recommence work two days later. Although I had already arranged to again reside at The Almorah Hotel – which only reopened that weekend after the winter break that many such establishments on the island took – I knew that, as this time I was likely to be at The JEP for considerably longer, I would need to find a flat.

The most significant news I learnt on my first day back was that Graeme Currie had left the paper shortly before Christmas after a falling out with Chris Bright. Relations between the two of them had always been a little strained – mainly as a result of Graeme's tendency to speak his mind and query instructions – so while I found his departure disappointing from a social point of view, I was not totally surprised.

I placed a free advert for a flat in three consecutive editions of The JEP, but knew finding somewhere might not prove straightforward as there were limitations on where non-Jersey folk, without what were known as housing qualifications, were allowed to live. I certainly didn't expect to get a positive response as quickly as I did.

A Maureen Chapman contacted me, saying she had a top floor flat available in her own St Helier home. When I asked whether the island's housing regulations would allow someone from the UK to take the property she said there would be no problem as whoever lived there would share her front door and therefore, technically, counted as a lodger, even though the flat was totally self-contained.

So at the end of my second week back I took up residence at what, in most parts of England, would have been considered a high rent, although some of my colleagues assured me that I wouldn't find anything cheaper in Jersey and, on what I was getting paid, I could certainly afford it.

I soon settled back into the routine at The JEP, again mainly compiling the world news pages and helping out on sport, and despite such an eventful seven months back in the UK, on the work side of things it was almost as if I had never been away. It was outside of the office that I started to notice a marked change.

Socially things got off to a reasonable start with a retirement party for the Features Editor Gordon Young on my first Friday back and a bowling night on the second Saturday, but these were one-off events. The previous year sometimes as many as eight or nine JEP editorial staff congregated at a St Helier pub called The Lamplighter after work on Wednesdays, but by now the only regular attendees were Neil Bradbury and a sub called Chris Lake with other former participants having either left the paper or simply stopped going.

There were no longer any regular after-work pub trips on Fridays – something I found more than a little surprising as one of the social conventions of the island seemed to be that all office workers flocked to a hostelry at that time of the week – and what with Graeme Currie having departed, there was no longer anyone guaranteed to watch Sky football with on a Sunday afternoon as Neil usually only went to the pub when his team, Manchester City, were being shown.

Having found myself with a lot more solitary time on my hands, outside of work, than I would have liked, one weekend activity I expanded was my preparation for a 49-mile round-the-island sponsored walk, set for mid-June, which I decided to enter after hearing about the annual event the previous year. Many of my colleagues expressed doubt, given my drinking and smoking prowess, as to whether I would stand a chance of completing the full distance, but I had always been a natural-born walker. I had completed 20-mile sponsored events in consecutive years when aged 11 and 12 – although doing more than double that distance would certainly be a challenge.

I never had my own computer during my first spell at The JEP – as a temporary freelance I simply moved from week to week to the work station of whoever was on holiday or otherwise absent – but having now replaced a retiring staff member I now had my own permanent berth and couldn't help notice the apathetic and insular existence of most of the downtable subs around me. A couple of them never spoke to anyone unless they had to on work matters, while others talked of nothing but television programmes, the routine of their own family lives and running down other people in the office providing they were well out of earshot.

Rarely was a word spoken on news, current affairs or sport, the mainstays of casual conversation in most if not all of the previous offices I had worked in. Indeed the only previous occasion I had been forced to listen to such dull and trivial diatribes had been at Dawlish where because of the cramped and crowded office, journalists had the misfortune of being able to hear accounts of the daily lives of their non-editorial colleagues. It was strange that I hadn't been aware of this situation during my first stint at The JEP – perhaps because I kept moving about the office and possibly, also, because I was the new boy and was too busy concentrating on getting the work done.

The round-the-island walk took place on the third Saturday in June, at the end of a week's holiday I had taken to coincide with the opening days of the 1998 World Cup in France. After a promising start, I felt shattered by halfway and although I struggled on, by the time we reached the 30-mile mark at Grosnez I was unable to walk uphill any more and withdrew. It was a blistering hot day and around half of the 500 participants failed to complete the full distance, but I was nevertheless disappointed.

Several people at the office commented that given my lifestyle and the fact that I had spent much of the preceding week watching football in various St Helier pubs, I had done well to achieve 30 miles. However a more likely explanation for my failure to go further came from a friend of Neil's, who drank regularly with us in The Lamplighter and had completed the walk several times before. He pointed out that I shouldn't have covered eight miles the day before, when I walked from St Helier to St Aubin and back as a 'final warm-up', but instead should have taken it easy in the 72 hours leading up to the main event.

A few weeks later, on August 7, came another illustration of the mindset of many of the middle and lower-ranking journalists at The JEP. Part of my job, in editing the world and national news pages, was to keep a constant watch on breaking stories, via the Press Association and ceefax, so that each day's edition was as up-to-date as possible.

That morning reports started coming through of simultaneous terrorist attacks on the United States embassies in Tanzania and Kenya. I immediately informed Chris Bright and as we moved towards our deadline it became clear that hundreds had been killed and many more injured in the truck bomb explosions that brought Osama bin Laden to the attention of the general public for the first time.

The breaking story, not surprisingly, filled almost all of the two world news pages and was trailed on the front of the paper -- something fairly unusual for a non-Jersey event – but it was the reaction of some of my immediate colleagues that truly amazed me. After some initial eyebrow-raising at the unfolding events, within an hour, before that day's edition had even gone to print, the conversation had returned to EastEnders, what arrangements the married ones had made for picking their children up from school and what they were going to have for dinner that night.

This non-journalistic culture, as I later described it to Lis Perchard, was partly down to Jersey's employment laws which stated that permanent staff positions could only be filled by non-islanders if no-one resident could do the job (I was on a fixed-term renewable contract and therefore unaffected by this rule).

However the consequence was that the majority of JEP subs had never been reporters, while none of them, unlike the vast majority of senior UK journalists, had worked at another newspaper office. They came from a variety of backgrounds: Channel Islands television or radio, magazines, teaching and some were ex-production employees switched to editorial when redundancies loomed (a growing trend in newspapers it seemed).

Moreover the fact that many of them did not become sub-editors until they were in their 30s or 40s inevitably meant they were set in their ways and were either oblivious to or had no desire to indulge in the traditions of the profession, whether constantly keeping in touch with, and reflecting upon, what was happening locally, nationally or internationally or going to the pub after work.

Unfortunately the generally-younger members of the news desk, some of whom were also late entrants with no formal journalistic training, were, with a couple of exceptions, little better, so there was no escape route for me there.

Offsetting this situation was the fact that I was enjoying the work, that with the passing of each month my bank balance rose by an additional £500, despite my going to the pub almost every day and paying a large amount in rent, and that I was quite settled in my accommodation which was handily situated for both the office and the town centre.

I was now on a year's contract until the following April, which I hoped to extend to have another crack at the round-the-island walk, and despite the vagueness and strange priorities of many of my colleagues, I had no intention of returning to the mainland before I was good and ready.

There were, at this stage, still enough positive social happenings to prevent me becoming too downhearted by the office environment. That summer saw a couple of leaving dos – including Chris Lake who, despite returning to teaching, continued to turn up at The Lamplighter on Wednesdays – and at the end of September I spent a busy week's holiday back in Truro after eight months away. In November Dave Ball, a friend of mine from Cornwall who had lived and worked on Jersey in his younger days, came over for a week's break and we enjoyed several drinking sessions. The following month saw my third week's holiday of the year when I again returned to the mainland for the Christmas period.

It was during late 1998 that the Wednesday evening drinking circle was boosted by one with the arrival of Mel Warrs on the subs desk. Originally from Yorkshire, he was a former JEP journalist who had left the paper a few years earlier due to what we were told were personal problems which he had now put behind him and was ready to return to work.

He was interesting to converse with and, on occasions, quite good company, but it soon became evident that he had a serious drinking problem. While Neil, myself and one or two others in the office were heavy drinkers, we never indulged while at work – there were no lunch hours anyway, only a 15 to 20 minute break after the paper went to print – and, it is fair to say, never let our outside-the-office consumption affect the way we did our jobs.

Mel, however, regularly turned up to work reeking of alcohol and still obviously under the influence from the previous night and later started sneaking off to the one nearby pub (a downmarket establishment rarely used by anyone from The JEP) for a top-up.

His appearance showed that his long-term lifestyle had taken its toll: despite only being in his mid-40s he looked at least 60 with completely white hair and a haggard face while an extremely-scruffy appearance added to his negative demeanour. Several of the younger staff members, who were not at the paper during Mel's first spell there, asked who the 'old bloke' was shortly after he recommenced work.

On some days he was fine, doing the work satisfactorily and being perfectly amiable, but on others simply sitting in a drunken stupor and unable to do anything. Sadly but inevitably his contract was cancelled in early 1999 and although he continued to turn up at The Lamplighter some Wednesdays, the state in which he appeared was as unpredictable as it had been at the office.

Before he left The JEP Mel had been responsible, presumably on one of his better days, for my third and final nomination of the decade to the shortlist of The UK Press Gazette's Headline of the Month competition. Again a pop song was the inspiration: Bob Geldof's commencement of legal action against The Sun newspaper being accompanied by 'Tell you why I don't like Sun days'.

I had signed an extension to my contract, keeping me at The JEP until late September, and was by now spending much of each weekend training for the rapidly-approaching round-the-island walk, covering up to 12 miles most Saturdays and Sundays, mainly along the island's south west coast from St Helier to St Aubin and up to the Five Mile Road before returning via a couple of pubs.

It was also around this time that I had my first experience of the internet. One of The JEP's computers had the rising-phenomenon installed and Deputy Editor Rob Shipley spent 15-minute sessions, during the quieter afternoon periods, showing each editorial department member how it worked.

Even at this relatively-early stage of what many were already calling the alternative media, there were some concerns that the internet could, in the long term, pose a threat to newspapers, but after the matter was discussed at a meeting of The JEP's senior editorial staff, the consensus was that people would always want a permanent record of certain events – be it a football match, wedding or obituary report – and the future of our industry was secure.

Saturday June 19, the day of the royal wedding between Prince Edward and Sophie Rhys-Jones, saw my second attempt at the 48-mile trek around Jersey's coastline. Because of the distance involved, the event began at 3am – to ensure that everyone, no matter how slow, would finish before darkness fell the following evening – and the mid-summer date was chosen to ensure the maximum amount of daylight hours.

There was an early hiccup when my pre-ordered taxi failed to arrive and I had to walk around a mile-and-a-half to the start point at St Helier harbour before my participation officially got under way. This made me late and meant setting off behind the rest of the field which, in a way, was an advantage as I spent the entire day catching up and overtaking walkers slower than myself rather being drawn into 'race' situations with the faster participants and consequently wasting energy.

I had not repeated the mistake of the previous year by practicing too close to the day, having done no serious walking since the Wednesday evening, and felt relatively-comfortable throughout as I completed the full distance in around 15 hours and 50 minutes, a time safely within the fastest 100 of the day, I was reliably informed, although official finishing positions were not released because of the organisers' policy that the event was a charity fund-raiser and not a race.

Lis Perchard had asked me, beforehand, if I would be prepared to write a feature for The JEP on the walk from a personal perspective and I readily agreed providing I completed the 48 miles. My subsequent piece was well received by all – including one of the walk's organisers who rang me at the office to congratulate me on 'a lovely piece of writing' – and the article provided me with my first by-line on any newspaper since leaving Dawlish six years earlier.

The JEP had, by now, become short-staffed again and following a plea from Lis Perchard I agreed to a third and final contract-extension up until Christmas when, I made it clear, I would definitely be returning to the UK as by then my second spell at the paper would be close to two years and that, I felt, was long enough to be away from the mainland in one go.

After the walk, very little happened outside the routine of work during July and August, but on the first Friday of September Chris Bright asked if I would mind being seconded, for three weeks, to The Guernsey Press, which was changing from a broadsheet to a tabloid format and had asked for help, being owned by the same parent company as The JEP, during the transitional period.

I had been chosen as the most suitable person because of my experience of working for different papers whereas none of my colleagues had been subs elsewhere. I agreed to go providing I did not finish out of pocket and was told I need have no worries as The Guernsey Press had already agreed to pay for my flights and accommodation.

By an ironic twist, I had been due to make my first visit to Guernsey the following day for a reciprocal social event between the two papers which saw JEP staff as guests of the Guernsey counterparts at a barbecue to be held a sports club hired for the day while the England v Luxembourg European Championship qualifier would be shown live in the bar.

This event, I understood, had no official connection with The Guernsey Press's re-launch, but had been arranged some months earlier. However it provided me with a fitting opportunity to meet my new temporary colleagues informally two days before starting work with them.

True to form, very few of The JEP's editorial staff took up their invitations, even although the ferry fares were being paid for by the company and all food and drink at the clubhouse would be free. I was the only sub to attend and was joined by Neil, Sports Editor Ron Felton and four or five younger members of the news desk with the rest of the travelling party being made up by members of advertising, administration and production.

Our hosts were very welcoming, despite the well-known fierce rivalry between the two islands, and after watching the football, I made myself known to several Guernsey Press editorial staff members who said they looked forward to seeing me on the Monday.

On the return ferry journey Neil and I reflected on the hardly-unexpected poor turnout by JEP editorial members, agreeing, quite loudly after a day's free drinking, that if they weren't prepared to attend an all-expenses-paid day out like that, what hope was there for such 'boring and lifeless' individuals.

I returned to Guernsey, this time by plane, two days later and, after a none-too-taxing first day's work, was accompanied to my accommodation, a nearby pub which was also the paper's 'local', by Deputy Editor Richard Digard who stayed for a couple of drinks after I had checked in.

He informed me that The Guernsey Press were not only prepared to pay my bed and breakfast costs but evening meals at the pub and I was also given the paper's account number with a taxi firm so I could travel to and from the airport without cost. Basically the only money I needed to spend those three weeks was on drink and cigarettes –

although, of course, I still had to pay rent on the flat in St Helier.

The editorial staff in Guernsey were, as had been indicated the previous Saturday, a breath of fresh air, both socially and spiritually, after the lifelessness of most of my immediate colleagues at The JEP. The tone and content of casual conversation was what I would have expected any newspaper office and almost every evening at least a couple of people from the office would drop into the pub for a drink or two with Fridays seeing quite a gathering.

Paradoxically it has to be said that The Guernsey Press, as a finished product, was a far inferior publication, both in design and content, to The JEP, although the paper seemed to be successful – the amount of money they were prepared to spend to accommodate me was an indication of that – and there was a lively but pleasant atmosphere throughout the office.

Richard Digard was very much the day-to-day boss with the much-older Editor so anonymous that he remains the only person I have worked for holding that position whose full name I can't remember, although I think his surname might have been something like Machon.

One minus point, outside of work, were Guernsey 's archaic licensing laws which prevented pubs opening on Sundays, other than between midday and 3pm, while supermarkets were not allowed to sell alcohol at all on the Sabbath. This presented a problem during my second weekend there as Tottenham were scheduled to appear on Sky, away to Bradford City, with a 4pm kick-off. I therefore flew over to Jersey to watch the game in the Sports Bar – the only time I have ever flown anywhere to watch a football match.

On my final day Richard Digard inquired what my future plans were and I confirmed that I would be returning to the mainland at Christmas, but thereafter I wasn't too sure. He requested my Cornwall telephone number in case he urgently needed a freelance at any point in the future – confirmation, if any were needed, that I had made a positive impression at The Guernsey Press.

I returned to my flat in St Helier to find, among the backlog of unopened post, a letter from Naomi, informing me that her first child, a boy named Ralph, had been born in early August. Like me she was now in her late 30s, so I suppose if she wanted a family the matter couldn't have been left much longer. We had maintained occasional contact during my time in Jersey – I had sent her a copy of my article on the walk earlier in the summer – but I wondered whether she might see becoming a mother as one hurdle too many to justify remaining in contact with a long-term 'ex'.

While I was welcomed back to The JEP by the likes of Chris Bright and Lis Perchard, who were keen to know how I got on in Guernsey and how the working practices of the two papers compared, there was a more-muted reception from certain other people in the office who spoke to me even less than before. I later learnt, via the smoking room gossip, that Neil and I had, that evening travelling back on the ferry, talked a little too loudly about some of our colleagues' aversion to socialising and our comments had been passed on to those we had criticised.

Some of the individuals on the subs' desk and elsewhere in the editorial department almost adopted an 'I'm boring and proud of it' defence of their lifestyles outside of work, saying they had family responsibilities and labelling the likes of Neil, Graeme Currie and myself as 'alcoholics' – even though we never drank during working hours or turned up at the office under the influence – who weren't really typical of journalists at all. Of course, such an argument would have been laughed out of any UK newspaper office, but they probably didn't even realise that. To some extent we were talking about a Jersey v mainland culture clash, although it was ironic that the same situation did not exist at The Guernsey Press.

All this led to a slightly-strained but largely-uneventful final few weeks on the island. So as not only the year, but the decade and indeed the century drew to a close, so did my first substantial spell with a daily paper and the most financially-profitable period of my career so far.

On my final day Chris Bright, like Brian Cooke at Kingsbridge two years earlier, said I could come back whenever I liked providing there was a vacancy. However while I had no regrets whatsoever about returning to Jersey for a second, longer period, unless it was a case of 'needs must' my gut instincts told me I would not be taking up his offer.

17 Round of applause for The Indy

1999 had been the first time I had been away from Cornwall for a full year from Christmas to Christmas – a situation brought about by the uncertainty of exactly when I was leaving Jersey and the round-the-island walk preventing any return during my main holiday in June – so there was an awful lot of catching up to do, with family and friends, that festive season.

With nearly £15,000 in the bank and no debts there was certainly no financial urgency to find work quickly, but I knew that once the novelty of being back on the mainland wore off, I would soon start getting bored and was determined not to remain inactive for any longer than was necessary.

Around a month before leaving Jersey I had rung Brian Cooke – considering The Kingsbridge Gazette to be a paper where I had 'unfinished business' given my earlier, happy stay had been cut short by the financial lure of a return to The JEP – but he had no vacancies, adding that he would let me know if the situation changed.

In order to try and establish some sort of continuity in working for daily titles, I also sent speculative letters to The Herald Express and The Express & Echo, in that part of Devon I was so familiar with, but only got 'we'll keep your name on file' replies.

In mid-December I rang Steve Crossman at The Cornishman, informing him that I was about to return, and picked up several interesting pieces of information, not least of which was that Richard Van Hinsberg's ill-conceived fad to bring in an outsider to replace Nigel Salmon had not worked out with Richard Wardle having parted company with the paper, for what Steve would only say was 'a temper problem', earlier in the year.

He had been replaced, as a full-time member of staff, by the former production worker who had taken over from me as relief sub and subsequently my old job was vacant.

Even more interesting was the news that the entire Northcliffe newspaper empire was in the process of switching to a new subbing system called Tera and that The Cornishman would be the first title in the county to make the change in March with The West Briton and The Cornish Guardian following later in the year.

The spring changeover, followed by the usual office summer holidays season, meant a lot of freelance work would be available between March and September, although there would be nothing foreseeable available before that time, and Steve Crossman suggested that, providing I was not otherwise employed, I get in touch again towards the end of February.

Socially things had once again clicked back into place in Truro as if I had never been away with very few friends' personal circumstances and lifestyles having changed significantly during my longer-than-usual absence from my home town. The Wednesday quiz team at The Globe was still going strong, by now being in its seventh year, and while the similar Monday night event at the football social club had folded the previous year, my team had relocated to another, new quiz at a pub called The City Inn on Sundays.

I rang Steve Crossman again in late February and was told Richard Van Hinsberg was finalising plans for the spring and summer and would be in touch soon. Around the same time, in order to keep my options open, I applied for the role of Deputy Chief Sub-editor at The Basingstoke Gazette in Hampshire after seeing the job advertised in The UK Press Gazette.

I was invited to attend an interview on the first Friday in March and decided to make a weekend of it in the South

East by staying in Basingstoke overnight after the appointment and going on to London the following day for a long-overdue visit to a Tottenham Hotspur game. Mainly through being off the mainland, I had not been to White Hart Lane for more than four years and the match, against Bradford City, was ironically the return fixture of that I had flown from Guernsey to Jersey to watch six months earlier.

The interview at The Basingstoke Gazette went, I felt, very well, but a fortnight then passed before I heard anything from the Editor Bill Browne. His letter said the standard of applicant had been very high and the task of picking out the most suitable candidate had been 'no easy task', but ultimately I had been unsuccessful. A few days later I was phoned by Richard Van Hinsberg –asking me to start work the following Monday, initially for three days a week rising to five once the staff holidays began but with nothing guaranteed beyond the end of August – so, for the time being, I would be remaining in Cornwall.

A lot more than the subbing system had changed at The Cornishman. Firstly the paper had moved from its old office in North Parade to a smaller outlet called Alverton Manor on the outskirts of the town centre. Also there had been several staff changes, particularly on the reporting side, and the fresh surroundings coupled with the new faces generated a completely different atmosphere to that I had been used to between 1994 and 1997.

The Tera method was not too difficult to grasp – it took most of us two to three weeks to reach the same speeds we had previously achieved on Applemacs – but rather than being a revolutionary step forward in newspaper production technology, it seemed unbelievably antiquated to me, with no on-screen subbing possible and the use of weird signs that reminded me of the by-now archaic pre-computer 'casting off' method of writing instructions for typesetters.

When I remarked as such to Richard Van Hinsberg, he agreed with me, describing Tera as 'a backward step' which

Northcliffe was imposing on its titles as a 'cost-cutting' measure. This emphasis on saving money seemed a little strange as the expense of installing the new computers in every office in the country, along with the retraining of existing staff and bringing in freelances like me to help during the transitional period, must surely have been substantial.

Although I soon got into the routine of things at the 'new' Cornishman, and spring and summer passed quite quickly, far more irritating than the slightly-odd subbing system were the intake of young reporters since my previous spell at the paper, who ranged from slap-happy to downright incompetent and who would simply shrug their shoulders when told they had done something wrong and then repeat the practice a few days later. Steve Crossman admitted that the often-poor standard of copy was 'a nuisance', but no action was taken to change the situation.

I completed my five-month stint in Penzance on the last Wednesday in August. Thereafter nobody with subbing responsibilities had holidays booked before the new year and Steve Crossman said he had 'no idea' when they would need me again.

I heard, on the grapevine, that The Sunday Independent was looking for a sub-editor although they had not, to my knowledge, advertised. This, you might recall, was the Plymouth-based regional title where I had been interviewed for a reporter's job shortly before going to Dawlish in early 1988.

My recollections of that day were fairly vague – perhaps because I preferred to remember my more positive visit further up the south Devon coast a couple of weeks later – but I did recall that the Editor who interviewed me that day was male, so when I rang the paper's switchboard to find out who the present incumbent was, I knew that there must have been a change when informed that the current Acting Editor was a Nikki Rowland.

I sent off a speculative letter to The Sunday Independent, known simply as The Indy by many in Devon and Cornwall, and while I was awaiting a reply received an astonishing, out-of-the-blue letter from Richard Van Hinsberg relating to my final Friday at The Cornishman when, due to a lack of work, I finished at lunchtime.

It seemed that, after I departed, one of the young pretenders on the newsdesk had decided to play a practical joke on a colleague by inserting a swear word into one of his stories before it had been subbed and, in order to avoid detection, had done so on a computer other than his own – the one I had been using earlier that day.

Anyone who has ever worked in a newspaper office during the electronic age will know how ridiculously easy it is to gain access to other people's computers. Even when passwords are used they are usually common knowledge as freelances and part-timers rarely have their own permanent desks and move around the office depending on who is absent. Yet here I was being asked by Richard Van Hinsberg if I 'knew anything about' the incident.

I wrote back saying I had no recollection of even reading the story in question (I would have had no need to given it was not allocated to one of my pages and copy-subbing was not a working practice at the Penzance office), reminding him that I had finished early that day and obviously expressing dismay that someone of my age and experience could be questioned on such a matter.

I never learnt whether Richard Van Hinsberg got to the bottom of the incident and discovered who was responsible – there were three or four prime candidates, but without the availability of CCTV cameras irrefutable proof would be almost impossible to establish – but even before I received his bizarre communication I think I knew, deep down inside, that my six-year on-and-off association with England's most-westerly weekly newspaper was at an end.

For the second time in my career I had learnt the validity of the 'never go back' saying.

There was soon better news from The Sunday Independent when I received a phone call from the General Manager, a Simon Dixon-Phillip, who gave me a lengthy spiel on the paper's latest owners Newsquest, an American company who were relative newcomers to the British newspaper industry, before moving onto the more important matter of whether I could work the following Friday and Saturday – inevitably the two busiest days on a Sunday paper – on a freelance basis as the first step towards a possible staff position.

I spent a largely-enjoyable first couple of days at The Indy, working on news during Friday and Saturday afternoon before taking on a couple of football pages on a hectic deadline night. Nikki Rowland and the Sports Editor Kevin Marriot were obviously happy with my efforts as, before departing, I was asked to work Thursdays to Saturdays from the following week until further notice.

One slightly-peculiar happening during that first Friday at the office came midway through the morning when Simon Dixon-Phillip summoned everyone from editorial and production into the advertising department where he excitedly announced that a new sales rep, named Tracey, had exceeded her targets during her first month at the paper, concluding by saying 'I think that calls for a round of applause for Tracey'. The non-journalists present heartily responded and while I knew that, what with it being my first day, I had to keep a straight face, some of my new editorial colleagues were struggling to achieve a similar respect for the proceedings.

'I hope you don't think we're all raving mad after witnessing that,' said Nikki Rowland after we returned to our department. I asked whether such events were normal practice and was told that, until recently, they hadn't been.

'Knowing Newsquest it's probably some new national initiative that has to be implemented,' she added.

In addition to being lively and friendly, the atmosphere in the editorial department contained an element of mischievous irreverence towards senior management that I had not really experienced since my days at The Dawlish Gazette. Simon Dixon-Phillip was referred to by all, providing he wasn't present, as 'Dixie' and following events in the advertising department on my first day, anyone carrying out the most menial of tasks, even getting a round of coffees from the machine upstairs, was greeted upon their return by someone shouting out 'round of applause for…'

Unfortunately my second week at The Indy coincided with the Hatfield train crash in Hertfordshire which plunged the entire national rail network into chaos until the end of the year with speed restrictions, coupled with the arriving winter weather, meaning massive delays to services on almost a daily basis. Subsequently it was sometimes taking me up to three hours to complete journeys in each direction between Truro and the office, which was about three miles from Plymouth station, by train and bus. Although I was only working three days a week, those days were proving to be so long that I certainly felt as if I was employed full-time.

I was, on one occasion, able to turn the railway chaos to my advantage. On a wet and windy Saturday night in late November, having finished at the office at the usual deadline time of around 9pm, I arrived at Plymouth station to learn that the last train down to Truro had been delayed by an hour on its journey from London Paddington.

Such a scenario was not unusual in the post-Hatfield climate, but when the train finally limped into the station at about 10.45pm those of us waiting were suddenly told not to get on while those already aboard were ordered off. We then learnt that reports of thunder and lightning down in

Cornwall meant the train would be going no further and a fleet of taxis had been ordered – no doubt at some considerable cost to the Great Western rail company – to enable us to reach our destinations.

Out of a mixture of anger and journalistic instinct I decided to turn the situation into a news story, getting quotes from several of my equally-frustrated and willing-to-talk fellow travellers and handing the completed article to Nikki Rowland the following Thursday. It subsequently appeared as a page lead, under the heading 'Slow as lightning', and earned me £25 and my first by-line on a mainland paper for more than seven years.

The Indy's unashamedly downmarket tabloid style suited me down to the ground and I was receiving nothing but praise from all corners for my efforts. The paper was already editionalised for Devon, Cornwall and Somerset and, in the new year, there were plans for a fourth edition, solely for Plymouth, when a new reporter and sub-editor would be taken on to help with the increased workload. According to Nikki Rowland it would be a formality that I would be offered the latter role.

On the last Wednesday before Christmas I travelled up to the office on a day I was not scheduled to work to attend the editorial department's festive lunch. While I was waiting for everyone to finish what they were doing and decide who was travelling in what car with whom to the pub, Simon Dixon-Phillip asked to see me.

Never one to use five words when 50 would do, he began by telling me the latest news on the appointment of a new Editor. Nikki Rowland, I was already aware, did not want the job on a permanent basis through having three school-age children and an advert had been placed in The UK Press Gazette the previous month. A new Editor, I was told, would be in place by February.

Our General Manager, dressed as always in a bow-tie and braces, then moved onto my future at the paper. The much-vaunted Plymouth project, as he called it, would not now be happening (there had been rumours to this end circulating around the office during the previous week) and he would not now be taking on any new full-time staff members.

However because they had all been so impressed with my work to date, he was prepared to continue employing me three days a week and additionally full-time whenever anyone with subbing responsibilities, whether news or sport, was on holiday. I quickly calculated that this would mean at least 30 five-day weeks each year and accepted the offer while readily agreeing to move to Plymouth – I had already experienced enough of Great Western and the tedious weekly travelling schedule – as soon as I could find somewhere suitable to live.

I gave the news to my colleagues as we made our way to the Christmas lunch – another event which illustrated the slightly-archaic disregard for authority that generally existed in The Indy's editorial department.

A directive had been given that everyone working that day should return to the office once the meal ended at around 2.30pm, but apart from Nikki Rowland and Kevin Marriott no-one did – choosing instead to remain in the pub for a lengthy drinking session which did not conclude until the early evening.

The following day I witnessed a lengthy procession of editorial staff members being summoned, one at a time, into Simon Dixon-Phillip's office to be told how thoroughly naughty they had been. Seemingly the most severe dressing-downs were reserved for the more senior journalists involved – Deputy Chief-sub John Collings and Chief Reporter Anthony Abbot – who were informed they should have been setting an example rather than 'leading on' the youngsters.

We returned to work after Christmas to be told that the paper's new Editor was Andrew Kelly, latterly in charge of the Bedfordshire on Sunday title, who would be joining us at the end of February. Shortly afterwards Anthony Abbot gave notice to take up a (presumably better-paid) public relations job and we subsequently learnt that he would be replaced by a new Chief Reporter who would be accompanying Andrew Kelly from the Home Counties.

By mid-February I had found a suitable flat in the Mutley Plain area of Plymouth, within walking distance of the office and also on a direct bus route for whenever I didn't fancy the mile-and-a-half stroll, and left the family home in Truro as an indefinite resident for what turned out to be the last time (and some might say it was about time, although the nomadic nature of my career rather than financial necessity had led to my spells of residence in more recent years).

After a slow start, my first post-Jersey year had turned out to be quite eventful and I waited to see what the remainder of 2001, under the new regime at The Sunday Independent, would yield.

18 Look away from Dixieland

Andrew Kelly, who took over at The Sunday Independent shortly after my move to Plymouth, was about the same age as me – a sign, perhaps, that I was getting older as all my previous editors had not only been older than me, but in most cases by some considerable margin.

The new Chief Reporter who accompanied our new boss from Bedfordshire on Sunday was also his girlfriend, Alex Peake, who was about 10 years his junior. Although it soon became apparent to all at the office that neither of the newcomers had a habit of over-extending themselves, on a personal level they soon fitted into the slightly-mad environment, quickly catching on to Simon Dixon-Phillip's nickname and extending the banter further by regularly referring to our workplace as Dixieland.

The day-to-day office scenario at times resembled the 1990s television programme Drop The Dead Donkey. Relations between the editorial and advertising departments were not particularly good (not the first paper I had worked for where that had been the case) and as the sales reps made their way past the news and sports desks to deliver details of their adverts to the production room, they nearly always became known by nicknames of a largely-derogatory nature which were occasionally mentioned a little too loudly or before they had completely left the room.

On one occasion Graham Hambly – a veteran sports writer whose name I had known since my teens as for many years he covered Plymouth Argyle matches for The Evening Herald – described a tarty-looking, middle-aged recent female addition to the advertising department as a 'legover job' as she started to disappear into production.

Unfortunately she had forgotten something and turned back into our room just as the words were loudly leaving his lips.

Simon Dixon-Phillip's enthusiastic implementation of Newsquest's jargonistic Americanisms were constantly the subject of ridicule. At meetings, attended by department heads and their deputies, banned words included 'problem', which had to be replaced by 'issue', and 'cuts' which were really 'cost savings'. Rounds of applause were also regularly proposed – including one, ludicrously, for a young sales rep who was celebrating her 21st birthday – with Dixie seemingly oblivious to the contempt with which the paper's journalists treated his style of management.

A regular Friday evening drinking circle evolved, usually meeting at the Hogshead pub in Mutley Plain, with John Collings, Graham Hambly, reporters Kirsty Turner, John Couch and Mark Sullivan and myself the most regular members, although we were occasionally joined by Andrew Kelly and Alex Peake.

Being only a 45-minute train ride away from Dawlish, I had re-established the contact with Colin Wallace and Mike Taylor that had been lost while I was in Jersey and the three of us met up at Newton Abbot races two or three times that year. I also went down to Truro, where I was still an occasional member of the Sunday night quiz team at The City Inn, about every third weekend, and was feeling quite settled at The Indy until it started becoming apparent, during the second half of the year, that the paper was having financial problems.

The first sign, from my own perspective, was that I was being asked to work full-time less and less whenever anyone with subbing duties was on holiday. When I complained to Nikki Rowland, and she in turn raised the matter with Dixie, his untruthful reply was that he had 'no recollection' of guaranteeing me more than three days a week work when taking me on the previous Christmas.

In the late summer a raft of 'cost savings' were announced which not only included the axing of several contributed columns and a reduction in the use of photographs from freelances, but the non-retention of Mark Sullivan and Jon Couch, the paper's junior reporters, when their two-year contracts expired a few weeks later. This would leave Alex Peake and Kirsty Turner as the only full-time staff reporters, which seemed ridiculous for a regional paper, although Dixie did indicate that one new junior might be taken on at a later date.

The full-time editorial staff members were in the process of forming a National Union of Journalists branch – legislation introduced by the Labour government, which had won a second term of office a couple of months earlier, made it easier to do so than had been the case for many years, although such bodies still had very little power – and an unofficial meeting was held at The Golden Hind pub to discuss the cuts and particularly the dismissals.

I was invited to attend as an observer, but unfortunately the date chosen for the gathering was the early evening of Tuesday September 11 when the unfolding news of the terrorist attacks in the United States made the atmosphere a little unreal – someone present indeed commented 'that puts our problems into perspective' – although it was still abundantly clear to me that any new NUJ chapel could do nothing to prevent Dixie, whether or not he was simply following orders from higher up the Newsquest chain of command, from cutting whatever he liked.

During an informal conversation with Andrew Kelly, at another pub a few weeks later, I made it clear that my position was unsatisfactory; that I was using the money saved from Jersey to subsidise what, most weeks, was a part-time income and unless something changed I would have to look to move on again. He told me not to worry and that if I could hang on until after Christmas, he had expansion plans which would include me as a full-time, staff sub-editor.

His words sounded convincing and I assumed he must have been given the green light by Dixie to make such promises, so for the closing weeks of 2001 I held fire. Remarkably it had been the first time for a decade that I had only worked at a single newspaper office during a calendar year, but unless Andrew Kelly was true to his word, there would be little chance of that statistic being repeated in the 12 months to follow.

One positive development, from a work satisfaction point of view if not a financial one, came when Nikki Rowland invited me to write The Indy's leader column for the new year edition – something I had not done for any publication since my days as Editor of the student paper at Middlesex – and so impressed was everyone with my efforts that I was asked to permanently take on the role which previously had been done largely on the basis of whoever had the time before we went to print each Saturday evening.

In February Andrew Kelly called a meeting of the editorial staff to confirm, we thought, his much-vaunted expansion plans which, we had been told, included the editionalising of far more news pages to go hand-in-hand with the new full-time staff members including myself.

Instead all we were told was that a new trainee reporter would be starting shortly while the experienced Nigel Walrond – another journalist whose name I was familiar with but had never met – was rejoining the paper to fill a vacancy that had recently arisen on the sports desk and would also deputise for Kevin Marriott, thus allowing John Collings, who usually sat in for Kevin, to remain on news subbing all year round. No mention was made of increasing the editionalising, as had been promised, or of my becoming a staff member.

Dixie had obviously scuppered most of Andrew Kelly's proposed expansion plans and while our Editor had tried to come across as upbeat and enthusiastic, we all agreed afterwards that he had looked sheepish and embarrassed.

A few weeks later he and Alex Peake went off on holiday together to the United States. One Thursday, the first of my guaranteed three days at work each week, I went into the office to be told that Alex had called in two days earlier – to the astonishment of everyone present as she was not supposed to be back in the country for more than another week – and had subsequently left the company with immediate effect following a meeting with Dixie.

Although I never heard the full story, she and Andrew Kelly had a massive bust-up during the early days of her vacation and the relationship now being over, Alex obviously considered that working at The Indy was no longer an option.

Shortly afterwards came another round of 'cost savings', some of which were so petty that, as I remarked to someone at the time, they were literally penny-pinching (for instance cutting the number of national papers we received at the office from three to two each day) and rumours began that Andrew Kelly's days at the helm were numbered.

By now I had, not surprisingly, decided to apply for other jobs, the first suitable vacancy spotted being at The Farnham Herald. Despite my past connections with the town, this was not a paper I knew a great deal about, other than it being Tindle Newspapers' flagship title, as it had not been in direct competition with The Aldershot News, despite the close proximity of the two places, and I couldn't remember Naomi, or anyone else there, ever mentioning it.

While I awaited a reply to my application, we heard that Andrew Kelly was leaving The Sunday Independent in a month's time and the fact that he was not working the three-month notice period usually required of editors indicated some harsh words had been spoken at a meeting he attended with Dixie shortly before his departure was announced.

Neither Andrew Kelly nor Alex Peake were immediately replaced with the entire news editorial staff now consisting of Nikki Rowland, who again became Acting Editor, John Collings, Kirsty Turner and the recently-appointed trainee – at a paper, don't forget, that was supposed to cover three counties and several large towns and cities.

I attended an interview at Farnham on a Monday afternoon in late June. That my meeting with Editor Peter Thompson went well is probably best summed up by the fact that, before I left, he refunded my full train fare in cash (for a Tindle paper to pay interviewees' travel costs was almost unheard of).

Apart from the two of us seeming to be on the same wavelength journalistically, I stressed my first-hand knowledge of Farnham, albeit only as a weekend visitor more than a decade earlier, and I think being single also helped as, if appointed, I would not be bringing a family in tow to a town where available accommodation was neither plentiful nor cheap.

As I made the round trip from Plymouth in a day, I had very little time in Farnham either side of the interview and no opportunity to re-explore the town beyond the route between the railway station and the centrally-situated Herald office, much of which seemed unfamiliar although there were one of two landmarks that reminded me that this was somewhere I had been before.

Peter Thompson rang Nikki Rowland for the clinching reference three days later and despite not being a member of staff, I decided to give a month's notice in writing as I would not be required to start at The Herald until the second Monday in August.

Dixie's initial response to my resignation was, ironically, to ask me to work full-time those final four weeks – partly because Nikki Rowland had a fortnight's holiday booked during that period and also, I suspect, because the recent cutting of the wage bill made it possible for him to uncharacteristically increase expenditure for a strictly-limited period.

During my penultimate week at The Indy, Dixie called me into his office and after congratulating me on the quality of my belatedly-full-time work during the previous fortnight, said he had been going through the company's finances and that 'it might be possible' to offer me a full-time staff position.

This suggestion I immediately rebuffed without even needing any time to think it through. I had already given notice to leave my flat and accepted, in writing, Peter Thompson's offer of employment. 'Why should I let the people in Farnham down – they've done nothing wrong,' I said.

To this Dixie had no immediate answer but I later learnt, from Nikki Rowland, that once I had departed he informed everyone at the office that my exit was no fault of his as I had turned down a staff job – without mentioning, of course, that he deliberately made the offer far too late for there to be any chance of it being accepted.

I had not heard from Naomi since Christmas 1999, shortly after the birth of her first child. When my card to her the following festive season went unanswered, I believed that my earlier assumption – that motherhood, rather than marriage, would finally end communications between us – to be correct.

However given the ironic twist of my pending return to the scene of our downfall, I now felt there was a pretext to re-establish contact and sent off a letter after first discovering she and her husband had a new address through the 192.com website on the one Sunday Independent computer to have internet access.

While I had no journalistic regrets about my latest career move, as the weeks ticked down to joining The Farnham Herald I found my mind increasingly flashing back to my previous time in the town, not only the long-held regrets about not having moved there, which would inevitably now resurface more intensely, but also more obscure incidents that had been buried in my subconscious for several years.

The most peculiar of these came on a Sunday afternoon two weeks before I left Plymouth. I was watching Star Trek Generations on television – the film where Picard and Kirk join forces to save a star from destruction – which included a time-warp scene when the latter decides to propose marriage to the love of his life, rather than undertake the next Enterprise mission, only to then realise that the scenario is not real and therefore he cannot change the past as he had hoped. Picard, in turn, in transported to a parallel universe Christmas gathering where he is welcomed by the children he never had.

That these scenes ignited thoughts of how different my own personal life might have been was perhaps not surprising, but what followed certainly was – a vivid but hitherto long-forgotten recollection of something Naomi said to me in the pub near Waterloo station on the day we effectively split up in June 1987.

She described a dream, a few nights earlier, during which the doorbell rang at her house in Farnham and she answered the door to be greeted by an older version of me saying 'it's 2002 and I've come back to put things right'.

I even recalled some of her more minor observations, such as I hadn't looked as old as I would have been by that year and, with a slight hint of disapproval, that I still had fairly long hair. While her part-premonition had been spot-on in terms of the date of my return to the Surrey town and my appearance, I couldn't see how I was putting things right other than making the gesture of finally moving to where I should have been a decade-and-a-half earlier.

The present-day reality was that, with just a couple of weeks to go before I began the next stage of my career, I still had nowhere to live in Farnham. On Peter Thompson's advice, I had arranged through Sue Cansfield, his personal assistant, to place a box-number advert for a one-bedroom flat in three consecutive editions of The Herald. This strategy had worked well in Jersey, the last time I had sought accommodation outside my own part of the country, and I was hoping for a repeat performance.

But by the time my last day at The Sunday Independent arrived, on the first Saturday in August, I had received only one, less-than-serious reply. I was due to spend a week's holiday in Truro before travelling up to the South East and asked to be contacted there should there be any further responses to the advert. In the meantime, I provisionally arranged to take up residence in a Farnham guest house from the Friday before starting work.

Those final two weeks at the Plymouth office epitomised the way things had gone there during the previous few months. With Nikki Rowland ill and Kirsty Turner on holiday, it had been left to John Collings and myself, aided by the new trainee reporter, to fill the news pages which we somehow did, albeit with some unashamed 'lifting' of stories from other West Country weekly papers.

Such was the extent to which The Indy's editorial staff had been depleted that my leaving 'do', at a new Wetherspoons pub on Mutley Plain close to the flat I was about to vacate, was attended only by John Collings along with Graham Hambly and Nigel Walrond from the sports desk with Kevin Marriott, rumoured to be leaving the paper himself shortly, sending his apologies.

The week in Cornwall yielded no further replies to my advert, so indeed it was the guest house where I spent my first night in Farnham for 15 years after arriving there during the early evening of Friday August 9.

19 Finally Farnham

It had become a tradition that whenever I had started work in a location I knew very little about – the Isle of Wight, Teignmouth/Dawlish and Jersey the first time – I travelled there on a Friday and spent the weekend familiarising myself with the new surroundings before my first day at the office on the Monday.

I had once again decided to pursue such a course in Farnham, although this time it was more a case of re-familiarising myself with the town rather than getting my bearings from scratch.

After a quick look around the not-particularly-large town centre after breakfast on the Saturday, I found myself being drawn, like a magnet, towards Ridgway Road. I could remember the route, from the railway station, involved cutting up a slip road and then negotiating a fairly steep hill on top of which, to the right, lay what should have been my temporary home a decade-and-a-half earlier.

Front doors are usually made to last, not being replaced very often on most residential houses, and it was this unchanged feature of number 23 that enabled me to recognise the dwelling immediately, without having to look for the number. I instinctively wanted to walk up the short pathway and ring the doorbell, half expecting Naomi, as she was in 1986 or 1987, to answer.

However I also knew that my return to Farnham was not primarily about rekindling sad memories of lost opportunities in the past, but helping to make the next stage of my career a success by settling into a town that had lost none of its charm and style from when I had been an all-too-infrequent visitor in days gone by.

I spent the rest of the day exploring or rediscovering parts of my new base. Unsurprisingly, I was unable to pinpoint the exact location of Naomi's second home, which I had only visited twice, and could not remember the house number, although I was sure I got the road right.

Later I tried out a few town centre pubs, none of which seemed remotely familiar and were generally old-fashioned with small, separate lounge and public bars. On the Sunday I watched the FA Charity Shield football match at the much more modern and spacious Hogshead hostelry, which I was sure had not existed in the 1980s, and decided this would be my 'local' unless my new colleagues introduced me to somewhere better I had not yet discovered.

Earlier that day I had paid my first visit to Aldershot since 1987 – and the self-proclaimed 'Home of the British Army' had, like Farnham, not changed a bit; being as dirty, grimy and run-down as it had been 15 years earlier. The contrast between the two towns, especially as they are less than three miles apart and almost joined together, was, I reminded myself, truly remarkable.

The situation at The Herald, during my first week there, was a little confusing. Although I was warmly welcomed by Peter Thompson, the Chief Sub-editor, Sandy Baker, was in hospital and another sub, Joyce Sharland-Brown, was on holiday. The paper had five editions – Farnham, Haslemere, Alton, Bordon and Petersfield – and I was given the latter, where the Chief Reporter was also on holiday and I had to spend the next three days liaising, by phone, with a branch office occupied by an elderly parish-pump-orientated female part-timer and two inexperienced juniors.

None of the trio of reporters seemed to be in charge of the office and collectively they had little idea of how to fill a paper, although we got there in the end, thanks mainly to stories I lifted from other editions.

Peter Thompson asked to see me on the Thursday morning and said he was impressed by what I had done that week in circumstances that were, as he admitted, not ideal. He explained that there was currently a lack of continuity at the paper: Sandy Baker was off for three weeks and he was retiring in the October (something I had been aware of since the day of my interview) and was still involved in the process of finding a replacement – something that was not proving as straightforward as at first anticipated.

For the next few weeks, he added, I would take over the Bordon edition with Joyce Sharland-Brown returning to resume control of Petersfield, Deputy Chief-sub Tony Short doing Alton, Corina Larby editing Farnham and Graham Collier – a freelance who was shortly to retire to, would you believe, Kingsbridge – taking charge of Haslemere until Sandy Baker returned.

The same day also saw a breakthrough on the accommodation front. The previous afternoon I had been handed a long-overdue second response to my box number advert, a communication I had been too busy to read until I got to The Hogshead after work. It informed me of the availability of a small annex flat in a road about half-a-mile south of the railway station and on the Thursday morning I rang the owner, Geoff Swann, and arranged to see him and the property that lunchtime.

After talking for about half-an-hour I was offered the flat, subject to Peter Thompson confirming that I was who I said I was, at £450 per-calendar-month including bills. This rent, all at the office confirmed, was very reasonable by Farnham standards.

My new landlord – a blunt, talkative, semi-retired Yorkshireman who reminded me a little of the Charlie Hungerford character in the 1980s Jersey-based television series Bergerac – added that there was no problem about me smoking in the accommodation and that I would see very little of him providing I paid the rent on time.

The flat, in a well-heeled road named Menin Way, was within comfortable walking distance of the office and, in another direction, just a 10-minute stroll from Ridgway Road – the two locations being separated by a leafy thoroughfare containing massive detached houses with long drives known as Great Austens. The irony of my return to Farnham, in terms of where I was to live, was already complete.

I moved my belongings into my new accommodation before starting work on the Monday and my latest home was not the only era to begin that day. Immediately upon arriving at the office I had to make myself known to the Bordon office's editorial staff -- Chief Reporter Kelly Frank and her sidekick Julie Minter. Little did I know it, but this was the start of a partnership that would remain in place, unbroken other than when I was temporarily switched to other duties, for almost two years.

I hit it off with the Bordon duo from the first week. Both were in their early 20s with Kelly, I soon discovered, on the same wavelength as myself, being highly organised with a remarkable memory and a wicked sense of humour. Julie was quieter, but extremely hard-working with nothing ever being too much trouble.

It was, in a way, a strange working relationship as all our contact was by telephone and what with Bordon being 10 or 12 miles away from Farnham, they rarely came over to head office and it would be several weeks before I met either reporter in the flesh. An amusing factor was that both had similar high-pitched voices and, at first, it was impossible to tell who was answering the phone when I rang their office. I therefore began each conversation with 'is that Kelly or Julie?' and long after I had mastered the art of immediately recognising who was speaking, that phrase remained the subject of much banter.

Among the first raft of redirected post to arrive at Menin Way from the South West was a letter from Naomi who, at the age of 40, had just given birth to her second child, a girl. While noting the irony of my latest career move, she expressed surprise that I wanted to return to Farnham (strictly speaking I wasn't 'back' in the town as I hadn't actually lived there the first time around) and gave me the quite believable news that she had been largely out of contact with her parents for some time, following some sort of row over where the wedding would be held, and they had not yet even met her husband of six years.

As the weeks went by I was feeling quite settled in both my job and accommodation – all that was missing was some sort of social life outside of work. The other subs were, apart from Joyce Sharland-Brown, all a fair bit older than me and did not mix outside of the office. None of them had any interest in football or pub-going, preferring hobbies such as bee-keeping, running a cub pack and Cajun dancing, whatever that was.

None of the three Farnham office reporters lived in the town, and subsequently were never to be seen outside of working hours, while Kelly and Julie both commuted to Bordon from Portsmouth, so there was no possibility of getting to know them socially.

I still went to The Hogshead most days after leaving the office and on Sunday afternoons to watch live football. On Saturdays I visited places like Guildford and Woking and towards the end of September, with my financial position improving now I was back in guaranteed full-time work, went up to London to watch a Tottenham home game for the first time in two-and-a-half years (going from Plymouth had never really been an option as I working every Saturday and the cost of going to top-flight games was proportionately much more expensive than it had been in my younger days).

A condition of my appointment at The Herald was that I would deputise for Carl Obert, the Sports Editor, when he was on holiday. Previously whenever my namesake was away, Peter Thompson had compiled the sports pages but as he was about to retire it had been mandatory that the new sub taken on that summer had some experience of sport.

My first opportunity to fulfil this obligation came when Carl Obert took a fortnight's holiday in late October. Filling the three broadsheet pages was straightforward enough, but the job also included reporting on Aldershot Town home games. A Football League club until the early 1990s (I had been to a couple of their home games with Martin Creasey during the 1986-7 season), the Shots then hit hard financial times and had to reform as a non-league club. However they had by now climbed several divisions and were pushing for promotion to the Conference from the Ryman Premier League.

I had not reported on a football match, at any level, since covering a pre-season friendly between Dawlish Town and Watford 10 seasons earlier and admittedly felt a little nervous when entering the press box at what had been a Football League ground during my last visit. However it was, as they say, like riding a bike: once the match got under way it was if I had never been away from covering games and my report was widely-praised the following week by Peter Thompson and others at the office with an interest in football.

Peter duly retired the week after my first stint as Acting Sports Editor and at his leaving 'do' I met Julie for the first time (Kelly was on holiday and unable to attend). The Herald's new Editor was Vic Robbie, a Scotsman who didn't seem much younger than his predecessor and whose past experience included a spell as Assistant Editor of The Daily Mail.

I had no problem getting on with the new man at the helm, even accompanying him to the nearby Wheatsheaf pub a couple of times after work during his early days at the paper. I readily accepted his invitations partly because of the novelty factor of someone from the office actually wanting to go for a drink at the end of the day.

Vic Robbie was quite guarded, as we talked in the pub, on what he thought of his newly-acquired staff, although I formed the impression that he did not have a very high opinion of certain individuals. The feeling of dissatisfaction was not one-sided: I discovered, as the weeks went by, that some of the subs, in particularly Sandy Baker, were less than endeared to their new Editor.

Part of the resentment, I learnt, was down to Vic Robbie's stance that, unlike Peter Thompson, he would not be subbing an edition during the 25 weeks or so a year when a sub was on holiday. Corina Larby explained to me that when I was taken on it was a new position, rather than replacing someone who had left, in order to eliminate the additional workload when the office was one sub down. 'We thought we had taken one step forward, but now we're back to square one,' she said.

This situation was then compounded by Joyce Sharland-Brown being struck down with a serious illness which would keep her away from the office for several months.

Vic Robbie decided to fill the vacuum by using freelances, but unfortunately the only replies his adverts attracted were from individuals with magazine backgrounds, of which there seemed to be a bottomless pit in the South East, probably because that is where most national magazines are based.

Each of the temporary sub-editors he took on proved to be as hopeless as his or her predecessor as they struggled to bridge the gap between magazine and newspaper journalism.

Part of the problem was that The Herald did not use formatted templates and subs began their week's work with blank pages on which any adverts were drawn before the remainder was filled with news. Straightforward enough? Not to our magazine-trained visitors who were used to a graphic designer compiling their pages before they simply subbed the copy to fit the boxes and typed in a headline.

Furthermore these freelances were largely used to working to monthly schedules and had no experience of reaching the speeds required, particularly on our hectic Wednesday deadline day at the Farnham office.

Joyce's first replacement lasted only three or four weeks and proved to be such a slow worker that I had to start the Petersfield edition, in addition to my Bordon duties, each Thursday and Friday to give the freelance, who worked Monday to Wednesday, a head start. However he still struggled to finish much before 8pm on deadline day when the rest of us usually completed our editions between 5.30 and 6.30pm.

He was replaced by someone who, after one week, decided such work was not for him and then by a female self-employed landscape gardener, with some experience of magazine subbing, who proved to be little better, but who was still employed at the office as Christmas approached.

In early December I again deputisied for Carl Obert, who obviously hadn't taken much holiday during the first half of the year, for a week and was then moved onto Sandy Baker's Haslemere edition for three weeks over the festive period while our Chief Sub took a pre-booked three-week foreign holiday.

This meant we were two subs down for the best part of a month and even when Vic Robbie belatedly decided that he would sub the Farnham edition with Corina Larby taking over Bordon, it still proved to be a frantic few weeks.

I quite enjoyed subbing the Haslemere edition. Working with the long-serving Chief Reporter Sue Carter, and second year trainees Jenny Clarke and Sam Rkaina, again created the situation of being in constant telephone contact with people I had never seen. So curious were the trio to put the face to my name that one Thursday afternoon Sam arrived at the Farnham office, primarily to see Vic Robbie about something, armed with a digital camera with which he promptly took my picture. Sue and Jenny, he claimed, were 'desperate' to see what I looked like.

The one time I almost lost my rag, during those first few months at The Herald, came on Christmas Eve. Because of the way the days fell, I could not travel down to Cornwall until December 24 itself and after almost completing the Haslemere edition the previous day, anticipated simply finishing the front page that morning before beginning the seven-hour, three-train journey to Truro.

However it became clear by 10am that the freelance allegedly subbing the Petersfield edition had not only failed to turn up, but had left two pages, including the front, not even started. My anger at having to stay and help finish somebody else's work (subsequently not arriving at my destination in Cornwall until after 9pm) was exceeded only when I returned to the office after Christmas to discover the 'journalist' in question was still being employed by Vic Robbie.

For the first time, at any office where I had worked, there had been no Christmas 'do' involving members of the editorial department. This summed up the non-existent social scene at The Herald caused primarily by the paper's strangely-fractured set-up whereby subs hardly ever saw the reporters they were working with (other than whoever was doing the Farnham edition). An additional problem was that of the entire editorial staff, only Corina Larby and myself lived in Farnham with the remainder being scattered around various locations in Surrey, Hampshire and Sussex

Somehow, and I was not really sure how at this stage, my life outside of work was something I was determined to improve in 2003, but overall, as the year ended, I had no regrets about leaving The Sunday Independent for journalistic pastures new.

I had, after all, left the Plymouth title primarily because they would not employ me full-time and I had not abandoned a thriving social life there as, by the latter stages, there were so few journalist left that there was barely anyone to socialise with.

Despite the feuding in the Farnham office, along with the seemingly-endless staff shortages and poor quality of freelance replacements, I felt quite settled in my work there, enjoying working with both the Bordon and Haslemere reporters and having the occasional stint in charge of sport.

Moreover there was still a strange mystique about being back in the town, especially living so close to Ridgway Road. Rather than reviving bitter memories of what could and should have been, instead I consistently felt a feeling of contentment that, by being there, I was, in some small spiritual way, partly righting the wrongs of 15 or 16 years earlier.

Perhaps Naomi's dream did have a meaningful significance after all.

20 House of cards

2003 turned out to be one of those very rare years in my career where not only were there very few significant happenings in my own life, but neither did anything of real consequence happen at my place of work. Yet it all could have been so different had it not been for a major policy change at a certain national newspaper.

Shortly before Christmas I had written a speculative letter to the Chief Sub-editor of The Daily Star inquiring about the possibility of weekend shifts. Attempting to get a foothold, subbing-wise, on the nationals had been part of my larger plan when I took the job at The Herald and I always intended, once I had settled into my 'day job', to make contact with the paper with which I had past family and freelance connections.

However the reply I received in early January stopped any such ambitions in their tracks. The Daily Star, I was informed, was in the process of transferring its subbing operation from London to a new, purpose-built centre in the North West – I think Ormskirk was the precise location – and they were therefore unable to offer me (or presumably anyone else based in the South East) weekend shifts.

At The Herald, meanwhile, everything chugged along in its new-found routine after the personnel changes during the second half of the previous year. There was still a simmering tension between Vic Robbie and Sandy Baker, which eventually exploded in a furious row one Friday in the spring, but nobody left as a result and indeed there was not to be a single editorial change during the entire year. Apart from my second and fourth years at Dawlish (where only four staff journalists were employed anyway) I could not remember that happening before at any office where I had worked.

Everyone was pleased when Joyce Sharland-Brown eventually returned to work, not only because she had recovered from her serious illness, but it also meant there would be no more need for the incompetent freelance subs we seemed to attract. I continued to work happily with Kelly and Julie and, while deputising for Carl Obert, fulfilled a long-held ambition by reporting on a Tottenham game, albeit only a pre-season friendly at Aldershot but a goal I was nevertheless pleased to have achieved.

The nearest we came to staff changes was during the summer when Vic Robbie decided to reshuffle some of the reporters. The Bordon office was unaffected, but Jenny Clarke moved from Haslemere to Farnham with Caroline Bullock travelling in the opposite direction. Despite having been at The Herald for almost a year, I had only seen Kelly twice and Julie once, so it was perhaps of no surprise that, despite many telephone conversations, I had never set eyes on Jenny until her first morning at her new place of work.

She immediately knew who I was, presumably from the photograph taken by Sam Rkaina a few months earlier, and informed me that she had recently moved to Farnham, taking a flat on Firgrove Hill, the previously-mentioned route between the railway station and Ridgeway Road, and therefore was based in the same part of the town as me.

Not long after this I learnt that Neill Barston, another Farnham office reporter, had moved into the town from an outlying village, meaning there were now three of us in the editorial department who were living where we worked and were all single.

I can't remember exactly how it started, but in the late summer Jenny, Neill and myself started going for a few drinks after work on Wednesdays, when the frantic nature of press day dictated that alcohol was a much-needed pickmeup.

At first we tried out different pubs each week before finding ourselves roped into a quiz at The Wheatsheaf where we did so well that it became our regular Wednesday evening outing. We then began occasionally going for a few drinks on Friday evenings as well and, after waiting a year, I had finally found something approaching a social life involving colleagues from The Herald.

The paper's reporters were not well paid – a trait at Tindle titles that I had experienced first hand at Dawlish and witnessed at Kingsbridge – and Neill, in particular, was constantly short of money. This, combined with his regular visits to his parents' home at weekends, meant that often it was just Jenny and I who frequented Farnham's pubs on Friday evenings and we became increasingly friendly.

Apart from a scattering of alcohol-fuelled one-night stands, women had not played a significant part in my life since the Pauline Jonas debacle eight years earlier, mainly through those females I might have been interested in being already spoken for or, increasingly as I had grown older, being too young.

At 27 Jenny was more than 10 years my junior and had a long-standing boyfriend from her student days in Liverpool who was still living in that city and rarely travelled south, which suggested the relationship was perhaps petering out.

One Friday evening Jenny and I embarked on a mammoth drinking session, starting at The Wheatsheaf before moving onto another Farnham pub called The Nelson and as the amount of alcohol consumed increased, so did our honesty with each other. Jenny began by confessing what I had suspected for some time – that her relationship with her Liverpool-based partner had been in decline for some time and was about to end.

She added, however, that while there was undoubtedly a mutual attraction between us, any relationship between us could never work, partly but not totally because of the age gap. I found myself agreeing with her and, having had a 'clear the air' discussion, we were able to maintain our friendship without the risk of either of us misinterpreting the situation and making an embarrassing first move. In short, I think we both realised that while we both liked each other, it was never going to extend beyond that.

An excellent festive editorial 'do', one Friday evening at a Guildford pizza house, ended 2003. The event was organised by Neill and attended by around 15 of us, although the only senior staff members present were Vic Robbie, Carl Obert and myself. The other subs went to an alternative lunch, organised by Sandy Baker earlier in the day, which showed that, despite a fairly quiet and stable year at The Herald, divisions and personality clashes still existed.

In January Sue Carter gave a month's notice. She had been at The Haslemere Herald for many years and was approaching 60, but nobody was totally sure why she had picked this particular time to go.

Sue was given quite a send-off at a Farnham pizza restaurant and it was a tribute to her popularity that almost every editorial member of staff attended the Thursday afternoon function and management's uncharacteristic offer to foot the wine bill was abused by many of us ordering a bottle each rather than the one-per-table-of-four that Tindle Newspapers had in mind.

More significantly, the resignation seemed to trigger off – as is often the case at newspaper offices – a succession of departures and staff changes in stark contrast to the preceding 15 months or so of total stability. Sam Rkaina soon left to go to a weekly paper in Somerset and in March Neill Barston informed us he was joining the features desk at The Kent Messenger.

Kelly was appointed Chief Reporter at Haslemerre – admitting that she didn't see the move as a serious promotion but it was a bigger paper and, most importantly, a larger salary – and Vic Robbie followed my recommendation by promoting Julie to succeed her. Alex

Farrell, Michael Willey-Harris and Steve Baker were the new reporters at Bordon, Farnham and Haslemere respectively.

One of my subbing duties at The Herald was to compile a business page for all editions each Thursday and Vic Robbie sometimes passed onto me items that the company bosses wanted to include in this section of the paper.

On Thursday morning that spring he handed me a press release and said 'wasn't that your last paper?' and I read that Tindle Newspapers had purchased The Sunday Independent from Newsquest.

I had called in at the Plymouth office while on holiday in the South West the previous summer and knew that The Indy had continued to struggle financially since my departure. Neither Nigel Walrond, who had left just after me to join the BBC, or myself had ever been replaced. Kevin Marriott followed soon afterwards, to become Sports Editor at The Cornish Guardian, and was succeeded by John Collings, whose old position of Deputy Chief-sub was done away with. How they managed to keep producing a regional paper with such a skeleton staff was amazing.

I spoke to both John Collings and Nikki Rowland by phone that week and both said they were relieved to be leaving Newsquest rather than thinking too far ahead to what life might be like under the new regime.

I couldn't help wonder how a company used to running small weekly papers in small to medium-sized towns – and not renowned for spending large sums of money – was going to cope with running a regional title covering such a large geographical area. Still, it was no longer a problem that directly affected me.

Back at The Herald, the next departure came in July when Jenny, whom I knew had been looking to move elsewhere, departed to join a weekly paper in North East London, which meant another drunken, well-attended send-off, this time at The Wheatsheaf. The Wednesday night quiz team at the same pub managed to survive the changes with Steve Baker having replaced Neill and Michael Willey-Harris, both a Farnham resident and a heavy drinker, now succeeding Jenny.

Then, in the September, Julie left The Bordon Herald, after only a few months as Chief Reporter, for a better-paid job at The Basingstoke Gazette. Alex Farrell, though quite a capable operator, had decided that newspaper journalism wasn't what she wanted as a long-term career and departed at about the same time.

This left me with two new trainees at Bordon, Zoe Wright and Shane Brock, and until they got used to the town and the amount of copy required each week my role became as much as a news editor as a sub as I guided them along. Both new recruits were keen and eager to learn, but with no senior reporter at the office it was down to me to sort out priorities and page leads for the first few weeks.

Zoe had worked at the Farnham office for a couple of weeks before going to Bordon and this placed me in the so-far unique position of knowing what a branch office reporter looked like before starting work with them. She was a strikingly-attractive woman (and pleasant and mature with it) in her mid-20s and we got on very well from the start. Not for the first time with a younger female at The Herald, I was left wondering what might have been had I been 10 or 15 years younger.

Shane, who more typically I did not see until several weeks after he joined the company, hailed from Northampton and not only was he the first black reporter I had ever worked with, but according to the long-serving Carl Obert, the first journalist of such a colour ever to be employed at The Herald.

Then, just as we thought the 'all change' year of 2004 simply couldn't yield any further comings and goings, Vic Robbie announced his resignation after two years at the helm. He told the editorial staff that his departure was due to the expansion of a publishing company he was involved with meaning he no longer had enough time to commit to The Herald. There followed, of course, the inevitable rumours that he fallen out of favour with The Tindle Newspapers high command, but nothing along those lines was ever confirmed.

Some of the subs couldn't contain their delight at his pending exit and happiness at the parting of the ways appeared to be mutual as during Vic's last day at the office, while I was on holiday in Cornwall, he shook hands only with the reporters and Joyce Sharland-Brown, ignoring the rest of the subs present. His fiercest critic Sandy Baker took over as Acting Editor, making it clear to everyone that she wanted the job permanently.

Such had been the merry-go-round of staff changes that it was perhaps not surprisingly that no festive editorial shindig was formally arranged, so several of us, past and present Herald journalists, held our own unofficial gathering in Guildford the Saturday before Christmas.

A lunchtime meal, followed by an afternoon and early evening in a couple of pubs, was enjoyed by Jenny, Neill, Michael Willey-Harris, Steve Baker, Caroline Bullock and myself with several others who had been invited being unable to attend.

One of the topics of conversation that day were everyone's increasing concerns over the health of James Bowman, The Farnham Herald's Chief Reporter, who had been away from the office for more than a month and was currently in hospital.

It had always been common knowledge that James, who was 30, suffered from cystic fibrosis. This had been his first significant period off work during my time at the paper, but according to some of the longer-serving journalists, there had been lengthy absences in the past from which he had always returned.

True to form, Jenny and I were the last two to leave the pub that evening and after exchanging season's greetings I promised to keep her informed of any news on James, whom she had known quite well during her time at the Farnham office, although partly because of his medical condition, he rarely socialised outside of work.

On the Monday afternoon news started filtering through at The Herald that James' condition had deteriorated during the weekend and that the end might be nigh. Someone pointed out that 30 was almost a respectable age for someone with cystic fibrosis to reach, but even that couldn't detract from the sense of disbelief that time was almost up for a colleague so young.

We were informed of James' death shortly after arriving at the office on Christmas Eve morning, a Friday. A tearful Sandy Baker arranged for the branch offices to be informed, one by one, and I agreed to contact Neill and Jenny, getting hold of the former almost immediately but having to leave a message for the latter, whose mobile phone was switched off.

She got back to me on my mobile while I was making the long train journey down to Cornwall and like everyone was shocked despite what we all knew to be the inevitability of the situation. Although some, much older, journalists I had known had died after we no longer worked together, James was the first-ever current colleague of mine to pass away.

I arrived in Truro to be shown a death notice, in The Western Morning News, stating that my father's second wife had died, after a long illness, a few days earlier at the age of 69. We had not been in contact since shortly after my father's funeral, more than 12 years earlier, and her passing, it was fair to say, would not be causing me any lost sleep – but it had certainly been a bizarre Christmas Eve.

Including James, eight journalists, around 40 per cent of the editorial staff, had departed The Herald during 2004 and

I wondered what the following year – with either Sandy Baker confirmed as Editor or another outsider arriving on the scene – would have in store. Could there possibly be another 12-month period with such a lack of continuity?

In the words of the popular 1970s song by Bachman Turner Overdrive, it was to be a case of 'You Ain't Seen Nothing Yet'.

21 End of the beginning

James Bowman's extremely-well-attended funeral took place at St Andrew's Church, Farnham, on the first Friday in January, two weeks after his death, and in some ways that day marked a watershed in my time at The Herald.

Peter Thompson, Jenny, Neill and Julie (though strangely not Vic Robbie) were among the many former colleagues who travelled to the service where some bad feeling was caused by company owner Sir Ray Tindle making a speech just weeks after his underlings had stopped James' wages because of the time he had already been absent from work through illness.

Most of the editorial staff made only a token appearance at the official wake – dominated by Sir Ray and his hangers-on and where sherry was the only alcoholic drink available – before retreating to the Wheatsheaf where Jenny, Neill, Kelly, Julie, Zoe, Michael Willey-Harris, Steve Baker and myself drank well into the evening. With around half of those present already being ex-Herald journalists, I somehow sensed that this would be the last time we would all be together under one roof – and so it proved to be.

Later that month Sandy Baker was officially confirmed as the new Editor and she quickly reshuffled her pack. Corina Larby was moved from subs back to her old position (from before my time at The Herald) of Chief Reporter as James' replacement, Tony Short became Chief Sub-editor, taking over the Farnham edition from Corina, and I became Deputy Chief-sub with responsibility for the Alton paper and co-ordinating the three East Hampshire titles.

This meant a £500 a year pay rise and the parting of the ways with the Bordon office after two-and-a-half years. I felt a quiet satisfaction at my promotion as, of course, Deputy Chief-sub was the position I had falsely been promised at The West Briton nine years earlier. Now, on a similarly-sized multi-edition weekly, I felt that particular wrong had finally been laid to rest.

With Sandy Baker and Corina Larby no longer working as subs, two additions were made to the team: Kayleigh Close, a quiet but competent young Australian, who took over the Bordon edition, and Roz, a middle-aged and somewhat excitable South African, who was placed in charge of Petersfield with Joyce Sharland-Brown stepping up a notch to assume control of Haslemere.

Steve Baker then gave a month's notice to pursue a non-journalistic career and was quickly followed by Michael Willey-Harris, who somewhat surprisingly departed to work for a London-based magazine specialising in coverage of air-conditioning systems. The three of us – with the occasional guest appearance from Shane and Zoe – had kept the Wednesday quiz team going since the previous summer, but now this double departure surely signified the end of that particular social era.

The new Farnham office reporter was Dee Hutchings, a local woman in her mid-20s who accompanied Michael and I to our Friday night rendezvous at The Wheatsheaf at the end of his last week at the paper and thereafter replaced him as my new pub partner.

She was obviously an experienced drinker, matching me pint-for-pint in a way that none of The Herald's male reporters had been able to do, and as winter turned to spring we became increasingly friendly, mainly outside of work as I was not directly involved in the Farnham edition.

Around that time I was contacted by Julie, who had resigned her position at The Basingstoke Gazette following a personality clash with the News Editor. We met at The Nelson pub in Farnham one lunchtime shortly before Easter when she informed me that she had a couple of interviews lined up, but if these proved unsuccessful would I recommend to Sandy Baker that she be allowed to return to

The Herald once there was a suitable vacancy. I, of course, was happy to do so and given the current turnover of staff, somehow did not think she would have too long to wait.

One area of my life where change was imminent was accommodation. I had known since the previous year that Geoff Swann was planning to sell his house, which included my annex flat, so he could move somewhere smaller. I had half been expecting to be asked to leave when my latest contract expired in the February, but was told I could have another six-month stint which would almost certainly be my last.

And so it was as I was informed in writing, at the end of May, that I would have to move out by the third anniversary of my arrival in August. This gave me two months to find a suitable alternative in a town where, I have stated more than once before, affordable, rented one-bedroom flats were extremely difficult to find.

One emerging possible solution was Dee 's family. On a Saturday evening I was invited to meet her mother and older sister at The Bat and Ball pub on the outskirts of Farnham. My only previous visit to this establishment had been with Naomi 18 years earlier and my return must have set some kind of record for the length of time between my first and second visit to any tavern anywhere.

I learnt that night that the Hutchings family home, which was not far from the pub, had its own annexe flat currently unoccupied and I agreed to keep them informed should my search for new accommodation continue to be as unfruitful as it had been so far.

It was an enjoyable evening, although an understandably-protective Mrs Hutchings did question me, while Dee was outside making a lengthy call on her mobile, as to my intentions towards her daughter and seemed relieved when I replied that it was a professional and social relationship only and I would be stepping on dangerous ground indeed if I started looking for anything more with a trainee reporter around 15 years my junior.

A more tempting possibility would have been her older sister Trudy who, at 35, was much more in my own age group. Seemingly like all her family, she was anything but a shrinking violet and spelt out in no uncertain terms, at the end of the evening, what her desires would have been towards me…if, of course, she hadn't been married.

The following week Sandy Baker informed me that Julie was not only returning to The Herald, but would again be working directly under me. She had been assigned to join Moira Howells, the long-serving Chief Reporter at the Alton office, with Peter Carline, the junior there, moving over to Farnham.

While I was more than happy to see Julie return, I was a little puzzled by these moves as I didn't think there was a vacancy at the main office. However such had been the turnover of staff, and the moving of people from one office to another, during the past year or so that it was getting difficult to keep track of just what the overall numbers situation was.

Unfortunately, my first instincts were correct. After another week had passed Dee was absent from the office one Tuesday morning and nobody knew her whereabouts. It was known that Sandy Baker had asked to see her at 5pm the previous day, just as everyone else was leaving the office, but as our Editor was absent herself at a dental appointment, confusion reigned until she arrived, mid-morning, and informed us that the evening before Dee had been told she would not be kept on after her probationary period and had then left the office in a flood of tears, refusing to work the offered three-week notice period.

In seemed a harsh decision. Dee was by no means without her rough edges as a reporter, but was certainly no worse than several other juniors who had been employed by The Herald during my time there. The usual procedure for trainees who did not immediately come up to scratch was to extend their probationary period from three to six months as had been the case with Shane, at the Bordon office, a few months earlier.

Since becoming Editor, Sandy Baker had performed better than many of us expected. There had been concerns about certain aspects of her background – being one of the growing number of late entrants into journalism, she had never worked as a reporter and subsequently had no training in the profession's legal requirements – but most people were impressed by how she had kept on top of the job. Her premature sacking of Dee had, however, cost me a friend, a growing number of social contacts and a possible solution to my pending accommodation worries.

Dee's departure – as she understandably broke off contact with everyone at the Farnham office thereafter – left me without a regular after-work drinking partner for the first time in nearly two years, but there was, during May, a brief resurgence in quiz nights at The Wheatsheaf. I joined up with Peter Carline and a friend of his in a second reincarnation of The Herald team, but after winning twice in three visits they seemed to lose interest and that particular social era finally ended for good after more than a-year-and-a-half.

Another month passed and still I was no closer to finding a new flat. I obviously scoured the accommodation pages of The Herald each week, but the few one-bedroom properties advertised were either too expensive, in out-of-town rural locations or asked for non-smokers only.

As we reached the end of June, with me now having little more than a month to find somewhere new, I decided that the best course of action would be to again put a box number advert in the paper in the hope that this would solve the problem in the way it had previously.

I approached Sue Cansfield, the person who dealt with such matters, about placing an advert to be informed that she and her husband owned a one-bedroom flat that would soon be becoming vacant and would I be interested in moving in? She subsequently drove me over to see the property in Weybourne, an outlying district of Farnham bordering on Aldershot and about two miles from the office.

The flat itself seemed fine and a two-mile walk to work each day would, of course, be no hardship to me. It was the rent – at £600 a month, £150 more than I had been paying Geoff Swann – I found staggering. At this point I must hold my hands up and admit that I should never have taken the property. Many people, at the time and over the years since, have commented that such a move was financially impractical considering that, even after my elevation to Deputy Chief-sub, I was still earning slightly less than £20,000 a year.

I suppose I was taking what seemed the easy way out after weeks of fruitless searching. I had to find somewhere and short of moving into Aldershot itself – where the inevitably cheaper rents would be counter-balanced by the less-than-salubrious environment of a crime hotspot – I could see no other solution.

I vaguely knew Sue Cansfield's husband, Peter, as he was a village correspondent to The Alton Herald and I had met him briefly at a couple of social functions. The couple were nicknamed The Old Colonials, by many at the paper, because of their unashamedly stuck-in-the-1950s right-wing political views and the deserved nature of that title was soon apparent when I met Peter in The Nelson to discuss my move into his flat and for both of us to sign copies of the contract.

It was Thursday July 7 which, as many of you will recall, was the day terrorist attacks on public transport in central London left 52 civilians dead and more than 700 injured. Inevitably such an atrocity was the subject on everyone's lips, but Peter Cansfield's contribution to the debate was to say 'confirms what I've always said – that people of a certain skin colour shouldn't be allowed in this country'.

When I pointed out, as diplomatically as a I could, that many of that same skin colour were probably among the victims, he was unresponsive and continued to make derogatory references to ethnic minority groups, including Jews, during our stay at the pub, as well as making loud, disapproving comments about a young woman, seated a couple of tables away, who was sporting tattoos.

Two days later I travelled up to London to meet Jenny and Neill at a gathering arranged before the bombings. Amid tight security, including a massive police presence, we drank at a couple of pubs close to Victoria station, where Neill, who was reluctant to use the underground that weekend, had arrived from Kent.

I informed them of my pending change of abode and they described my new rent as 'obscene', even allowing for Farnham being an expensive place to live, and that I must have been mad to agree to pay it. I replied that the move went against my gut instincts, but could only reiterate that I had to move somewhere.

It was, in fact, another three weeks before I left Menin Way for Weybourne – the reason I met Peter Cansfield so far in advance was down to him and Sue being away on holiday at the time of the changeover – and during that period Zoe gave a month's notice to leave the Bordon office to join a magazine in London.

As usual I was the only sub to attend the obligatory leaving 'do' at The William Cobbett pub in Farnham the following month. As the evening drew to a close, with a reasonable amount of alcohol having been consumed, the departing reporter's tongue became sufficiently loosened to impart some interesting and largely-flattering information on how I had been perceived by all the young female reporters to grace The Herald's offices those past three years. Much of what I was told, it has to be said, I was already generally aware of, but it was pleasing to hear certain things confirmed.

A few days later I went down to the South West for a week's holiday and fully anticipated that this would be my last visit to the region until Christmas. However, it would be just three weeks before I returned as, in early September, I had a call from Mike Taylor informing me of the death of Colin Wallace at 69.

The news was not entirely unexpected as I had received an e-mail from Colin, earlier in the summer, saying he had been in hospital in France (to where he had retired two years earlier) and reading between the lines of what he wrote, the outlook did not seem particularly optimistic.

As the funeral was on a Friday, I was able to travel down to Dawlish for a service that was poorly attended by past and present Gazette employees. Apart from Mike and myself only two minor non-editorial former colleagues turned up with there being no sign of Cedric Clough, Pat Betts or Chris Russell, all of whom had worked with Colin for many years and still lived in the area. David Banks, I was aware, had been suffering from Parkinson's Disease for some time, so his presence was not really anticipated, but the overall turnout was disappointing to say the least.

The wake proved to be a far more fitting send-off. Held at The Lansdowne pub – a recently-refurbished and enlarged tavern next to the Gazette office and run by Ray Martin, formerly of the now-closed-down Prince of Wales – it attracted a reasonable attendance including several people who had been unable to get time off work to attend the service.

Members of Colin's family expressed the pragmatic view that given his lifelong addiction to alcohol, cigarettes and lack of exercise, he had done extremely well to get to within a few months of his 70th birthday.

I stayed that night at Mike's new rented home in Newton Abbot which he shared with his girlfriend, Gail, whom I met for the first time. In the 17 years I had known Mike this was the first time he had been involved in what could be described as a serious relationship and his new partner had achieved what many of us saw as the impossible – getting him to move out of his parents' home where he had lived happily for 35 years since being born.

A couple of weeks later came an incident that perhaps summed up cluelessness of many of the senior management staff employed by Tindle Newspapers. Overnight on the Wednesday, after we had officially gone to press, a serious road accident in the Alton area saw four or five teenagers killed. Because The Herald's three East Hampshire editions were not printed until Thursday mornings, it was possible, in circumstances such as these, to submit a new front page providing senior production operatives and the printing centre were kept informed.

Moira Howells and myself quickly took control of the situation. Information on the accident was still limited, but she put together a seven or eight paragraph account which I inserted into a panel on a new front page and that was it, job done – or so we thought.

Unfortunately, Sandy Baker was away on holiday and for some unknown reason The Herald's General Manager Rosie Prior – a loud, overweight middle-aged individual from an advertising background who rarely involved herself in editorial matters she did not understand – suddenly got the idea into her head that she was in charge of the operation. She told first me, then Tony Short as Acting Editor, that we had to have more on the story, even though at that point in time there was no further information available. In the end we managed to get the message across and sent the new front page as it was, but it was an episode that was to lead to a lasting frostiness between middle and senior management at the office.

Sandy Baker returned and did her best to smooth things over, saying that the free-for-all would never have developed had she been present, but the whole business increased my feeling that it was time to move on again.

Apart from the fact that I had now been at The Herald for just over three years, and all the colleagues with whom I had mixed regularly outside of work had now departed, the overriding concern now was financial. While at Menin Way I never managed to save any money, neither did I have to dip into savings as I consistently managed to survive on what I earned.

Now, however, the Cansfields had their snouts so deeply stuck into my financial trough that I was losing money – a ridiculous scenario considering I was a single non-car driver and now the editorial number three at one of the country's larger paid-for weekly newspaper groups. What added insult to injury, of course, was the fact that the two people ripping me off were colleagues.

The Old Colonials' defence of what they were charging was that it was 'a Farnham rent', even though the flat wasn't really in Farnham and the amount was £150 a month more than I had been paying at Menin Way (albeit for a much-smaller residence) which unquestionably lay in the most affluent part of the town.

To compound matters, they only informed me after I moved in that I was responsible for the property's 'council tax', although the subsequent correspondence from Waverley District Council was addressed only to 'the occupier' so such unwanted communications were immediately discarded.

Moreover the Cansfields were, quite simply, the most disagreeable landlords I had encountered since my undergraduate days – tutting and sighing when I pointed out that the washing machine didn't work and having an overriding attitude that they were under no obligation to spend any time or money dealing with any difficulties that might arise at the flat they owned.

As their own home was in Alton, around 12 miles from Weybourne, personal visits to my abode were thankfully very rare, but Peter Cansfield still had the cheek to send me e-mails at work, reminding me that the rent was due, when he only had access to my office computer's address because of his minor, part-time role at The Herald which he was clearly abusing.

I scoured Holdthefrontpage – the website which by now had largely superseded The UK Press Gazette as the medium for journalists seeking jobs – that autumn, but saw nothing particularly appealing. Then, one Friday, I happened to be glancing through The Surrey Advertiser, a Guildford-based weekly that was mailed to our office, when I noticed an advert for a sub-editor at The Reading Evening Post, a vacancy which had not been circulated nationally.

I was asked to attend an interview on the first Friday in December and travelled to the Berkshire city in a reasonably-confident frame of mind given that the post had only been advertised regionally. A youngish, affable Editor (whose name I can't recall, possibly because all the day's arrangements had been made with his secretary) seemed quite impressed with my cv, saying he was aware of the success of The Jersey Evening Post and the wide area covered by The Sunday Independent and the day ended with a tour of the building, which was always a good sign.

My new prospective employer informed me that as he was on holiday the following week, leave he had to use up before the end of the year, it would be 10 days to a fortnight before I heard anything.

The Reading Evening Post, I had been told, was part of The Guardian's national company whose titles in the South East included The Aldershot News and The Surrey Advertiser (hence why the vacancy appeared there). The wages would not, the Editor made clear, be on a par with what I had been paid in Jersey, but this did not unduly concern me. The time was right for a move and, in a city the size of Reading, I was sure I would be able to find accommodation at the market rates rather than what the Cansfiields and some others in the Farnham area were charging.

Three weeks went by and as I travelled down to Cornwall on Christmas Eve still I had heard nothing from Reading. Because of the way the days fell that festive period, I only had 48 hours or so in Truro, having to return the day after Boxing Day to recommence work on the 28th.

It was during a cigarette break that first morning back in Farnham that I received a message on my mobile from The Reading Evening Post Editor informing me, almost apologetically, that one of The Guardian group's other centres, somewhere in the north, had recently made two sub-editors redundant, as part of round of cuts, and he been ordered to accommodate one of them. The reason for the delay in contacting me, he added, was through having to wait to hear whether either of the out-of-work individuals would be prepared to move to another part of the country.

My hoped-for, and I might say, overdue return to daily newspapers had been scuppered by events completely beyond my control.

22 The 'tax' man cometh

There was to be no let-up to the turnover of staff at The Herald during 2006 – if anything it intensified further, particularly in the reporting ranks.

First to go, in February, was Kelly who joined The Chichester Observer as a reporter. As far as I was concerned she was capable of working at a much higher level, but because she was getting married that year I think her main priority was staying within daily travelling distance of Portsmouth.

Contact between us had inevitably been less frequent since she moved to the Haslemere office, but we said our farewells at a leaving 'do' she shared with Judith Clay (the trainee who had replaced Steve Baker) who departed the same day.

Shane Brock gave a month's notice in May and around the same time Julie announced that she was quitting the company for a second time, this time to join the Hampshire Constabulary press office, where she would no doubt be paid more than anyone at The Herald, probably including Sandy Baker.

What I was finding increasingly disturbing about the exodus of young reporters was that none of them were moving onto daily papers – where you would expect them to go after a couple of years if they were ambitious – but to other weeklies, magazines, PR jobs or dropping out of journalism altogether, which suggested their lot at The Herald was not a happy one.

From this point onwards the comings and goings at the branch offices intensified to the point that I really did lose track of who was working where. Even at Alton, the edition I subbed, Julie was followed by a succession of trainees, some of whom stayed only a few weeks and most of whom

I could not now name. It was a similar tale at Bordon, Haslemere and Petersfield, where some juniors stayed for such short periods that I never got as far as speaking to them on the phone, let alone meeting them.

Outside of work I now had no consistent social life. There were a couple of one-off charity quiz nights in which The Herald entered a team and most Thursday evenings I went to The William Cobbett with Chris Joint – the Farnham office trainee who replaced the person who had replaced Dee – but any attempts to explore new avenues were thwarted by the money the Cansfields were siphoning from my bank account each month as my savings continued to dwindle.

Relations with my landlords continued to be a little strained, particularly when they gave my name to Waverley Council regarding the 'council tax' bill they should have been paying. Sandy Baker, aware of the mounting tensions between the Old Colonials and myself, made her view known that to rent a flat from a work colleague(s) was a bad idea from the outset and that all of us involved should have known better. She was right but unfortunately, in a town like Farnham, I could find nowhere cheaper to go.

One oasis of enjoyment, as a not-particularly-exciting year reached its midpoint, came when I took a fortnight's holiday to coincide with the World Cup in Germany. I spent a busy 10 days or so in Cornwall before stopping off in Newton Abbot for a couple of days on the way back, again staying with Mike and Gail.

I also visited the new home of The Sunday Independent, which since being purchased by Tindle Newspapers had been moved from Plymouth to Liskeard in South East Cornwall, where it shared premises with the weekly Cornish Times. Nikki Rowland was the only person present I knew when I called in. Kirsty Turner was out of the building, John Collings, like me, was on holiday, but the rest were completely new faces.

The vacation's success made me start seriously thinking about a return to the South West if I could find a suitable vacancy. I had now been in Farnham for almost four years, longer than anywhere apart from Dawlish, and given the bewildering turnover of staff at The Herald and the ludicrous rent I was reluctantly paying, surely I would be better off once again backtracking to my own region?

These plans were momentarily put on hold, in the late summer, by another new arrival at the Farnham office. Roz, the South African sub, left to join a magazine and was replaced by Lorna – not the first attractive woman to be employed at The Herald during my time there, but at 36 the only such female broadly in my own age group.

But like all those who had gone before her during my time in Surrey, both inside and outside of the office, she fell into one of two categories: already spoken for or too young. Ironically she had only recently wed (surprisingly, given her age, for the first time). Nevertheless we became good friends, sitting next to each other at the office and regularly seeming to bump into each other outside of work.

However I was now becoming more and more resigned to the probability, given the age I now was, that my 16-year quest to find someone capable of stepping into Naomi's shoes was doomed to failure - and it was, of course, the irony of ironies that this realization should come about in Farnham of all towns.

Each week I scoured Holdthefrontpage for possible alternative employment, particularly in the South West, but times, in the world of provincial newspapers, were very much a-changing. The relentless march of the internet was continuing to hit advertising revenues hard and a trend was quickly emerging whereby departing journalists were either not replaced or superseded by a part-timer or freelance.

Redundancies, compulsory or otherwise, were increasingly becoming commonplace – as I knew to my cost after what had happened at The Reading Evening Post

– and all these factors meant, of course, that there was much more competition for those vacancies that did occur.

The Herald was not bucking the trend. Lorna, a three-days-a-week freelance, had replaced the full-time Roz; the Bordon office was in the process of being closed with the edition's one remaining reporter set to be re-housed in the Alton office, and each time a journalist left the company Sandy Baker had to get permission from Brian Doel, Tindle's national Managing Director, before the vacancy could be filled.

In early October The Herald's entire editorial department showed exactly what they thought of the way their company was being run by boycotting Tindle's 80th birthday dinner, to which everyone at the office had been invited.

Sandy Baker, luckily for her, was on holiday at the time - otherwise she would never have got away with not attending - while Tony Short subsequently claimed, with some justification, that he was too busy. There was, of course, a 100 per cent turnout from the advertising and administration staff, all of whom considered it was a great honour to have been asked to attend so prestigious an event.

Later that month I saw my chance to escape the world of cost-cutting, ever-changing faces and extortionate rent. Archant, a company I had not worked for before, advertised for a full-time sub at their Exeter centre where they produced several weekly titles for towns in East Devon such as Exmouth and Sidmouth.

It was another sign of the times that this was the first occasion when I had been required to apply for a job by e-mail rather than traditional letter. As I only had work computer access, I was careful to keep my communication well hidden, although apart from when I was on holiday it was rare for anyone else in the office to use my terminal.

I was duly invited to travel down for an interview one Thursday in early November. The Archant centre was on an industrial estate several miles from Exeter city centre and close to the airport. This meant that, should I get the job, I would be relying on public transport or lifts to get to and from work for the first time since my last spell at The Cornishman.

That, however, was the day's only negative aspect. My meeting with the Group Editor went very well and as I returned to Farnham in the evening I felt the same sense of satisfaction I had when making the same journey in the opposite direction, after my interview at The Herald, more than four years earlier.

Around a fortnight passed before I heard from Archant again. This time I received a letter, rather than an e-mail, which stated that I had 'presented myself well' but that the successful candidate had 'more experience', which I took to mean he or she had been a longstanding senior journalist at a daily or even a national newspaper given my own by now quite considerable experience with weeklies.

As Christmas approached my frustration at the unchanging situation was increasing. The only way I could see myself staying at The Herald for a significantly longer period was Sandy Baker's pending retirement the following April. If Tindle Newspapers followed its usual practice of promoting from within, Tony Short would become Editor and I would be in line to be the next Chief Sub-editor, the pay rise involved possibly enabling me to be able to afford the rent that the Cansfields, and others in the Farnham area, were charging.

Given my less-than-perfect relationship with Rosie Prior, who would have a considerable say in the matter, such a promotion would not be a formality, but there was some sort of light at the end of the tunnel as a largely-disappointing 2006 ended.

As it turned out, any hopes of the new year bringing a resurgence to my fortunes in Farnham ended after just five days. Since the Cansfields had 'grassed me up' to Waverley

Council, I had at first ignored the subsequent 'council tax' letters and then returned them marked 'no longer at this address', backing up this information by 'forgetting' to fill in the electoral registration form the previous autumn.

I was not the first Herald journalist to have a Farnham landlord who believed they didn't have to pay the rates bill on their own property. Jenny and Neill – who, as reporters, were paid considerably less than me and could only afford to occupy 'flats' that were little more than bedsits – had been similarly inconvenienced with the former being pursued by Waverley parasites for months after leaving the paper.

On the first Friday in January I returned home from work to find a piece of paper stuffed under my front door. This in itself was quite unusual as there was a communal letterbox on the building's outer entrance from which I and the other residents collected our mail.

I switched on a light to read a communication from a bailiff, who had called earlier that day, demanding between £500 and £600 in 'council tax' arrears. For two greedy work colleagues to put me in this position meant, from that moment on, that my position at The Herald had become untenable.

As the weekend progressed, my thoughts moved from disgust and almost physical sickness that I could be legally pursued for not paying someone else's bill to practical planning of how I could escape the situation and return to the South West as quickly and smoothly as possible.

The holiday year at The Herald ran from May to May and having only taken only a fortnight so far, mainly because of the constant staff changes and shortages the previous year, I was owed three weeks off. Giving a short period of notice would not, therefore, be a problem.

A more immediate issue was that, as a non-driver, I would not be able to move all my belongings in one journey. On the Sunday I rang Mike Taylor and he agreed I could leave a couple of bags, containing things I would not need in the short to medium term, at his Newton Abbot home the following weekend.

On the Monday evening I rang my mother, said I was returning to the region to work as a freelance – remaining vague about which papers I would be working for as, of course, I didn't have that information yet – and added that I would be back on holiday for a week or so while I sorted out accommodation for the new venture.

Although the Cansfields had relieved me of around £2,000 in savings during the 18 months I rented from them – this loss, remember, came on top of spending every penny of my £19,000 a year salary during the same period – I had no immediate money worries as I returned to my home region and time would be on my side, for a limited period, in attempts to find work.

I left The Herald on the third Thursday in January, arriving back in Truro less than 24 hours after putting the Alton edition to bed for the final time. My departure from Farnham, after four-and-a-half years, was similar to the way I had ended my only longer stay at a paper, in Dawlish – hardly unexpected given the events of the preceding months, but quite sudden in its execution.

My first priority was to sort out somewhere to live. On the Monday of my first full week back in the South West I travelled up to Plymouth, deciding this would be the best place to make my base both in terms of familiarity and being within daily commuting distance of most main towns in Cornwall and South Devon.

I called at a small, independent letting agent I knew of through my previous stay in the city and arranged to move into a one-bedroom flat, ideally situated very close to the main railway station, once it became available during the first weekend in February.

This arrangement was very much a case of 'normal service resumed' as the rent was the market rate £300 per month with everything included except electricity. However while the Cansfields and their money-grubbing ways were now out of my life, the smell was to continue for a little longer.

True to form, the female half of the Old Colonials abused her position as Editor's assistant by obtaining my mother and stepfather's address from The Herald's company files (where it had been stored in case of an emergency, next-of-kin situation) and passed it onto her other half who wrote to me demanding additional rent as I had not given a full month's notice to leave their flat.

My reply began by pointing out that I was not living at the family home in Truro, giving a fictitious address in Newton Abbot should he wish to contact me again, and ended by stating that he 'stood about as much chance of receiving further money from me as he did of being appointed The Herald's next Editor'.

I did not hear directly from the Cansfields again, although they did – surprise, surprise – pass the Truro address onto Waverley Council, whose letters were returned unopened and quite truthfully marked that I was not living there. After a while they stopped, but I still took my revenge against the Old Colonials.

The day I fatefully agreed to take the Weybourne flat, in July 2005, I remembered Peter Cansfield boasting, while under the influence of alcohol, that he did not declare his income from the property to the Inland Revenue. I therefore wrote to the relevant office giving this information, although because I did so anonymously I never discovered whether my handiwork yielded the deserved repercussions for my unscrupulous ex-landlord.

Past and present accommodation issues resolved, the next item on the agenda, as my unofficial holiday entered its second week, was to start seeking work. While visiting The Sunday Independent's new office while on holiday the previous summer, I recalled Nikki Rowland saying John

Collings was 'always' looking for Saturday night subs on the sports desk and decided that this would be my starting point.

I rang JC, as he was commonly known, on the Tuesday morning, explained my situation and asked about Saturday nights. 'I might be able to offer you more than that this week,' he replied. 'I've got Graham (Hambly) on holiday, so we could do with someone all day Friday and Saturday.'

I made my return to The Sunday Independent on Friday February 2, four-and-a-half years, almost to the day, after my departure from the title's former Plymouth office with its new Liskeard home becoming the 14th newspaper office where I had been employed. My time out of journalism since leaving Farnham had totalled just 15 days.

The only unfamiliar face on the sports desk was JC's deputy Richard Hughes. Graham Hambly, while rapidly approaching retirement age, was still on staff part-time and Nigel Walrond was back in the South West and employed two to three days a week as a freelance.

I also learnt that day that there would soon be plenty of full-time freelance work available as both Nikki Rowland and Kirsty Turner were going on extended maternity leaves. Although the former wasn't much younger than me, she had recently remarried and, to the surprise of many at the office, had chosen to take this route.

That evening, the penultimate night of my brief stay back in Truro before moving into the Plymouth flat, I was watching an episode of Midsomer Murders, featuring the 1970s rock star Suzi Quatro, entitled The Axeman Cometh. As theme music ended the programme I started reflecting on the week's events and somehow sensed, at that moment, that the latest adventure in my eventful career was now up and running.

And I was right – although because of the rapidly-changing world of the newspaper industry it would sadly prove to be the last, the longest and ultimately the most frustrating.

23 Maternity magic

My first three months back at The Sunday Independent were steady rather than spectacular as I worked every Saturday along with Thursdays and Fridays if anyone else with sport subbing duties was absent, which was the case on five or six occasions in 12 or 13 weeks.

While The Indy's payment to freelances of £100 a day was the same as The Farnham Herald and most other weeklies in the South East, it was considered generous for the South West where the going rate was usually £70 to £75. So while I was not working full-time, the fact that I was being paid without deductions. and having to shell out only half the amount in rent I had been losing to the Cansfields, meant. in real terms. I was no worse off than I had been during the latter stages of my stay in Surrey.

Modern maternity leave regulations meant that Nikki and Kirsty would be away from the office for up to a year, but because their jobs had to be kept open for them and they did not have to state when they would be returning if at all, permanent staffers could not be taken on which meant several months' ready-made employment for freelances such as myself.

The Indy's Editor John Noble shuffled his pack, promoting an existing staff member to Acting Chief Sub in place of Nikki and moving Andy Pyle, a trainee who was earmarked to replace Graham Hambly on the sports desk when he retired later in the year, onto news for the duration of the maternity period. A freelance was taken on to replace Kirsty as a senior reporter and I had my days upped to Thursday to Saturday each week with Tuesdays and Wednesdays added if anyone from sport was on holiday or ill.

I couldn't really complain about earning, in real terms, more than I had been in Farnham while working a three-day week and considerably more when employed full-time. Of course, I knew this rate of earnings would not last indefinitely but for the time being I was quite happy with my lot and quickly settled into the routine of commuting from Plymouth to Liskeard, about 20 to 25 minutes by train, and going from the office down to Truro on a Saturday night, to spend the rest of the weekend there, about once a month.

I was still in regular contact with Mike Taylor, although he and Gail had left their rented house in Newton Abbot shortly after I had moved to Plymouth, buying their own place, with some generous help from her parents, at Hennock, a small and remote village on Dartmoor.

This inevitably restricted the frequency of how often Mike and I saw each other socially, but in the June I met up with him and a few friends at a Monday meeting of Newton Abbot races and he gave me the news that David Banks had died a few months earlier (he had forgotten to inform me at the time).

The former Dawlish Newspapers Managing Director, who was in his late 60s, had of course been suffering from Parkinson's Disease for several years and his passing was not considered a surprise. Never one to mix socially with the staff outside of work, he had become something of a recluse upon retirement, with nobody from the paper having seen him for several years prior to his death.

In July Richard Hughes gave a month's notice to leave The Indy. A single man in his mid-30s, he had decided to seek his fortune as a freelance in London, informing us that he had a friend in the capital who would put him up for nothing, although JC and one or two others at the office labelled him 'a dreamer' for making such a move (I, of course, could say nothing as I done exactly the same thing, only in the opposite geographical direction, just a few months earlier).

John Noble decreed that Richard would not be replaced until the matter of if and when Nikki and Kirsty were returning was resolved. Nigel Walrond (who had been Deputy Sports Editor under Kevin Marriott when the paper was in Plymouth) would cover for JC when he was on holiday and I would now work full-time every week until further notice, subbing not only for The Indy but also The Cornish Times when required.

The upshot was that I was now earning £500 a week and my bank balance began to rise, during the final third of the year, at a rate not seen since my time at The Jersey Evening Post. Because I knew this situation would only last a few months, I decided it was very much a case of 'making hay while the sun shines' and took no holiday. I did base myself in Truro for a week in the September, commuting to Liskeard by day while catching up with old friends by night, and also spent the Christmas period in my home town, but as 2007 ended I suddenly realised that I hadn't had a full week off work since the first few days after leaving Farnham in the January.

The situation continued unabated during the first half of the following year. Only in the July, in fact, was it finally confirmed that Nikki and Kirsty would not be coming back. The latter had been expected to return, even working a couple of 'buddy days' during the spring, but then her partner obtained a well-paid job in Southampton and that was that.

Nikki, several people at the office suspected, never had any intention of taking up her old position, but had deliberately dragged out her maternity leave to make as much money as possible following some sort of dispute with Jan Eagle, The Indy's General Manager, shortly before my second spell at the paper began.

The upshot was that Richard Hughes would still not immediately be replaced: Nigel Walrond would continue to deputise for JC, who would train Andy Pyle – who finally arrived permanently on the sports desk a year later than he originally expected – as his new assistant. During an initial three-month transitional period I would work Wednesdays, Fridays and Saturdays (full-time if anyone was away) while Graham Hambly, who had retired as a member of staff the previous Christmas but still did some freelance work from home, would not be replaced.

Having worked full-time solidly for more than a year without a full week off, and with my bank balance almost as high as it had been when I left Jersey, I was quite happy with the new arrangement for the time being. At first I enjoyed having up to four days a week off, but by the autumn the novelty started to wear off and while I had no intention of leaving The Indy at this point, I began to look around for additional freelance subbing, at other papers in Devon and Cornwall, preferably on Mondays and Tuesdays of each week.

I had maintained regular contact with Mike Taylor, despite his being out on a limb geographically. Apart from our attending another couple of Newton Abbot race-days, he had helped out at The Indy, at my suggestion to JC, when we were short of Saturday staff a few times earlier in the year – the first occasion we had worked together for 15 years – before deciding that a six-day week was not for him.

In the August we were talking in a Newton Abbot pub, prior to the racing, when he mentioned that one of The Mid-Devon Advertiser's senior subs was off long-term with a serious illness and would I, subject to the Editor's agreement, be interested in working Mondays and possibly Tuesdays for them until he returned?

I of course agreed and a couple of weeks later received a message to ring the MDA's General Manager, a woman whose name I can't remember, who subsequently asked me if I would be interested in employment each Monday until further notice. This was fine, but she then added that her accountant had advised against employing me as a freelance, so would I be prepared to come as staff?

This was a financially-unworkable proposition. As I pointed out, we were talking about one day a week for a limited period at £70 and by the time tax, national insurance and train fares were deducted I would be left with very little.

So for the second time I almost returned to the world of Dawlish Newspapers (in production terms, now completely merged with The MDA), but not quite. At Kingsbridge a decade earlier I had briefly worked at another title within the same Devon group before the financial lure of a return to Jersey intervened; now I had to decline an offer I would have liked to have accepted were it not impractical.

Meanwhile it was gradually becoming clear that Tindle Newspapers had not been as successful in turning around The Sunday Independent's fortunes as they had hoped when acquiring the title four years earlier. During the second half of the year, rumours started circulating that the paper was losing money and that cuts would have to be made and shortly before Christmas a raft of measures were announced that included my guaranteed days being cut to Fridays and Saturdays, although I would continue to be used full-time during holidays and illnesses.

Other freelances were affected. Nigel Walrond, who had his own agreement with John Noble to produce The Cornish Times' sports pages, was told this arrangement was being stopped with immediate effect and JC and Andy Pyle would now have to take on the extra work. There were also reductions both to the number of submitted columns and articles used and the number of casual staff employed on Saturday nights.

There was a definite sense of déjà vu to all this – a different office in a different town owned by a different company, but the same paper being cut and chopped as it lost, or was not considered to be making enough, money.

As 2008 ended, I had no financial worries after a very profitable first two years back in the South West, but I was beginning to feel that, unless there were to be further unexpected staff departures, the bubble had burst and the days of my earning very good money at The Indy on a regular basis were probably over.

A strangely-stagnant few months were to follow. I saw no part-time freelance or permanent staff jobs advertised anywhere in Devon or Cornwall. I was not, at this point, looking to move away from the South West as I was still almost breaking even at The Indy and had accumulated quite a bit in savings during the previous two years.

In the June I attended my first ever wedding when my brother finally tied the knot at the age of 41. This was only the second time any of my mother's five children from her two marriages had wed, the previous occasion being a private registry office affair to which nobody had been invited, and weddings in my family were generally so rare that this was definitely the stand-out social event of 2009.

In the late summer my patience in waiting to find additional work seemed about to be rewarded when The West Briton, no less, advertised for a part-time, freelance news sub-editor on Mondays and Tuesdays.

There had been huge changes at my home town paper since I last worked there 12 years earlier. Like many provincial titles it had moved out of its long-standing home in the centre, which was now a Wetherspoons pub, and relocated to a modern, purpose-built office on a riverbank road leading out of the city, where all the subbing for The Cornishman and the Cornish Guardian was also now done.

The likes of John Pearn, Richard Van Hinsberg and Gary Kaye had all long-since retired or moved on and although Rod Mitchell and Kevin Marriott were still sports editors for The West Briton and The Cornish Guardian respectively, I had no senior contacts left on the news side of things. Even Jeremy Ridge, who eventually became Editor, had, I learnt on the grapevine a few months earlier, taken voluntary redundancy despite not being much older than me.

The new man at the helm was a Richard Best, a complete outsider to the Cornish newspaper scene who did not know me from Adam. Still, I thought, my overall experience and past connections with the paper would make me a strong candidate for the position as I applied, emphasising my Truro background and stating that I would return to the city to live if employed (I could easily commute to Liskeard, which was only 50 minutes away by train, on the days I was working at The Indy).

Unlike Chris Bright at The JEP a decade earlier, Mr Best, sadly, did not live up to his name. Not only was I not selected for interview, but my application was never even acknowledged. Possibly the new Editor had a 'new broom' philosophy, and wasn't interested in employing senior figures from past regimes, but to not even receive a rejection letter defied belief.

Perhaps my real 'crime' was to apply by post rather than on-line as had been requested. Because I shared a computer with other freelances and part-timers at Liskeard - and sometimes spent several days at a time away from the office - I had decided that to contact The West Briton via the work terminal was too risky. What had things come to, I asked myself, when candidates were discriminated against for using the Royal Mail? However this would prove to be the last occasion that lack of on-screen privacy would potentially hinder my jobseeking efforts. Shortly afterwards, on the advice of a friend, I opened a private e-mail account, which could be accessed on any computer anywhere, including those in public libraries.

After peaking at the beginning of the year, my bank balance was now starting to decline each month, albeit only very slightly, and although I had no short to medium term financial worries, I began to wonder whether it was time to move on yet again.

I worked full-time at The Indy probably around 20 weeks that year, but most of the rest of the time was only there on Fridays and Saturdays. The novelty of having so much free time, after working without a proper break through almost all of 2007 and 2008, had long since worn off and after almost three years back in the freelance world my thoughts again started wandering towards the greater security provided by a full-time staff job.

Next year will be different, I told myself. If only I had known precisely in which ways it would prove to be different, I would never have wished so heartily for change.

24 Lost in space

Jan Eagle was one of a succession of general managers or managing directors I had encountered at Tindle Newspapers' titles who fitted a recurring stereotype.

Like David Banks at Dawlish Newspapers, Mike Roberts at Kingsbridge and Rosie Prior at The Farnham Herald series, the overall boss at The Sunday Independent and Cornish Times came from a non-journalistic background and despite her best efforts to pretend otherwise, it was clear to all that she understood nothing about journalism.

It therefore shouldn't have been a total surprise when, early in 2010, she announced that, as part of a raft of cost-cutting measures, a member of the production staff, with no knowledge or experience of journalism at any level, would be moved onto the sports desk with the amount of work available to Nigel Walrond and myself being reduced as a consequence.

A clearly-disgruntled JC spelt out to me, during the week that marked the third anniversary of my return to the paper, what this would mean: my only regular working day would be Saturday, and even that could not be guaranteed outside of the football season, and holiday cover would be reduced to maximum of two weekdays, usually Thursdays and Fridays.

Production workers transferring to editorial was, of course, nothing new in the provincial newspaper world. I had already seen it happen at both The Cornishman and The Jersey Evening Post, while Mike Taylor had originally been a 'comp' at Dawlish Newspapers but was now considered to be a sub at The Mid-Devon Advertiser even though he had no journalistic training and had never worked as a reporter.

The increasing trend had been for production operatives, as new technology and fewer adverts meant an increasingly smaller amount of work for their department, to fill editorial positions vacated by departing journalists. Fair enough, some might say, if compulsory redundancies were to be avoided. However this was the first time anywhere, that I was aware of, that subbing work had been taken away from journalists (freelance or otherwise) and given to people with no experience of or aptitude for the profession.

In earlier times this situation would have precipitated a hasty departure for me from The Sunday Independent to fields anew, but the pace of change in my profession had intensified still further during the previous three years and there were now very few full-time subbing posts advertised on Holdthefrontpage, with fierce competition for those that were given the large number of journalists being made redundant at papers around the country.

During the next three or four months I applied for three vacancies outside the South West - including one in Guildford - and although, unlike The West Briton, these papers at least had the courtesy to acknowledge my interest, I was not invited for interview at any of them.

An additional problem, I increasingly suspected, was my age. Given my perennial single person's lifestyle, gradually growing older had never been something that had unduly concerned me. I suppose I had officially reached the middle-aged landmark while in Farnham, but given that all my drinking partners there were considerably younger than me, if anything I became even more oblivious to how quickly the years were passing.

The tell-tale figure at the top of my cv would, however, present a somewhat different prospective to many would-be employers. I had now reached the stage where quite a few editors and deputy editors would be a fair bit younger than me and I had known for some years that many holding such positions were uneasy about taking on subs who were both older and more experienced than themselves.

In the June I spent a week's semi-holiday down in Truro, to coincide with the World Cup being played in South Africa, commuting to Liskeard during the three days I was employed. I again worked Thursday to Saturday the following week as a staff member was still on holiday, but was then informed by JC that I would not be required again, even on Saturdays, until the start of the new football season in the August.

Not working Saturdays, after only missing about three in more than three years, seemed peculiar at first and I was now effectively unemployed for around six weeks and living off ever-decreasing savings. I saw out the remainder of the World Cup, but thereafter life became increasingly boring. There were no suitable vacancies advertised anywhere and, in the absence of any other goals, I found myself counting down the days until the new season began.

My break down in Truro had been socially very active and, having caught up with so many people, I saw no reason to return for several weeks thereafter. However on the second Saturday in August, in anticipation of returning to The Sunday Independent the following weekend when the big kick-off finally arrived, I rang my mother to say I would be travelling on from Liskeard to my home town in seven days time.

In addition to arranging the following weekend, I was given the worrying news that my middle sister – the twin of the brother who had married the previous year – had discovered a lump under her breast and was awaiting the result of tests which she would receive the following Tuesday. I said I would ring again on the Wednesday to see what the situation was.

After a slightly anxious four-day wait came the good news that growth was not cancerous. The previous day I had been contacted by JC and asked not only to work Saturday that week but Thursday and Friday as well. The good news from home and my welcome return to work lifted my spirits and it was in a positive frame of mind that I travelled down to Truro on the evening of Saturday August 21.

Saturday nights in my home town had become something of a ritual during the past three-and-a-half years. Around every third or fourth week I would finish work at The Sunday Independent at 8.45 and catch the 9.07 train to the county's capital, arriving at my mother and stepfather's house at around 10.15pm, shortly before Match of the Day began. We would then watch the football highlights while catching up on the news since my last visit.

On this particular night we discussed Tottenham's efforts to reach the Champions League competition for the first time since 1961 when it was known as the European Cup. They were 3-2 down to Swiss side Young Boys after the first leg of the play-off round with the return match scheduled to be shown live on ITV the following Wednesday.

I asked my mother whether she planned to watch the game and she replied that she would before adding 'what a stupid name for a football team' Young Boys was.

The following day she and my stepfather had been invited out to a dinner in another part of the county, so there was no family roast, and as they left the house at around 12.30pm, I reminded my mother that, as the following weekend included a bank holiday, it would be one of the rare occasions when I travelled down to Truro on consecutive Saturdays.

'Yes, see you next week – same time, same place,' she said, adding to my stepfather, as they closed the front door, 'where did that saying come from again?'

I began to give that question some thought, and something told me the words 'to be continued next week, same time, same place' came at the end of the 1960s television programme Lost in Space, which I could vaguely remember watching as a young child. I made a mental note to impart this information the following weekend.

I remember nothing about the next three days other than watching Tottenham despatch Young Boys 4-0 on the Wednesday night. The following lunchtime I switched on my mobile phone to call Henry, a friend of mine from Truro with whom I still did the Sunday night quiz at The City Inn four or five times a year, usually during bank holiday weekends.

It was my intention to check that we were still on for the coming Sunday, but I was immediately distracted by flashing messages showing that various people had tried to contact me since I last checked the phone at breakfast time, even although I wasn't expecting any calls that day.

There were two recorded messages: the first, from my middle sister, tearfully asking me to ring someone immediately as there was 'really bad news about Mum' and the second, from my stepfather, asking me to call him urgently. Neither of them had spelt out exactly what had happened, but somehow I knew.

My mother was less than 18 months away from reaching 80 and had been a heavy smoker most of her adult life. She had also been diagnosed with bronchitis earlier that year, yet her death was totally unexpected. I later learnt she had spent the Wednesday in bed with a heavy cold and was awake the following morning when my stepfather left her to take the dog for a walk. When he returned an hour later she had passed away. The paramedics said it seemed the cold on top of the bronchitis had caused respiratory problems.

Not for 40 years had we experienced a sudden and unexpected death in any branch of the family. As I pointed out when we gathered in Truro the following morning, everyone knew this was something that had to happen one day and we agreed that such a quick and painless passing was preferable to a long, drawn-out illness, yet it was clear that everyone was in a state of shocked disbelief.

My mother had remained so young in spirit during her advancing years, in many ways acting more like someone in their 50s than a near octogenarian, that I think we had forgotten just how old she was getting. That and the fact that there had been absolutely no warning signs made the situation seem almost unreal for several days.

In addition to writing the obituary for The West Briton, I was asked to compose the eulogy for the funeral, which took place a fortnight later and, unlike my father's send-off 18 years earlier, was as positive as these events ever can be. A well-attended service was followed by an afternoon-long wake at The Victoria Inn, a pub at Threemilestone, on the outskirts of Truro, which my mother had regularly visited in her latter years with a former work colleague.

The final quarter of 2010 passed with there being some improvement to the amount of work available at Liskeard, though I was still not earning a living wage, and with no suitable vacancies being advertised elsewhere. I continued going down to Truro one weekend a month as my family had agreed to try and keep the routine of things, as far as was possible, as it had been before my mother's death.

My stepfather, who was 10 years younger than my mother and still worked part-time, stated that he had no intention of selling the family home for the time being and even Christmas, although inevitably a little strange, was organised in the same pattern as it had been for years.

As a year ended that all of us would always remember for all the wrong reasons, my main concern, as I attempted to look forward rather than back, was that I was now down to my last £2,000 in savings.

25 'Successfail' times

I'm not quite sure what happened to 2011. Unlike any other year in my career it came and went almost without incident. There were no changes to the amount of work I was given at The Sunday Independent – every Saturday as well as Thursdays and Fridays if anyone from sport was away – and no suitable vacancies, freelance or staff, were advertised for any paper in the South West.

The unsatisfactory employment situation did lead to one unwanted landmark: in the May I went overdrawn at the bank for the first time since immediately before going to Jersey 14 years earlier. The savings I had accrued there and then during those profitable first two years back at The Indy were now exhausted and I was now, as had been the case in the immediate pre-JEP era, relying on credit cards to supplement my meagre income

One piece of uplifting news, in terms of natural justice if not to my bank balance, was the departure of Jan Eagle from the Liskeard office. She was dismissed by Tindle Newspapers' high-command for what I was only told was 'financial mismanagement' – but her deserved demise changed little on a day-to-day basis at The Sunday Independent as she was replaced internally by another faceless character from an advertising background.

The first anniversary of my mother's death was duly observed and a second Christmas without her was noteworthy only for another unexpected passing: Peter Trevenna – a long-standing friend of the family whom I had known since I was a young child and had, over the years, spent many a drinking session with at the band club in his home town of St Austell – succumbed to a heart attack the day after Boxing Day and just four days before his 85th birthday.

After attending the funeral, ironically held on what would have been my mother's 80th birthday, there was at last some positive news, as 2012 got into full swing, when I was invited to attend an interview for a part-time, freelance sub-editor vacancy at The Express & Echo in Exeter.

This title had been one of several Northcliffe-owned dailies to be downgraded to a weekly the previous year as the cutbacks affecting the regional media continued unabated. I had known, or known of, several journalists at The Echo while at Dawlish, but all those names had long since departed.

The paper's present-day editorial management seemed over-concerned, when I met them, that all of my subbing experience in the previous five years had been on sport, when they were looking for someone to work on news. I pointed out that 15 of the 20 years I had been using QuarkXpress had been spent primarily on news, but they were not to be persuaded by such a logical and factually-correct argument and the rejection letter arrived in the post just four days after the interview.

I knew that I now had to consider once again applying for full-time vacancies outside of the South West, but subbing opportunities were becoming increasingly scarce as papers across the country tried to avoid replacing departing staff members. Also more and more titles were advertising for 'multi-media' journalists – those who were equally at home with editing websites as traditional news pages.

I had, during my last two years at Farnham, been required to copy the top five or six news stories from my edition onto the company's website each Friday, the day after we went to print – not a complicated task as articles on web pages could be of any length with none of cutting to fit skills required on a newspaper template – but I somehow doubted that this limited experience, between five and seven years earlier, would qualify me as the 'experienced multi-media' operator many employers were asking for.

One Saturday in July I arrived at the Liskeard office to be informed that John Noble had suffered a stroke a couple of days earlier and would be off work indefinitely. The Indy's long-serving Editor was, in any case, only a year or two away from retirement age and many at the paper privately expressed doubts as to whether he would return.

For several weeks there was no change to the situation. The senior news subs carried on bringing out the paper, the London Olympics came and went, and it was not until the October that it was announced that John Noble had decided to retire and that the most senior sub, Andrew Townsend, would – in line with Tindle Newspapers' national policy of promoting from within – be taking over as Editor.

However for the second time in as many years a change in the Sunday Independent senior management made absolutely no difference to my situation. The new man in charge, though quieter and less bombastic than his predecessor, nevertheless embarked on an immediate policy of steadying the ship and not changing anything – perhaps a little surprisingly given the paper's regional sales had fallen from over 30,000 when I was in Plymouth to less than 20,000, although to be fair, Andrew Townsend probably had his own strict directives from Brian Doel and Co up in Farnham.

As another largely-undistinguished year drew to a close, I knew I had to do something to increase my chances of finding additional or alternative work as the credit card bills continued to rise and the unhealthy amount time I spent watching daytime television showed no sign of lessening. Geographical location would no longer be important.

In late November, as I made my usual weekly glance through the vacancies advertised on Holdthefrontpage, an opening for a full-time sub-editor at The Express & Star, in Wolverhampton, caught my eye.

I was a aware that the Midlands multi-edition title, with a daily circulation of just under 100,000, was the highest-selling provincial newspaper in the country and competition for the position was bound to be fierce. Half of me was saying 'if I can't get a part-time job at a rapidly-declining outfit like The Express & Echo, what chance will I stand at a paper like that', but I also remembered my surprise selection and subsequent success at The Jersey Evening Post and I submitted my application shortly before Christmas.

On the morning of New Year's Eve, as I prepared to return to Plymouth following the customary week or so spent in Truro over the festive period, I received a phone message from a Diana Davies, Executive Editor at The Express & Star, asking me to arrange an interview for the following week.

As I made the train journey up to the Midlands I reflected that I had only ever set foot in Wolverhampton once before, on a day trip for a football match with two friends from Cornwall some 15 years earlier, and that this was, in fact, only my second venture north of London since that day.

The office was centrally-situated, within 10 minutes' walk of the railway station – rather than the out-of-town industrial estate location favoured by so many newspapers by this time – and this set the tone for a positive afternoon. The interview with Diana Davies and a youngish Sports Editor must have ranked among the best I have ever had, matching those at the likes of Dawlish and Farnham, in that I answered every question quickly and satisfactorily and not a single stumbling block emerged.

They were, I was quickly informed, considering putting the new sub onto sport, hence the presence of the desk's top man, and this immediately dissolved any fears that my lack of news subbing in recent times might again count against me, although my interviewers seemed quite happy with my general, all-round experience as, of course, I would have expected any competent would-be employer to have been.

Happy with the way things had gone, but still ever-mindful that there would be fierce competition for the position, I waited more than two weeks before hearing from The Express & Star again. The pleasantly-written letter from Diana Davies said a decision had not been easy, and thanked me for travelling up to meet her and her colleague, but ultimately they would not be offering me the position.

There was no immediate follow-up to this encouraging, if at the end of the day unsuccessful, start to 2013. A few weeks later I applied for sub's vacancy at The Bristol Post but did not receive a reply. I certainly hadn't had a lot of luck with Northcliffe publications since my return to the South West six years earlier – just one reply (from The Express & Echo) to three or four applications. I had regularly been informed, by those who were or had until recently been employed by the company, that it was not a happy ship – massive cost-cutting and redundancies and rumours of a takeover gathering pace – but in my present predicament it was a case of 'beggars can't be choosers'.

Better news came in early April when I applied for a vacancy at The Yellow Advertiser in Basildon, Essex. As the title would suggest, this was a long-established weekly newspaper which, I discovered from the internet, had been taken over by Tindle Newspapers around five or six years earlier.

After first checking that I would be prepared to move to the South East for a salary of just over £20,000 a year, the Editor Mick Ferris invited me up for an interview on a Monday afternoon which included my being asked to complete a page for that week's edition.

This I did satisfactorily other than when I was asked to finish off by importing a photo and had to admit I couldn't remember how to use Photoshop, a system for processing pictures which subs had to use, in the absence of dedicated picture desk staff, at some papers and which I had briefly used during my final spell at The Cornishman 12 years earlier.

That apart I felt the afternoon went well. Mick Ferris assured me that the cost of rented accommodation in Essex was nothing like the obscene Cansfieldesque amounts charged in Surrey and told me the position was between myself and two other candidates whom he had yet to interview.

A week or so passed before I heard from him again and my worst fears were realised when I learnt that Photoshop had proved to be the decisive factor. The other shortlisted applicants were fully versed in its use and this, he wrote, made them 'more suitable for the job'.

While in some ways I respected his honesty in stating precisely why I hadn't been offered the position, it was another sign of the changing times that I could lose out through something that, in days gone by, would not even have been considered a sub-editor's skill and, from what I could remember from my last summer in Penzance, any reasonably-competent journalist could learn in an hour or so anyway.

The next development, in what was proving to be a much more eventful year, was totally unexpected and, although short-lived, something of a throwback to the good old days of the 1990s when freelance subs prepared to travel could find work relatively easily.

After working at no less than 14 newspaper offices during the first 22 years of my career I had to wait another six for number 15 to arrive, but the long-overdue event finally happened during the first week of June when, out of the blue, I spent two days with the Somerset County Gazette in Taunton.

On a Saturday morning I noticed an advertisement from the paper, on Holdthefrontpage, desperately seeking freelance subs for short periods. I immediately applied by e-mail and, the following day, received a message on my mobile asking me to contact the Editor Alex Cameron. When I did so, on the Monday morning, he explained that the Newsquest company were expanding the pagination of many of their titles to offset a steep rise in cover prices. This policy had coincided with staff holidays at his office and would I be available to help out on Tuesday and Wednesday of that week and then possibly returning for the same two days the following week?

Although I would have contacted the Somerset County Gazette whatever the circumstances at Liskeard, my application coincided with negative news from JC just a week or so earlier when he informed me that, for the first time since 2010, he could not guarantee me employment, even on Saturdays, during the football close season due to the continuing need to make cutbacks. I had already been laid off for the whole of June and was told to await further contact in early July.

So it was with something of a sense of relief that I caught an early-morning train from Plymouth to Taunton on the Tuesday just three days after seeing the Somerset County Gazette's advert. I was aware that the paper's subs would not finish work until around 8pm that night, but Alex Cameron had already informed me that the paper would arrange and pay for hotel accommodation that night. It almost was like Jersey and Kingsbridge all over again.

I worked that day, and from 8am until 5pm on the Wednesday, before returning to Plymouth and at first it did seem a little strange to be editing news pages again after a six-year gap. However by the second day it was if I had never been away from such activities and both Alex Cameron and his Chief Sub-editor stated that they were totally happy with what I had done, although they added that the problems posed by the paper's increased pagination had not been as great as they had anticipated and, for that reason, they thought it unlikely that they would need me again the following week when one of their staff subs would be back from holiday.

On the editorial side there was no-one at Taunton whom I had previously met or even heard of before. However the centre's Managing Director was none other than Simon Dixon-Phillip, whom I renewed acquaintances with for the first time since leaving The Sunday Independent's Plymouth office 11 years earlier.

I had been aware that he had remained with Newsquest after they sold The Indy to the Tindle regime, but until now didn't know of his exact whereabouts.

Unfortunately the pay and expenses I received from the Somerset County Gazette, although quite generous, had no effect on my overall financial situation as the money simply replaced what I would have earned had I been working in Liskeard that month. I was recalled by JC at the beginning of July, initially for three days' holiday cover and thereafter every Saturday once again, and I was now back to exactly where I had been before the strange Taunton interlude.

There was, however, been one significant change. My financial situation had continued to decline to such an extent that my credit cards had reached their limit and I was now effectively only paying their interest charges each month. This meant I could no longer afford to travel to long-distance interviews (where expenses, unlike in the 1980s and 1990s, were rarely paid by would-be employers) let alone relocate to another part of the country. Consequently my work-hunting, whether for freelance or full-time positions, would now have to be restricted to the South West until further notice.

In the August I decided to try for a temporary position in the press office at Plymouth University. Like many long-standing newspaper journalists, this was precisely the type of job I swore, over the years, would never interest me. PR officers had long enjoyed a largely-deserved reputation, throughout the rest of the profession, of being overpaid, under-skilled and employed only to churn out upbeat propaganda or meaningless jargon on behalf the organisation they represented.

Yet as the position would pay the equivalent of £26,000 pa for the six months it lasted, it was something, in the circumstances, I had to consider, but after submitting the lengthy and extremely-bureaucratic application form I did not receive a reply, although the university did state, on its website, that only those candidates selected for interview would be contacted.

The Falmouth Packet was a newspaper I very rarely heard anything about, despite its proximity (just 10 miles away) to Truro. It had become Newsquest's only remaining title in Devon and Cornwall following their sale of The Indy some seven or eight years earlier, and for this reason it tended to operate as a lone ranger and had never been part of the 'gossip circuit' made up by the two counties' other publications which were all owned either by Northcliffe (now recently renamed Local World following the predicted takeover) or Tindle Newspapers.

I had, you might remember, attended an interview at The Packet for a trainee reporter's vacancy shortly before completing the NCTJ course way back in 1985, but had had no contact with the paper, or anyone who had worked there, since. So when, that September, they advertised for a full-time sub-editor, it was something of a step into the unknown, although one factor I viewed positively was the title being part of the same Newsquest regional group as The Somerset County Gazette, with Simon Dixon-Phillip the overall Managing Director, so surely my recent spell in Taunton would be to my advantage?

I was asked to attend an interview on the first Thursday in October and incorporated the day into a week-long stay in Truro (I didn't have enough regular work to undertake real 'holidays' but a pattern had emerged in the past three or four years whereby I would spend three weeks a year, including Christmas, in my home town and travel from there to Liskeard on whatever days I was required).

The Packet's office was, unsurprisingly, not the same one I had visited nearly three decades earlier, but in a business park on the outskirts of the town. I was greeted, at the entrance, by a smoking Paul Jordan - a senior production worker at The West Briton during my time there until his entire department had been made redundant and their function taken over by staff at the then new Western Morning News office at Derriford, Plymouth - and he seemed to remember a lot more about me than I did about him.

I was interviewed by the Editor Paul Armstrong and another senior journalist named Graham Smith, who were both at least my age, and this immediately lifted my spirits as I knew I wasn't going to come up against any 'generation gap' obstacles. And once again the proceedings went well from my point of view. Apart from the expected questions about my career history they asked about my Truro background and I emphasised that, because I had somewhere to stay in the city and did not have to give notice elsewhere, I could start work almost immediately if required to do so.

This seemed to please them as the person I would be replacing was leaving, I was told, the following Friday and they would be one person down thereafter. Paul Armstrong even said he had no problem with my continuing to work Saturdays at The Sunday Independent if I so wished – and for financial reasons I certainly would have to keep travelling to Liskeard once a week for the foreseeable future even if I was employed at Falmouth on weekdays.

The afternoon's only slight disappointment was the news that The Packet would only be paying the successful applicant around £19,000 a year. This was about the same as my final salary at Farnham but that, you must remember, was by now nearly seven years earlier. Another sign of the changing times, I thought, but then glossed over such feelings by truthfully telling my interviewers 'well that's more than I get at present'.

As at Wolverhampton and Basildon, several days passed thereafter and although my e-mail from Paul Armstrong started off by saying 'we were very impressed by the standard of your application' and 'it had not been an easy decision', for the third time in less than a year I had experienced what I started terming a 'successfail' interview.

In the month leading up to Christmas I found temporary work, via an agency, with Plymouth City Council. This was my first non-journalistic employment for exactly 20 years and at least enabled me to have a financially-untroubled festive period with my family remaining, for now, blissfully ignorant of my real situation which, as in the immediate pre-Jersey era, included massive credit card debts and rent arrears.

As I reflected that 2013, at least in comparison to the two previous years, had been quite productive in terms of near misses and increased job-seeking opportunities, I also had to concede that I was, not for the first time in my career, becoming engulfed in a severe financial crisis.

26 And then there were none

From quite an early age I had been familiar with the phrase 'life begins at 40', usually reflecting an optimistic outlook by those entering middle age, but a more appropriate slogan in my case, as the 21st century's second decade moved into its middle years, could have been 'journalistic life ends at 50'.

The industry's decline was gathering pace as the gamble undertaken by the larger companies - that of giving news away free on their websites before it appeared in their paid-for papers – was failing spectacularly.

The newly-renamed Local World. Newsquest, Trinity Mirror and the rest were beginning to realize that websites did not bring in anything like enough advertising revenue, but it was now a little late to start charging people to read news they had become accustomed to receiving for free.

Thus it was the traditional newspapers that suffered as these losses were offset with more and more redundancies, non-replacement of departing staff and the increasing trend of centralising offices which took many titles miles away from the communities they were supposed to serve.

Hence there was an inevitable decline in the standard of news, but journalistic 'dinosaurs' of my age group were not required to try and improve the situation. Instead the larger groups had a policy of taking on untrained youngsters to fill what editorial positions were still allowed – and only paying them around half of what would have been considered the normal rate just a few years earlier. Reporters became 'content curators' and news editors 'heads of audience' as traditional titles disappeared under the rising tide of jargonistic claptrap.

Vacancies for full-time sub-editors were inevitably few and far between, but one that was advertised on

Holdthefrontpage that spring was, ironically enough, at The Jersey Evening Post. In the 14 years since my departure from the Channel Islands' daily, this was the first time, as far as I was aware, that they had advertised for a sub, but I was aware that a great many changes had taken place at The JEP since my successful spells there in the late 90s.

No longer was the paper independent of all mainland titles - it had been owned by the same company as the Wolverhampton-based Express & Star for several years - while Chris Bright, I had read on Holdthefrontpage, retired the previous year to be replaced by someone not employed there during my era.

It was perhaps a sign of changed times that applications had to be sent to an 'administrator', rather than the Editor, and although I couldn't really afford to move back to the island, I duly made my pitch with a slightly-tongue-in-cheek letter; whether I was unsuccessful because of the small matter of an unpaid income tax bill from a decade-and-a-half earlier I will probably never know.

The JEP did, at least, have the courtesy to inform me of their decision, which is more than could said for both The North Devon Journal and The Bath Chronicle, two Local World titles who advertised vacancies later that year.

The irony of my rejection at the latter was that I had been selected for an interview there in late 1996 when it was an evening paper and I had no real experience of dailies other than my two short stints at The Western Morning News. Now (like many former Northcliffe dailies) it had been downgraded to a weekly and I was considerably more experienced than 18 years earlier. Was the problem my age or the ignorance (at least in their decision not to acknowledge my application)of the people in charge at these papers? The truth probably lay somewhere in the middle.

Meanwhile, back at The Sunday Independent, the main news of 2014 was a change of ownership. Tindle

Newspapers - whose speciality over the decades had been running small papers serving small towns and largely rural communities - had never quite known what to do with a regional title covering several counties and rumours of a sell-off had been rife for some time.

The new proprietor was Brian Doel, who had recently retired as Tindle's national Managing Director after many years' service and was given a controlling interest in The Indy as part of his severance package.

This meant a parting of the ways with The Cornish Times, after nine years sharing the same office in Liskeard with the rural weekly, and almost everyone connected with The Indy editorially, both staff and freelance, assumed the paper would return to what many saw as its natural home in Plymouth.

I vaguely knew Brian Doel from my time in Farnham, having attended several meetings he had chaired there and, shortly after his arrival at Liskeard, he said he remembered my face from that time and was, thereafter, quite friendly towards me.

The staff members at the office were duly divided between The Sunday Independent and The Cornish Times, with everyone connected with sport opting to stay with the former while Andrew Townsend and the rest of the news crew, all of whom lived locally, went in the other direction. Production and advertising operatives were likewise apportioned to each title.

Brian Doel was an extremely experienced newspaper man, and the initial reaction to his takeover was that he would 'shake things up'. It was therefore with almost disbelief that the journalists working there learnt, not long afterwards, that The Indy's new office would be elsewhere in the backwater of Liskeard.

This shortsighted approach had, we learnt, been taken so as not to upset the advertising staffers, all of whom lived locally but none of whom were particularly long-serving.

Any hopes we had of the paper entering a dynamic new era had dissipated almost before they had begun.

Editorial changes made by the new regime were not particularly significant. The paper had become even more sport-orientated since my second spell there began and the news coverage (with no reporters employed remember) had shrunk further and further.

Brian Doel accelerated this process still further by moving the news into the middle of the paper as a small supplement and having sport - which, of course, had been the paper's main selling point for many years - on the front page.

Frazer Cox - a former staff sub-editor from the Independent's Plymouth days who, ironically, I had replaced when joining the title the first time around - was taken on as a three-day-a-week freelance to compile the news supplement and Guy Channing, another name I was familiar with but had never previously met, was the new freelance photographer/picture editor. John Collings, while still Sports Editor, was given the additional title of Editor-in-Chief.

In the July I briefly returned to The Somerset County Gazette to work a Tuesday and Wednesday during the busy staff holidays period, but it would prove to be my last contact with the paper. A couple of months later I learnt that Alex Cameron had resigned to take up a PR job (a familiar destination for departing editors around this time) and that a significant shake-up of the editorial department followed.

In the autumn Andy Pyle resigned as Deputy Sports Editor at The Indy to take up the position of motoring website editor at The Plymouth Herald - such an excruciatingly-boring prospect for someone who, at that time, didn't even own a car that most at the Liskeard office believed he had succumbed to pressure from his girlfriend to take a 9 till 5, Monday to Friday job where he had Saturdays free.

In line with current trends he was not immediately replaced and this meant a welcome return to more weekday work for me after a dreadful year financially which had seen my debts, especially rent arrears, grow with my landlord threatening notice more than once and only refraining from doing so because of my long tenure which now stood at seven-and-a-half years.

The slightly-improved money picture did, at least, make it possible to once again be able to afford to travel to job interviews outside the South West. Paradoxically very few sub-editor vacancies in any location were, by this time, being advertised, but in early 2015 there was one at Newquest's Dorset Echo in Weymouth.

The job description on Holdthefrontpage certainly implied that they were looking for an older, more traditionally trained sub with there being no mention of websites or social media and, most interestingly, applicants were asked to top their cv with a headline summarising their career so far. I responded with 'Echo sounded out by much-travelled sub' and was duly asked to attend an interview in early March.

While pleased to have been shortlisted, I was aware that the vacancy was at one of Newquest's subbing 'hubs' which had received much criticism, nationally, for being unprofessionally run and remote from many of the titles they were serving.

It was, however, again a case of 'needs must' and my interviewees - Chief Sub-editor Andy Reed and his sidekick Carl Blackmore - painted a rosy picture of life at the Dorset office and I travelled back feeling the day had gone reasonably well.

As had been the case with my applications to Wolverhampton, Basildon and Falmouth two years earlier, there was a wait of well over a week before I received a letter thanking me for attendance and presenting myself well, but adding that my application had not been successful.

A couple of years later I learnt that the Weymouth hub had been disbanded and all employed there made redundant, so perhaps this latest 'near miss' wasn't such a bad thing. Symbolically, though, my trip across the south coast would prove to be the last time I would attend an interview at the office of a newspaper with which I had no previous connection.

In May a general election saw the Conservatives seize power after five years of coalition government. Nick Harvey, at one point Armed Forces Minister in the joint Tory-Liberal Democrat administration, lost his North Devon seat after 23 years and I sent him an e-mail of commiseration, having not previously been in touch since 2005. I hardly expected to be top of his list of priorities after so many years in parliament and serving the constituency, but the fact that I did not receive a reply at all illustrated that the 1980s were now a distant memory for those I had known in those faraway days of my early journalistic career.

Two months later The Independent finally completed the move to its new Liskeard home in a business park around three-quarters of a mile from the old office. In the autumn Andy Pyle was finally replaced, by a local youngster Liam Read, who, it was rumoured, was only being paid half the salary of his predecessor in what was, if true, certainly a sign of the times in the newspaper industry.

I was still in occasional contact with Mike Taylor at the Mid Devon Advertiser and, that October, we met up for a few drinks at the newly-opened Wetherspoons pub in Teignmouth.

His description of what journalistic life was now like at the MDA and the former Dawlish Newspapers titles now under its control seemed fairly typical of what was going on generally: three subs to produce news and sports page for all the group's titles and, more significantly, no freelance cover allowed when any of the trio were on holiday or ill.

As we talked about what was going on at South West offices generally, the conversion strayed onto South Hams Newspapers which, I was informed, was one of the few remaining Tindle outlets where freelance subs were still used on occasions. Would it, we debated, be worth my while seeking work there?

It was now 18 years since my short but happy stint at the Kingsbridge-based company, and there were, perhaps not surprisingly, no contacts from that time left. Brian Cooke, now long retired and aged around 80, had been suffering from dementia for several years while Ron White and Trevor Drew, the next two most senior subs in the late 90s, had both passed away at relatively young ages.

The day after meeting Mike Taylor I inspected the South Hams Newspapers website and amongst the names listed, the only one that rang a bell was Jackie Smith, advertising manager when I was there and now the Managing Director. The Editor, a Steve Harvey, I had never heard of before, but with nothing to lose I decided to drop him an e-mail.

A few days later I received a reply from Jackie Smith saying they sometimes used freelance subs for holiday cover and would I be interested in travelling up to discuss the matter further with the Editor and herself.

I did so the following Monday and Steve Harvey, an affable middle-aged character, seemed quite keen to use me in future. However the mood of Jackie Smith, who initially welcomed me warmly and said she vaguely remembered me from my previous stint with the company, changed somewhat when I admitted to not being a driver.

Kingsbridge, situated as it is in a far-flung rural corner of South East Devon, is not the easiest place to access from the outside world, but as I pointed out, there was an hourly bus service to and from Plymouth between 7am and 9pm each day, so I couldn't see a problem. I departed with Steve

Harvey saying 'we'll probably speak to you again soon' but the uncertain expression on Jackie Smith's face painted a less optimistic outlook. I left feeling it would be a case of who really 'ruled the roost'.

2015 soon became 2016 and as the ninth anniversary of my return to The Sunday Independent came and went very little was happening. It was now three months since my informal interview at Kingsbridge and by now I had already resigned myself to not hearing from them again. By now there were no subs jobs being advertised on Holdthefrontpage (apart, for some unknown reason, the occasional vacancy in Scotland) as all the major newspaper companies continued and indeed tightened up their 'non-replacement of departing staff' policy.

The early summer saw the European Union referendum and another dire performance by the England football team at a major finals as they crashed out of the Euros to little Iceland. In my life, however, there was little to get either excited or too despondent about as the same old routine continued unabated.

Then, one Monday in August, I received a copy of an e-mail, sent by JC to all the Independent's freelances, informing us that Brian Doel had died suddenly on the Saturday night. I remembered seeing him at the office on the Friday and was later told he had also been there early on the Saturday morning before departing and succumbing to a heart attack just a few hours later.

JC assured everyone that the paper would continue and within a couple of weeks it was announced the Brian Doel had left The Indy, in his will, to Sue Yates, apparently a business associate of his from his Farnham days, although I and no-one else at the Liskeard office had ever heard of her, and it transpired she had no previous experience of running a newspaper.

The new proprietor - a thin, bespectacled middle-aged woman - adopted an extremely low-key approach, rarely staying at the office for more than a couple of hours at a time and never present when the paper went to print on Saturdays.

Administration, it soon became clear, was not among her strong points. Payments to freelance subs and contributors - usually made three to four weeks in arrears under previous regimes - steadily were made later and later and matters were to come to a head at the end of the year.

Following complaints from a number of people when October invoices were not paid until early December, we were nevertheless assured that November payments would be in everyone's bank accounts in good time for Christmas.

Christmas Eve fell on a Saturday, which meant no Sunday papers, national or regional, were to be published and I planned to begin a rare weekend off by travelling down to Truro late on the Friday afternoon in good time for the festive period.

Having paid my rent in full at the start of the week I was totally relying on my November payment for the break in Cornwall and going to a cashpoint that Friday morning I felt so entitled to presume that the money would be there that I attempted to withdraw the cash I needed without even checking the balance first.

What happened next I'm sure, by now, you've already guessed. I nominally e-mailed JC, knowing that nothing could really be done as the admin/wages staff had already 'broken up' for Christmas. He replied that no-one had been paid, although why he still wasn't sure, and that he was being inundated with e-mails and phone calls from angry contributors and freelance subs.

Having now been reduced to working part-time only at The Sunday Independent for nearly seven years, and with no savings for the past three, I had long since been forced to adopt my own (to coin a political term in widespread use at the time) 'austerity' measures, such as drinking cheap supermarket cider instead of lager and smoking roll-ups -

two activities I had not been forced to undertake since my 20s.

And added to that list of unwelcome retrograde steps that weekend was travelling by train without paying. I knew all services into Cornwall would be full to bursting point the night before a Saturday Christmas Eve and not until my train had left St Austell, with only a few minutes remaining before I reached my destination, was I even asked to show a ticket.

My bank card, of course, was refused, but the guard blamed his antiquated ticket machine and told me to pay when I arrived at Truro station. However by now we were well into the evening and I knew (as he obviously did not) that the ticket office would be closed by then.

I borrowed money from my family to get through the next few days and payments from The Indy were finally received on Thursday 29th. I worked in Liskeard on New Year's Eve and learnt, from JC, that Sue Yates had simply disappeared before Christmas without signing off the invoices, later blaming an illness in her family.

While her incompetence might have led to my receiving a criminal conviction for fare dodging, there were more definite consequences for other freelances with one missing his mortgage payment and others receiving bank charges for unpaid standing orders and cheques.

Sue Yates was barely seen in Liskeard office during the early months of 2017, working almost exclusively from home amid rumours that she had received, anonymously, abusive e-mails following the festive fiasco. We heard, firstly, that she no longer wanted the paper and then, as we moved into spring, that if a buyer could not be found soon, the entire future of The Sunday Independent was in doubt.

By now the 10th anniversary of my return to the title had come and gone. Throughout my entire adult life - from my teens until my 40s - I had wondered how on earth anyone could stay with a single employer (whether in journalism or anything else) and work with largely the same people for periods ranging from one to as many as four decades. Thanks to a combination of the rapid decline of my once-proud profession and my own advancing years I had finally, albeit late in my career, experienced this for myself.

In March we were asked to submit our invoices at Liskeard a week earlier than usual, a request that puzzled most of those affected as no explanation was given as to why this was necessary.

We worked at the office as usual the following Saturday (not realizing until later the significance of the April 1 date) and everyone departed that night with the usual 'enjoy the rest of the weekend' and 'see you next week' niceties.

The following Wednesday JC sent an e-mail to everyone connected with The Sunday Independent stating that Sue Yates had failed to find a buyer and the paper had ceased publication with immediate effect after being in existence for some 200 years.

Around a sixth of that time, 33 years, was now the running total of my own wildly-fluctuating career. Was this really going to be the end in such inauspicious circumstances - or would there be one final twist in the tail?

27 Masters of incompetence

The Independent did not appear for two consecutive weekends in April and just as I was considering 'signing on' for the first time since 1993, JC contacted everyone connected with the paper saying a buyer, from Truro ironically, had been found.

Peter Masters was a name known to me as the taxi proprietor had, with a partner, saved Truro City Football Club from bankruptcy around four years earlier and the team, following a promotion, were now established in the National League South division.

Masters had, however, something of a reputation as a dodgy dealer as two long-standing friends of mine, both owners of rival taxi companies in the city, confirmed when we discussed his latest business venture.

Everyone, staff and freelances, were recalled to Liskeard and The Indy resumed publication as if nothing had happened. In those early days Masters managed the paper at arm's length. Being Truro based, some 40 miles away, he rarely visited the office and was never to be seen on Saturdays, when the paper went to print, because of his football commitments.

Even as a remotely situated proprietor, however, he soon gained a reputation as a headstrong 'bull in a china shop' operator, hiring two accountants in quick succession and then almost immediately firing each of them once they questioned his methods of running the paper's finances.

Then came a bizarre takeover of another newspaper company. The 'In View' series of weekly titles, based in Dorset and independently owned, had apparently been in financial trouble for some time. Masters, with no knowledge or experience of the media world, nevertheless abruptly purchased the group and attempted to merge it with

The Indy as a single concern. It was a bit like the 15 year old who, after getting seriously drunk for the first time, allows the unrealistic euphoria of the experience to take control and makes himself even more intoxicated the next time around.

It did not take long for the sober reality to dawn. After a few disastrous weeks of attempting to run the titles as a single operation, Masters decided he no longer wanted the 'In View' group and promptly sold the titles for £1 to an unfortunate individual who didn't realize that, by making the purchase, he was inheriting the company's debts.

The 'In View' papers soon ceased publication permanently and a protracted legal battle ensued, as to who was responsible for redundancy payments to staff, which was not resolved until 2020 when Masters' patsy was deemed liable, but The Indy's owner also received widespread and deserved criticism for his part in the fiasco.

Next on the agenda, that first summer he was in charge, was the sudden appointment of a new Editorial Director. Tim Dixon was a previous Editor of The Bristol Evening Post, so we assumed he knew what he was doing, and during the first few weeks he seemed a reasonable enough chap as he slowly got to grips with the workings of the Liskeard office.

There were soon mutterings of discontent, from JC and Frazer Cox, that the new man and Masters were 'freezing them out' by holding regular private meetings. Others wondered whether Tim Dixon's arrival would herald the long-overdue overhaul the paper's news coverage needed.

For a decade now it had consisted of little more than sterile and often out-of-date agency copy. Tackling this issue would not be easy without funds being made available to hire experienced reporters and possibly news subs. Was Tim Dixon's plan to improve the situation? We would never get the chance to find out.

With the Editorial Director having been in position for no more than four or five weeks, I arrived at the office one Friday, my first day there that week, and noticed that Tim Dixon wasn't present. When he was still absent at lunchtime, I enquired as to his whereabouts only to be informed, by JC, that he had resigned a couple of days earlier due to 'differences of opinion' with Masters.

Shortly afterwards JC confirmed he would be retiring in the autumn. Now well into his 60s, his pending departure had been rumoured for some time. The consensus of opinion at the office was that the arrival of Masters and his subsequent antics had been one change too many for our long-serving Sports Editor and he was glad to be getting out of it. Like Brian Doel, Father Time had caught up with him.

Options for a replacement were extremely limited amongst the existing sports desk staff. Chris Gray, the former production worker moved to editorial by Jan Eagle and now quite established in his new position, made it clear he wasn't interested, whether through lack of journalistic experience or because he wasn't much younger than JC we weren't sure, and that left Liam Read, who took on the role despite only being in his mid-20s.

Liam had already proved himself as mature, sensible and well-organised and I had no problem working with someone of that age providing they understood what they were doing (I hadn't been much older when bursting onto the scene as Chief Reporter at Dawlish, so I could understand, more than most, the ups and downs of having so much responsibility at such an age).

Masters was continuing to keep a low profile as far as the amount of time he spent at the office. I had still not met him and had only seen the proprietor in passing a couple of times, but the diminutive, scruffy 60-something did begin holding one-to-one meetings with Liam following his appointment and the new Sports Editor quite willingly informed the rest of us of what had been discussed.

Seemingly we all had six months to prove the paper was financially viable and thereafter, if that was so, the Masters' plan was to appoint younger people onto the editorial staff. This did not auger well for any of the journalists working at the office, both staff and freelance, as every single one of us was aged over 50, but someone as disorganised as The Indy's owner was likely to change his mind again before long, we anticipated.

After the hiring and firing of another accountant, Masters appointed a fourth person to the role in no more than six months. The new incumbent decided that a serious overhaul of the company's financial practices was needed and an upshot of this was that all freelances would be paid by cheque, instead of the much-quicker direct bank credit, until further notice.

The Indy's freelances had, since I rejoined the paper, been paid around three weeks in arrears from receipt of each monthly claim, but this had already slipped to more than a month under Masters' tenure and the introduction of cheque payments extended the wait for payments further to approaching two months.

This obviously caused cash flow problems for many of us, but as another year ended and 2017 became 2018 things didn't appear to be going too badly. The Indy's sports coverage, which of course was its selling point, had been well organised and comprehensive for many years and this continued under Liam's tenure. His previous role was predictably filled only on a part-time basis by Tom Farey, another youngster who had previously worked a few freelance shifts for us on Saturday nights, and was employed, during the early part of the week, by The Newquay Voice, an independently-owned title which had begun around the turn of the century and its infancy meant it was a publication I knew very little about.

Despite effectively now operating with fewer people on the sports desk, finishing times actually improved on

Saturday nights as Liam did away with some of the unnecessary and tedious checking procedures that had been in place on deadline day for many years.

Frazer Cox - having given himself the title of Acting Editor since JC's retirement, even although he was still only employed at the office three days a week - began having regular meetings with Masters and for a while they seemed to be getting on reasonably well. However as someone at the office prophetically remarked, when you get two headstrong and self-opinionated people working together, sooner or later they are going to clash and the one in the most senior position is likely to come out on top.

The two were by now regularly exchanging emails, as Masters was still spending far more time in Truro than Liskeard, and copies of these were automatically circulated to every other computer in the editorial department and these certainly made interesting reading.

Masters, as some people at the office had already informed me, was virtually illiterate, not even understanding the difference between 'there' and 'their' in his communications. This meant, of course, that he was incapable of analysing his paper's content, but that appeared to be the least of his worries.

On Friday in February I arrived at the office to learn that Liam had resigned his position the previous day and because of the amount of holiday he was owed, would only be working a week's notice. The story unfolded of a row with Masters, which started off about both staff and freelances not being paid on time and had then degenerated into further disagreements which culminated in the short-lived Sports Editor announcing his departure.

Masters had now been at the helm for approaching a year and had it not been for his lack of command of the English language he could well have written a book on the experience entitled 'how not to run a newspaper'.

Chris Gray was again offered the Sports Editor's job and this time he accepted, I was given an extra day, another freelance sub began working from home one day a week and things continued much as before despite several months with little continuity.

With money saved from Liam's departure, Masters then agreed to a full-time addition to The Indy's news desk and I was privy to an exchange of e-mails he had with Frazer Cox, in which the 'acting editor' recommended Guy Channing, a long-time friend of his, for the role, describing the paper's part-time Picture Editor as 'an experienced all-rounder, fully familiar with all aspects of the job, including newspaper law'.

Guy was a nice enough bloke with whom I had become increasingly friendly since he joined The Indy, and he seemed a sound enough photographer/picture desk man. However, 'experienced all-rounder' he most certainly was not, having no experience of reporting or sub-editing and whose knowledge of newspaper law was probably about the same as my understanding of nuclear physics.

Sadly, though perhaps inevitably, Masters succumbed to the misinformation he was fed and the first real chance in a decade to significantly improve the paper's news operation had been totally wasted with 'jobs for me mates' being well and truly the order of the day.

Yet as I was not involved on the news side of things, and with Masters still rarely visiting the Liskeard office during the business end of the week, things continued satisfactorily as the 2017-18 season drew to a close.

During the summer there were, as in previous years, reductions in the amount of material used by freelance writers working from home. This led to a disagreement between the sports desk and Nigel Walrond, after he voiced his opposition to the cutbacks, the upshot of which was that he would no longer be working at the office as a sub, only contributing articles remotely.

The World Cup finals were one of the more memorable tournaments for England as they reached the semi-finals and The Indy's Saturday shift watched the quarter-final win against Sweden, coming in a couple of hours earlier than usual and subsequently taking a two-hour break to see the game during the afternoon. The atmosphere was quite good and as the new season got under way there seemed little to be concerned about, despite the massive shortcomings of the person in overall charge.

Nigel Walrond's departure from the office meant I would now have complete responsibility for the paper's 'live' rugby pages produced on a Saturday night. For several seasons we had fulfilled this role between us when Nigel attended the office (about 50 per cent of Saturdays depending on the geographical location of which match he had covered that afternoon). So I was well used to such responsibility, but now for the first time this would be my role every week.

During the early months of the 2018-19 season things continued to progress satisfactorily as we continued to comfortably beat the deadline time week after week. Guy Channing, who since Nigel Walrond's departure had regularly given me lifts back to Plymouth on Saturday nights, even told me during one such journey that I been referred to as 'Mr Reliable' during one discussion at the office. The Sunday Independent's ruling clique, throughout my second spell at the paper, had never been renowned for praising others, even when they were safely out of earshot, with criticism far more commonplace, so, I thought, this was praise indeed.

Towards the end of the year rumours began to circulate that Masters was planning to move The Indy's production to Truro and in early December it was confirmed that this indeed would be the case.

He had recently sold his controlling interest in Truro City Football Club, who were heading for relegation, to the owners of the Cornish Pirates rugby club, with the long-term plan being for both entities to share a proposed new stadium on the outskirts of the city, which had been talked about for years, but didn't seem to be any nearer to fruition.

However with the football club off his hands, The Independent was very much set to become Masters' new toy and although it wasn't patently obvious at this point in time, that would spell disaster for many in the months ahead.

The move to my home city was originally supposed to taking place in January, but was suddenly moved forward to the December once the owners of The Indy's Liskeard office made it clear that any incursion into the new year would mean another 12 months' rent would become payable.

Saturday December 23 was the first press day of the paper's fourth home in less than 15 years and also the date that marked my working return to Truro for the first time since August 1997. The new, rented office, situated near the end of Newham Road a good 20 minutes' walk from the city centre, was certainly more spacious than either of its Liskeard predecessors and that first day everything seemed much as before as our deadline came and went.

Masters, now free of his football commitments, even called into the office during the afternoon, a happening not only unprecedented on a Saturday, but which also resulted in my first (albeit largely time of day) conversation with him some 20 months after he had first taken the helm.

What with it being Christmas, he even handed out a bottle of champagne to everyone working there that day and the festive season also meant that I would be spending a week or so in Truro and subsequently would not have to worry about travelling back to Plymouth late at night for the first couple of Saturdays.

Working from home for a least part of the week was becoming more and more common not only in journalism but in office employment generally and what with Chris Gray, Frazer Cox, Guy Channing and myself all being

Devon-based, it was agreed that we would only attend the new Truro base on Saturdays and work remotely for whatever other days we were needed.

This presented a potential problem in how I would get back to Plymouth on Saturday nights. We didn't usually finish until around 9.30pm, too late to catch the last train, and it was not really practical for me to stay in Truro every weekend because of the cost of the fares and the general disruption to my routine that would result from such a practice.

Guy Channing agreed to help out and as 2019 got under way, I started travelling with our Picture Editor to as well as from the office on press days.

Masters now began calling in at the office on Saturdays to the point where his presence was becoming disruptive. Still totally clueless as to the workings of a newspaper office, his one suggestion for improving, as he saw it, the editorial content of the publication was to introduce a 'page three girl', a suggestion greeted with a mixture of laughter and stunned disbelief once he had left the office, with someone commenting 'what decade is he living in?'

The owner's disagreements with Frazer Cox were becoming more frequent, louder and lasting longer. Listening to the two of them debating what they saw as the paper's future direction reminded me of two drunks in a pub each repeating, time and time again, their own views while deliberately ignoring the other's argument.

Towards the end of January came the news that The Indy would have find aa new printer as the centre at Weymouth, used by the paper since its Newsquest days, was ceasing weekend production. Masters had to look for alternatives, but the only one he could find was at a printing plant in Oxford owned by Reach.

Unfortunately, the slot available there had a Saturday deadline of 8.30pm, which meant finishing the paper around an hour earlier than had been the case and subsequently all reporters and correspondents had to submit material early enough to ensure this new cut-off point was met.

Saturday February 16 was the first day scheduled for the new arrangement and as the date approached I foresaw no problems: I had been producing the press day rugby pages single-handedly throughout that season without coming even close to missing the deadline and saw no reason why this shouldn't continue providing those submitting reports kept to the new deadlines.

Anyone familiar with my career will know that illness has rarely been something that has affected my attendance or performance. Apart from the occasional head cold, I rarely seemed to be affected in this way and the number of days I had missed work on health grounds, in the previous 30 years or so, could probably be counted on the fingers of two hands. Indeed, I could clearly remember going nearly 12 years, between early 1990 and late 2001, without having a single day off work for this reason.

But on Friday February 15 I knew something was badly wrong. From the time I woke up I felt totally devoid of energy and as the day progressed a severe and persistent cough developed and grew progressively worse into the evening.

There was no real improvement the following morning and I had to make a fairly-quick decision on whether to travel down to Truro with what was clearly some sort of flu. Had we still been working to the old 9.30pm deadline I would almost certainly have rung in sick - it would, after all, be the first Saturday I had missed on health grounds in 12 years - but what with it being the first day of a new, earlier deadline, I considered my absence would turn an already testing day into one of total chaos.

So I reluctantly went to work and it was obvious to everyone as soon as I arrived that I was not well. Like the previous day, my condition grew worse as we moved into the evening and while we just managed to make the new deadline, I had very little idea where I was by the final hour and Guy Channing had to physically help me out of the car when we arrived back in Plymouth that night.

Sunday saw little improvement but thereafter my condition gradually improved and by the time I was next scheduled to travel down to Truro, the following Saturday, I was fine apart from still having a bit of a cough.

When I arrived Chris Gray immediately informed me that I had missed a report out on one of my pages the previous week. Such omissions were hardly unprecedented during the mad rush to beat the deadline on a Saturday night and given my illness and the fact that we had finished earlier at the first time of asking, I was a little surprised that the matter was raised so abruptly

Indeed given some of my colleagues' appalling spelling mistakes in headlines that had punctuated the paper in the preceding months - 'Manor of defeat frustrates manager' (with no pun intended) being just one of the gems to reach the printing press unnoticed - I felt my own oversight, with plenty of mitigation, was mild by comparison, but a strange and negative atmosphere had already started to flow through The Sunday Independent's new offices.

The following week we learnt that Tim Dixon - the short-lived Editorial Director who had walked out on the paper 18 months earlier - was returning, although not in person, to edit the paper's news pages from home at a knockdown price. The rumours were that Masters had gone back to him, cap in hand, in a thinly-disguised move to oust Frazer Cox, but as the now soon-to-be former Acting Editor had moved from freelance to staff status a year or so earlier, and therefore would still have to be paid unless he chose to leave the company of his own free will, the change did not make total sense in financial terms, but then very little that Masters did involved any logic.

Frazer Cox was, understandably, uncharacteristically quiet that day, but the following Saturday was nowhere to be seen. I enquired whether he was still with the company to be told, by Chris Gray, 'at the moment'. Seemingly he was working from home editing features pages under Tim Dixon's instructions, but just how long that would last we weren't really sure.

That same day I was informed that, as part of cuts to the freelance budget, I would no longer be required other than on Saturdays, something that would make my already shaky financial situation totally unviable.

There was a definite sense that Frazer Cox'sr demotion was just the start of Masters' now-revived plan to replace most of the paper's over-40s, despite the fact that the new, earlier deadline was being comfortably met each week.

'I wonder if we'll both be here next season,' Guy Channing commented as he drove us back to Plymouth that night.

'I'm beginning to wonder that myself,' I replied, adding that making a 100-mile round trip to work one day a week was completely unacceptable anyway.

Tom Farey, being the only person now employed at the title to be Cornwall based, had, since the move to Truro, become a lone editorial figure in the new office on Fridays. Seemingly for reasons of geographical location only, Masters regularly began discussing the paper's future with this young novice who lacked Liam Read's maturity and had largely been a peripheral figure during his first year at The Indy, partly due to the number of pre-arranged vacations he had booked which earned him the deserved nickname of 'Holiday Tom'. Masters' second year at the helm was now complete and 'How not to run a newspaper (part two)' was the only accurate description.

Easter was late that year and the Saturday coincided with the last full day of the regular football and rugby seasons with all regional leagues completing their programmes. I stayed in Truro that weekend, seriously wondering what the future held with either non-journalist work or benefits (for the first time in a quarter of a century) looking an increasingly likely scenario for the summer. I would not have to wait long to learn my fate.

The following Friday I received an extremely-apologetic email from Chris Gray informing me that Masters had decreed that I was one of the freelances whose services would no longer be required. 'I am extremely sorry about this, but my hands are tied,' the sports editor wrote.

Apparently Masters, at a meeting with Chris, even had the cheek to mention the relatively minor errors I had made when going in to work while ill that Saturday in February, a full two-and-a-half months earlier and a day on which there had never been any dispute as to my poor health. The whole situation was such an obvious stitch-up that it was almost laughable.

The following week I learnt that Guy Channing had been told that he was surplus to requirements and as he had only been on staff for about a year, no redundancy money was payable. There would now, Masters ruled, be no Picture Editor with correspondents and subs that were left having to process photos themselves from now on.

I stayed in occasional contact with Guy for the next few months and, shortly after his departure, he informed that Masters had laid off what freelance subs remained (a handful who worked remotely on Saturdays) for at least the rest of the summer.

The Independent's sales had, even in its more successful days, dropped during this period when there was no football or rugby, and Guy's next piece of interesting information was that circulation figures had dropped below the 5,000 mark for the first time, about a fifth of what they were when I rejoined the paper in 2007 and around a seventh of the total during my first spell at the title. This, let it not be forgotten, was for paper whose circulation area stretched from Bristol to Land's End.

It looked as if my career had come to an ignominious end after 35 years (37 if you include my two-year tenure as Editor of the student paper) as I was, strictly speaking, leaving a title for the first time not entirely of my own free will, albeit at the behest of a complete clown who knew nothing about journalism or indeed the newspaper industry generally.

Yet despite my uncertain future, there was almost a sense of relief that such an unsatisfactory situation had finally come to an end. In truth apart from possibly the first two years, when effectively I was employed full-time, I had never felt totally comfortable working for the title, particularly after Brian Doel failed to reignite the paper's fortunes after his takeover.

I had experienced four different owners, five different editors (if you include Messrs Dixon and Cox) and three different offices, yet with each and every change The Independent's sales had continued to fall as it slipped further and further into the mire of mediocrity, especially as far as its 'news' coverage was concerned.

I suppose I drew some consolation from the fact that the decline in my own career (and indeed those of many others journalists aged over 40) had run on a exact parallel with the decline of the provincial newspaper industry generally, but I still felt frustration that I could have achieved so much more had I been able to escape the stale yet often infuriatingly-complacent set-up at Liskeard and then briefly Truro.

I saw Guy again later in the summer and he informed me that Tom Farey, seemingly now even more Masters' 'blue-eyed boy', was rumoured to be replacing Chris Gray as Sports Editor amid speculation of a merger between The Independent and the Newquay Voice title. Truly a case of 'the blind leading the blind', but who was the blindest of them all was open to interpretation.

****

I had for some time - particularly after the 'successfail' job application period between 2013 and 2015 and then Brian Doel's hugely-disappointing reign at The Independent - resigned myself to the fact that there was never going to be a spectacular 'bounce back' in my career, as there had been at Dawlish in the late 80s and Jersey in the late 90s, but during the late summer of 2019 there almost was.

I had maintained contact with Mike Taylor over the years, mainly by the occasional exchange of e-mails, although once a year or so we met up for a drink, and one such occasion came that July when we spent an afternoon at the Wetherspoons pub in Teignmouth.

Mike, now having spent 30 years with the Mid-Devon Advertiser/Dawlish Newspapers company, was eyeing retirement, despite being a few years younger than me, and he and his wife had, a couple of years earlier, bought a smallholding in Portugal which they were gradually renovating and planned to move into once the time was right

.I had regularly kept me former colleague informed of the shambolic decline of The Independent, and indeed my own departure, but he had, understandably given the chronic shortage of vacancies for older journalists, been unable to offer any help so far.

However that day in Teignmouth he, almost casually at first, informed of a MDA vacancy for a senior reporter shortly to be advertised via Holdthefrontpage.

'If we were looking for a sub I would have recommended you before the vacancy was even advertised,' he said, 'but the problem with it being for a reporter is that they want someone who can drive.'

I knew this would present a huge stumbling block, even though I had managed perfectly well without a car during my previous reporting stint with the company, but decided there would be nothing to lose by applying and even if my bid was unsuccessful, there would be a certain irony to my final throw of the dice (which is what it almost certainly would prove to be) taking place where I began my senior career three decades earlier.

Given that Mike was sure to provide a glowing reference, I had no doubt that I would at least be interviewed for the vacancy and sure enough I received an e-mail from Ruth Davey, the MDA Editor, asking me to attend an appointment one Friday morning in late August.

Accompanied by a middle-aged woman who, I think, was a regional manager with Tindle Newspapers, Ruth Davey began by saying she had 'heard a lot about me' from Mike Taylor, particularly my successful deputising for Cedric Clough, who had died, aged 81, in early 2017 following several years of post-retirement ill health.

My appointment continued briskly and constructively - pausing only briefly while my interviewers gasped in amazement after hearing of Masters' Page 3 Girl proposal at The Independent - with no stumbling blocks emerging (the driving issue was, perhaps diplomatically, not mentioned by either side, having been clearly stated in my original application so as not to waste everyone's time).

Ruth Davey was, I guessed, not a great deal younger than myself, and we found ourselves in total agreement on matters such as our dislike of companies like Reach filling websites with unsubbed press releases, many of which had no geographical relevance to the areas supposedly being served.

The MDA and its sister titles, she informed me, only gave priority to the website for fast-moving stories such as serious road traffic accidents. Everything else went in the printed titles first.

I left that day with a feeling that if this was to be my last ever journalistic interview, at least it had gone as well as could reasonably have been expected. Had the vacancy been for a sub-editor, I would have been supremely confident, but the driving issue, allied to the job being advertised nationally and therefore probably attracting good quality applicants who were younger and could drive, meant the odds were probably still against me. I was disappointed, but not really surprised, to receive an email from Ruth Davey a fortnight later, wishing me all the best for the future, but stating that my application had been unsuccessful.

Fewer and fewer newspaper jobs were advertised in the months that followed. Multi-media PR type vacancies appeared from time to time, looking for 'journalists' who could, amongst other things, 'support the delivery of marketing and communications plans by creating and curating content for online and offline activities.' Any 'journalist' writing such gobbledygook 20 or 30 years earlier would probably have been shown the door; now such people were in charge of recruitment. It was most definitely time to go.

The following year, of course, saw the arrival of the coronavirus pandemic and this inevitably accelerated the existing trend of many newspapers going online only or closing altogether. The various lockdowns saw the long-term suspension of most grassroots sport - without question The Sunday Independent's lifeblood for the past 10 to 15 years - and few in West Country media circles believed the already-ailing publication could survive such a body blow and indeed it ceased publication again, this time permanently, the following year.

Elsewhere the wind of change was blowing through many of my previous journalistic haunts. The Mid-Devon

Advertiser's Ruth Davey departed just a few months after my interview and was soon followed by Mike Taylor, who readily accepted a voluntary redundancy and made good his promise to move to Portugal, at the same time severing my last link with Dawlish Newspapers 32 years after we both began work there. The Gazette office closed down, following decades as the paper's focal point, with what reporting on the town that still remained now also transferred to Newton Abbot

The Farnham Herald had finally switched from a broadsheet to a tabloid format a year or so earlier and I had read, via Holdthefrontpage, of the passing of both Peter Thompson and, more surprisingly given he was only 59, Tony Short. An inspection of the company's website revealed not a single senior editorial member of staff remained from my era, unsurprisingly really as all of those concerned were in my own age group or a fair bit older

It was a similar tale of unfamiliar names at The Jersey Evening Post, which had recently left its Five Oaks home of several decades to occupy smaller premises in St Helier, while The West Briton had quit its Malpas Road headquarters in Truro with production work being moved to Plymouth and just a couple of reporters retained and located in a small industrial estate unit at Treliske on the outskirts of the city. With sales of what was once the country's biggest-selling weekly down to around the 5,000 mark, it was the first time in the paper's 200-year history that it had not had a town centre presence.

The sun, which had not really shone brightly since my departure from Farnham, would not be coming out again.

www.ingramcontent.com/pod-product-compliance
Lightning Source LLC
LaVergne TN
LVHW010052170826
845678LV00012B/2116

* 9 7 8 1 9 1 6 6 9 6 6 8 6 *